Criticism Without Authority

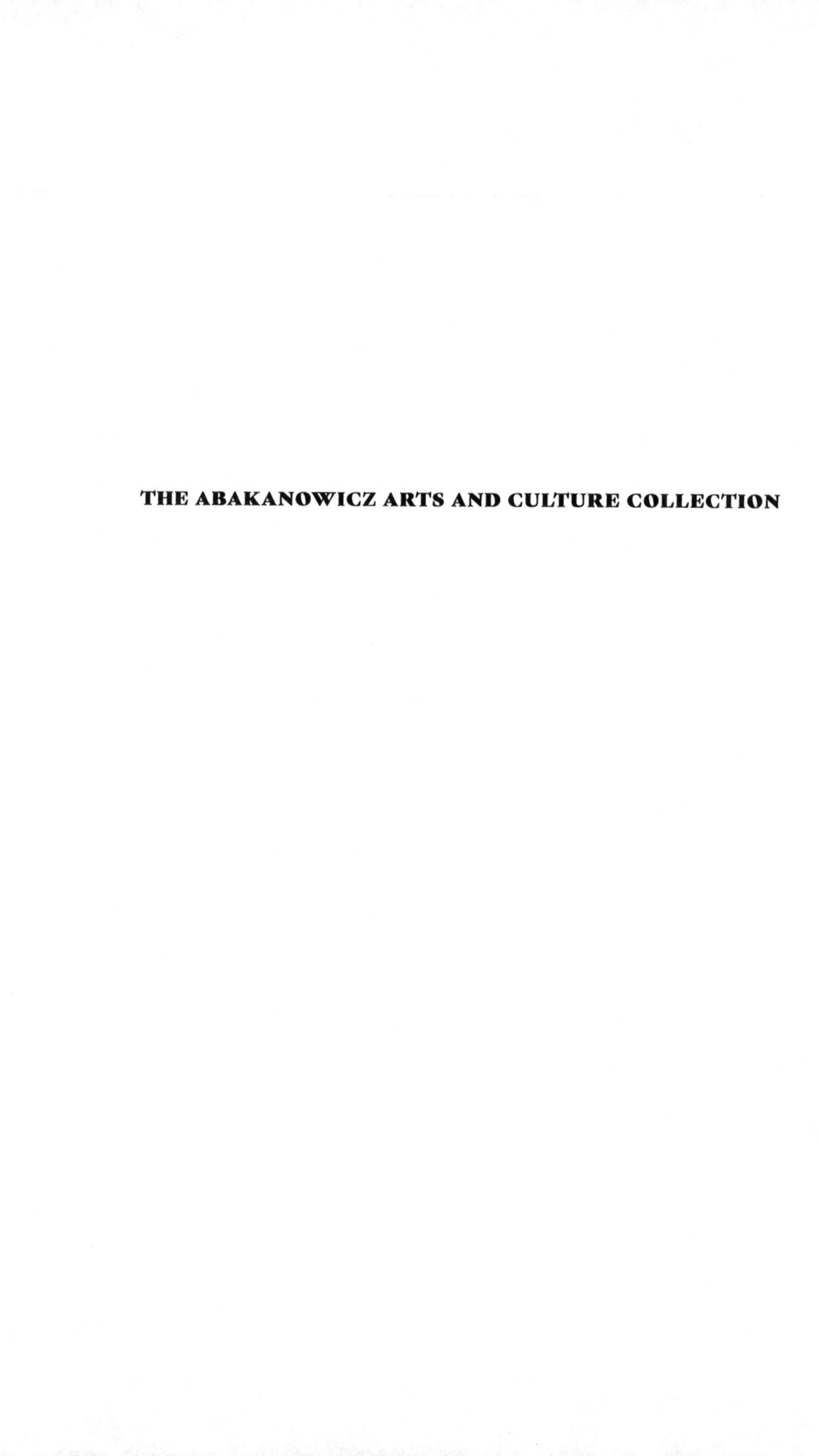

THE ABAKANOWICZ ARTS AND CULTURE COLLECTION

Criticism Without Authority

Gene Swenson's and Jill Johnston's
Queer Practices

Jennifer Sichel

THE UNIVERSITY OF CHICAGO PRESS

Chicago and London

The University of Chicago Press, Chicago 60637
The University of Chicago Press, Ltd., London

Published 2025
Printed in the United States of America

34 33 32 31 30 29 28 27 26 25   1 2 3 4 5

ISBN-13: 978-0-226-84282-0 (cloth)
ISBN-13: 978-0-226-84284-4 (paper)
ISBN-13: 978-0-226-84283-7 (ebook)
DOI: https://doi.org/10.7208/chicago/9780226842837.001.0001

The publication of this edition has been generously supported by the Abakanowicz Arts and Culture Charitable Foundation.

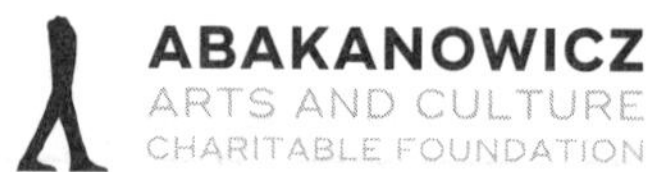

Published with support from the University of Chicago Department of Art History.

Library of Congress Cataloging-in-Publication Data

Names: Sichel, Jennifer, author
Title: Criticism without authority : Gene Swenson's and Jill Johnston's queer practices / Jennifer Sichel.
Other titles: Abakanowicz arts and culture collection
Description: Chicago : The University of Chicago Press, 2025. | Series: Abakanowicz arts and culture collection | Includes bibliographical references and index.
Identifiers: LCCN 2025009556 | ISBN 9780226842820 cloth | ISBN 9780226842844 paperback | ISBN 9780226842837 ebook
Subjects: LCSH: Arts, American—New York (State)—New York—20th century | Avant-garde (Aesthetics)—New York (State)—New York—History—20th century | Swenson, G. R. | Johnston, Jill
Classification: LCC NX511.N4 S52 2025 | DDC 704/.08664097471—dc23/eng/20250429
LC record available at https://lccn.loc.gov/2025009556

Authorized Representative for EU General Product Safety Regulation (GPSR) queries: **Easy Access System Europe**—Mustamäe tee 50, 10621 Tallinn, Estonia, gpsr.requests@easproject.com
Any other queries: https://press.uchicago.edu/press/contact.html

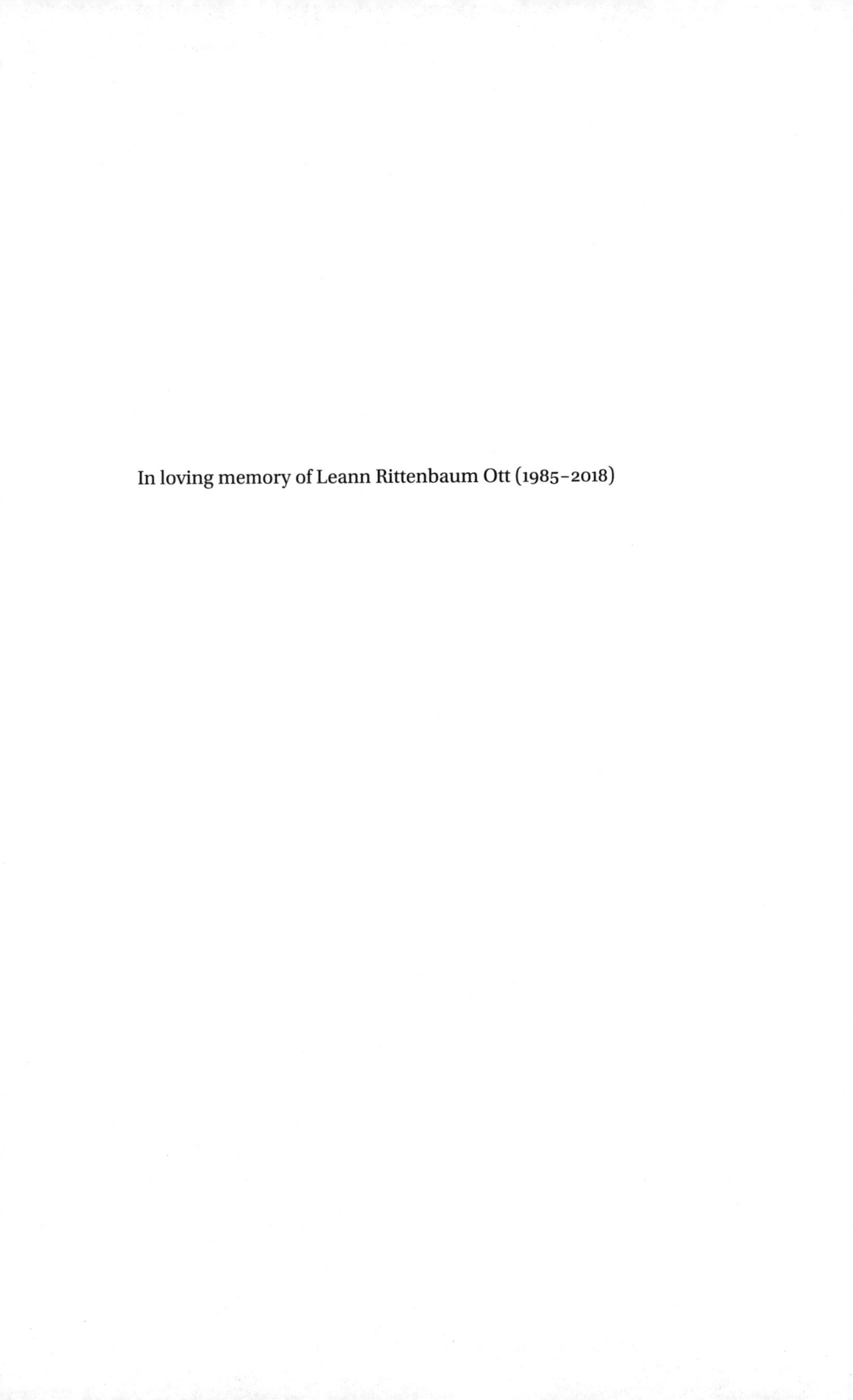

In loving memory of Leann Rittenbaum Ott (1985–2018)

Contents

An Impure Situation

Why bother with "modernist" originality if it is so easily defined?
GENE SWENSON, 1966[1]

Probably the world is too sure about its things. I like things that are certain about not being very sure about what they are.
JILL JOHNSTON, 1967[2]

This book is about things that are not sure about what they are. It follows the intertwined paths of Gene Swenson and Jill Johnston—art critics who were at the center of New York's art world in the sixties yet who tend to inhabit only the margins and footnotes of art history. There are two reasons why. First is a problem of genre: Swenson's and Johnston's writings and actions do not fit neatly into the category of either criticism or art, even when we consider the expanded field of sixties artmaking that encompasses happenings, environments, conceptual practice, and institutional critique. Second is a problem of tone: Swenson and Johnston reject conventions of discipline, coherence, and authority that often mark a cultural product as serious enough to anchor a scholarly monograph. So this book adopts a different tack. Rather than attempting to pinpoint Swenson's and Johnston's work, it starts from their entangled archives and traces connections as they unfurl. Things remain uncertain. Throughout, I use the phrase "queer practices" to convey how—in conversations, protests, and panels and on pages of underground newspapers—Swenson and Johnston reimagine intimacy and selfhood and posit ways of being ambiguous and unmanageable in response to a world that typically demands clarity and punishes difference.

In the sixties, Swenson and Johnston reinvented criticism as a capacious practice, rejecting modernist appeals to purity and coherence. They devised new ways to describe not only new experiments in art and performance but also new queer sensibilities: manners of feeling and relating that indulge wayward desires and indeterminacy. Attending closely to instances when Swenson and Johnston encounter others, reveal their influences, and reckon with the bigger picture of local and world events, I follow connections where they lead. Which means that this book's history is skewed, partial, and unruly—but that's the point. Swenson and Johnston often failed to effect change or to see a bigger picture beyond their own triumphs and struggles, so it goes. The point of this book is not to aggrandize success or inaugurate new heroes.[3] Rather, it tells a story of Swenson's and Johnston's historical situatedness in a radical political and artistic milieu filled with overlapping, contradictory concerns. It dwells in the mess, tracing the contingency and partiality of Swenson's and Johnston's vision in order, at least in part, to provide an alternative to ready-made narratives of liberal progress.

Beginnings

Swenson's and Johnston's lives as art critics began in near-perfect tandem in New York City around 1961 when they were writing short reviews for the same magazine, *ARTnews*.[4] "It was the magazine's practice to collect artists

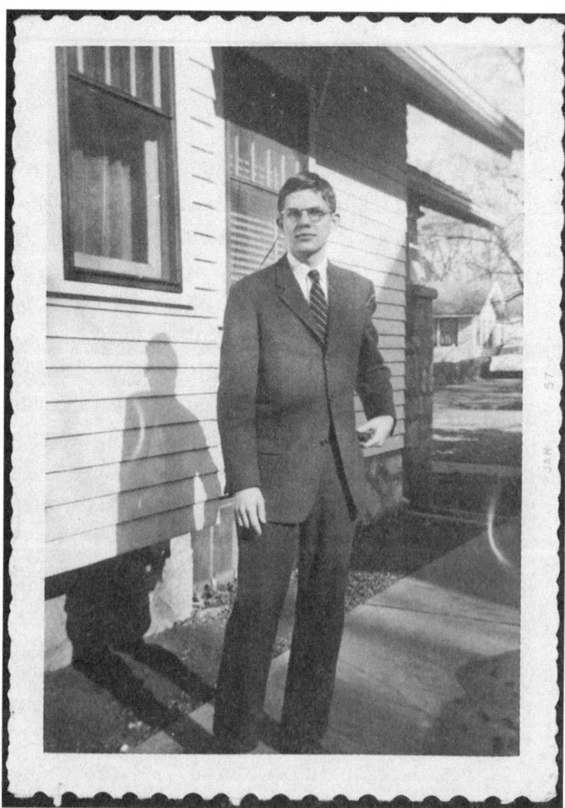

Figure I.1 Photo of Gene Swenson, January 1957. Gene Swenson papers, 1950–1969, Archives of American Art, Smithsonian Institution, Washington, DC.

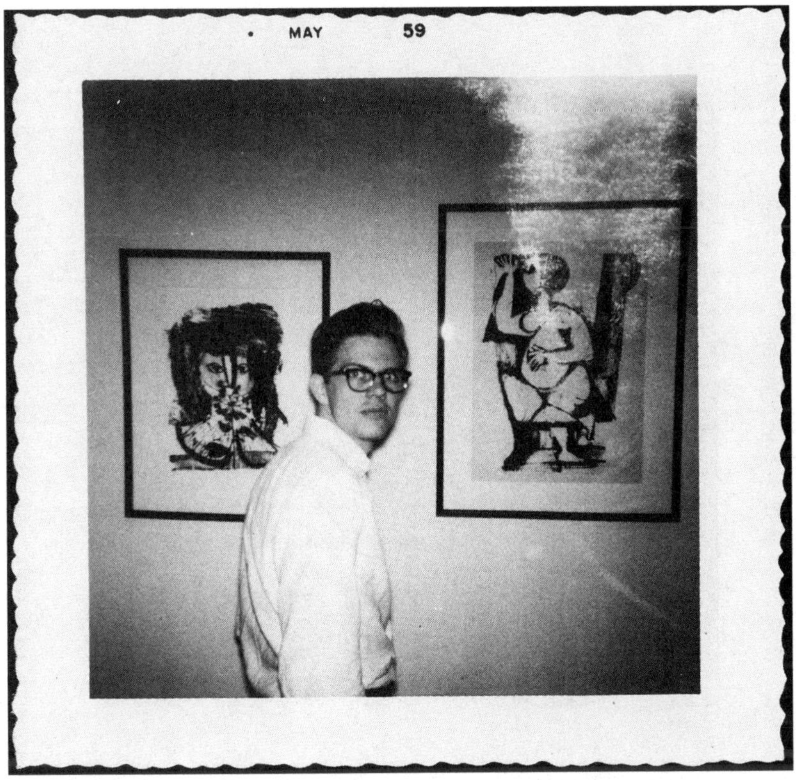

Figure I.2 Photo of Gene Swenson, May 1959. Gene Swenson papers, 1950–1969, Archives of American Art, Smithsonian Institution, Washington, DC.

in catch-all paragraphs, a single sentence allotted to each one. These were called 'junk reviews,'" Johnston writes, reflecting back. "This was easy work," she continues, "because I got three dollars per review whether I wrote one sentence or ten. Anyway, it was clearly pointless to damn an artist in one sentence, and I considered it a challenge to try and convey some essence of the work in a thumbnail description."[5] For Swenson and Johnston both, these "junk reviews" furnished proving ground for new ideas and experiments in terse, punchy descriptive language without judgment. They also furnished just enough money to eke by.

• • •

Swenson was born near Topeka, Kansas, in 1934. "I was brought up in a Kansas jerkwater, not even on a trunk line, and I've never been able to get over a fondness for melody," he would later write, mythologizing his rural past.[6] He arrived in the city by way of Yale University as an undergraduate and the

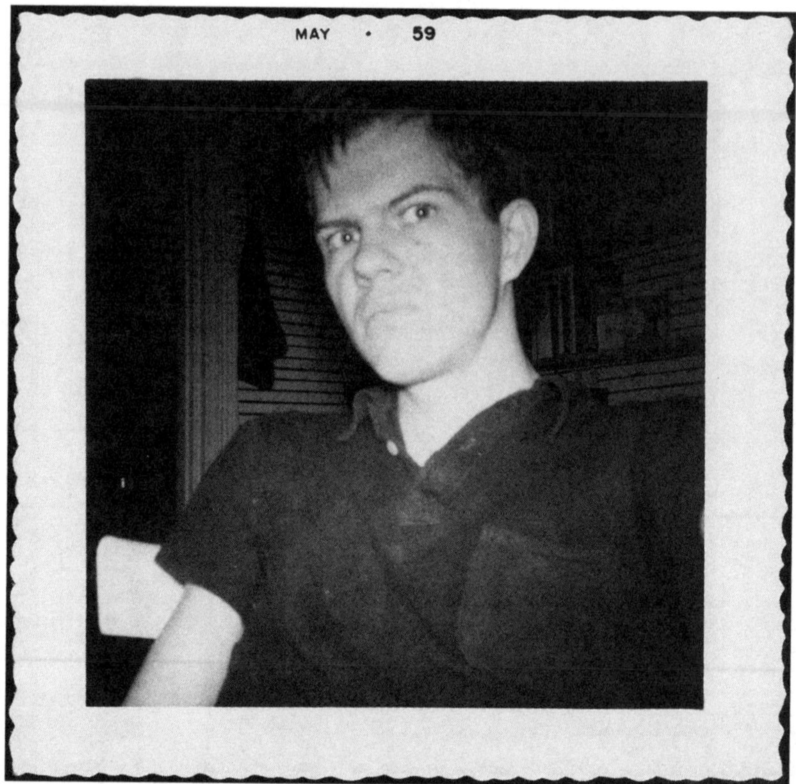

Figure I.3 Photo of Gene Swenson, May 1959. Gene Swenson papers, 1950–1969, Archives of American Art, Smithsonian Institution, Washington, DC.

Institute of Fine Arts at New York University for graduate school, though he didn't finish the program.[7] "In 1959, Gene Swenson was a nice-looking, tweed-jacketed, bespectacled boy from Kansas, very earnest," recalls critic Lucy Lippard, who was his friend and classmate at NYU. "He stuttered badly when delivering a graduate seminar report. . . . I was interested but not surprised by the change in the clothes and the attitudes with which he had arrived in New York. He became somewhat unkempt but never lost that American boyishness."[8] Snapshots in Swenson's archive chronicle the transformation. In a photo stamped January 1957, Swenson appears in front of a suburban house, looking very earnest, wearing a freshly pressed suit, wire-rim glasses, and an Ivy League haircut (fig. I.1). Two snapshots stamped May 1959 convey the new, New York look: his hair is messy, his shirt rumpled; there is a notable intensity in his stare (figs. I.2–I.3).

Swenson lived in a fifth-floor tenement apartment at 69 East 4th Street. His companion Ann Wilson describes the cramped space: "There was a bathtub in the kitchen, a bed in the air shaft, and a desk and two chairs under some bookshelves in the front room. The ceiling and walls were cracked—and on those walls was this splendid small collection of the work which was his life's involvement. The windows looked out onto 4th Street. Families with five and six kids lived in the other flats; it was noisy. He had no other possessions; he made less than enough to live on writing criticism."[9] Wilson played an important role in both Swenson's and Johnston's lives. Her relationship with Swenson was intense and complicated, and after his death she took care of the materials he left behind.[10] For her part, Johnston describes Wilson as "another sixties casualty down the block, trying to piece together the shattered fragments of herself." Johnston explains, "By the time I met Ann she was quite a well-known art-world character herself. With Bill [Wilson] she had twin daughters and a son, losing her standing with the artists by becoming a mother. She then lost her standing as a mother by falling in love with Gene Swenson ('a romantic escape,' she has described it, 'from the harshness and domestic responsibility of marriage') and running away from home. With Gene her standing was precarious because Gene was mostly homosexual."[11]

•　•　•

Johnston was born in England in 1929 as "the illegitimate daughter of an English aristocrat father and a rejected American mother," as one biographic note put it   or, in Johnston's words, "more orphan than not" (Johnston's search for "a father" would become a central preoccupation of her life and critical practice).[12] Raised in Littleneck, Queens, by her mother and grandmother, she returned to New York City in the mid-1950s to study dance with José Limón after graduating from Tufts University and the University of North Carolina at Greensboro for graduate school. After enduring a harrowing botched abortion followed by a broken foot, Johnston "suddenly stop[ped] dancing," as she would later write, and went on to "unaccountably take a musty job sorting out clippings and photos in the dance collection of the public library from which I was predicably fired . . . becom[ing] more completely than ever an isolated and alienated struggling young lost white middle class female unprotected in a big city." Regarding her abortion, Johnston recounts: "I think I nearly died significantly enough in the apartment of my friend Ruth Currier with whom perhaps I was still secretly in love anyway I happened to be in her place hemorrhaging over the spontaneous delivery of this four and a half or five month old fetus after a couple of weeks of visiting one of these abortionists who attach a device to the cervix to somehow electrically induce labor and I thought I was done for."[13]

Johnston began writing dance criticism in 1955 for the magazine *Dance Observer*. In 1959 she started writing for *The Village Voice*, where she would publish a regular column off and on (mostly on) until 1975.[14] Johnston got married in 1958, had two children, and by the early sixties was, by her own reckoning, "a stroller mommie in washington heights living in an $80 walkup near the river and across the street from the park"—as she explains in a 1972 *Village Voice* column titled "The Yearly Mellowdrama": a study of herself as a young, stressed-out mother trying to live and write "while," as she puts it, "everyone was screaming and looking at the [TV] box and eating tuna fish and falling and getting hit and generally going crazy including being unsuccessfully in love."[15]

The "stroller mommie" phase of Johnston's life ended around 1963, and she got divorced a year later. Around that time, she began a project of assembling a performative persona that would shift throughout the decade from ambivalent femme to iconic dyke (fig. I.4). As Johnston recounts, she was "a good-looking, athletic, well-built, straight-shooting sort of girl, no camp or swish, etc." with "a retiring, awkward, self-conscious personality except when drunk. Between '62 and '64 I went through an aberrant phase," she continues, "dressing up in high ladies' drag, looking more like a parody of some fixed idea of my sex than anything closely resembling it."[16] In 1963, Johnston moved to Houston Street to be "closer to this woman I'd fallen madly in love with and whom I was chasing around unashamedly."[17] Living and working downtown, she folded herself into a group of mostly Jewish artists, writers, and mothers who were "ethnically very different from me," as she puts it. "I was a failed bourgeois American," Johnston writes, "and

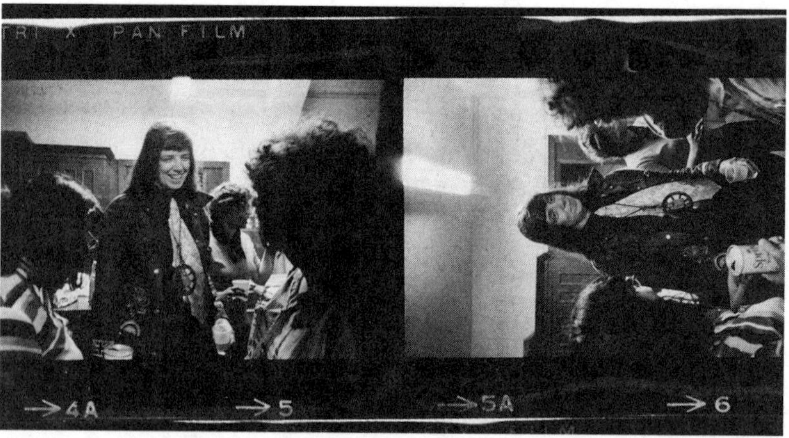

Figure I.4 Jill Johnston at GLF meeting, WBAI forum on gay liberation, 1970. Detail of contact sheet. Photograph by Diana Jo Davies. Manuscripts and Archives Division, The New York Public Library. © NYPL.

they were neither from bourgeois families nor from families with bourgeois pretensions. The Lower East Side society was very much a meeting ground for these two types of Americans."[18]

Downtown, 1963

This book's story begins, then, in 1963 when Swenson's and Johnston's lives converge in the complicated "meeting ground" downtown, as they moved into apartments just a few streets from each other in the blocks between Greenwich Village and the Lower East Side. Swenson was in his late twenties, and Johnston in her mid-thirties with two young children in tow. (Throughout the sixties and seventies, Johnston's children continue to "dot the printscape" of her *Village Voice* columns, as she writes much later, "like fugitive presences."[19])

Working independently but sitting at typewriters just a few blocks apart, in 1963 Swenson and Johnston began generating language that set the tone for avant-garde practices in painting and performance in the United States for years to come. Which is to say (and it's worth emphasizing), this book is not a story of isolated or quixotic curiosities. Rather, it provides a different approach to historicizing the development of art and performance in New York in the sixties and early seventies—an approach reoriented around the archival remains of a few unruly, queer practices that got purged in the long, ongoing process of historical streamlining. This book lingers with objects that do not quite fit into art history: things that fall between genres, often generated collaboratively in gaps and misunderstandings or in response to homophobic interferences or in harrowing circumstances so far from ideal that it does not make much sense to talk about artistic intention. As a result, this book's historical narrative sputters and spirals. But this book also makes a wager. By sacrificing forward momentum, by examining impurities that emerge when we pick at appearances, and by dwelling too long with messy objects, it is possible to write a new, queerer history of something we thought we knew inside and out: in this case, the development of painting and performance in New York City starting in 1963.

Around that time, Swenson published some of the earliest criticism on Pop Art for *ARTnews*, including "The New American 'Sign Painters'" (1962) and his defining series of interviews titled "What Is Pop Art? Answers from Eight Painters" (1963–64). Working in parallel, Johnston published some of the earliest and most perceptive criticism on happenings and the Judson Dance Theater. In a February 1963 review of Judson Dance Concerts #3 and #4, Johnston declares confidently: "The revolution in dance is upon us."[20] "Indeed," as historian Sally Banes notes, "this group would dominate postmodern dance for twenty years to come."[21]

Across the board, 1963 was an important year downtown. "In 1963 what we now call the Sixties began," Banes declares at the outset of her essential book *Greenwich Village, 1963: Avant-Garde Performance and the Effervescent Body*. In Banes's recounting, it was the year when "numerous small, overlapping, sometimes rival networks of artists were forming the multifaceted base of an alternative culture." These "groups of individuals," as Banes calls them, were making a kind of "political history that has nothing to do with states, governments, or armies, or with public resistance"; instead, they were "gently loosening the social and cultural fabric by merging private and public life, work and play, art and ordinary experience," Banes writes. "That loosened fabric fell apart by the late Sixties."[22]

Staying with Banes's apt metaphor: this book traces what happens as several threads in New York City's social and cultural fabric fray and become attenuated.[23] During the sixties, Swenson and Johnston developed idiosyncratic, confessional, energetic forms of writing that forged new ground, politically and aesthetically. Unimpressed by appeals to authenticity, rigor, and purity that dominated critical debates stirring around them, they stepped into the fray, refusing to cordon the intensity of social and political life off from their art criticism. For both critics, this entailed figuring out how to live a homosexual life and how to produce queer work in the context of a world (and an art world) that discriminated actively against homosexuals and that was hostile to queer ways of being. Rejecting critical distance and the benefits of hindsight, they embraced exigencies of their moment from positions mired in it. As a result, both Swenson and Johnston struggled with personal issues in highly public ways. They became, in a sense, real lived examples of the commitment to blurring art and life that many key artists and critics of the period championed but ultimately avoided when things got too blurry, intractable, excessive—or, in a word, too queer.

Chapter 1 opens with the question "What do you say about homosexuals?"—which Swenson jokingly posed on tape to Andy Warhol in 1963, in a previously unknown recording of Swenson's interview with the artist that I uncovered during my research. The chapter follows how Swenson moves from that question to assemble an expansive queer worldview. His professional career peaked in 1966 with an exhibition and essay titled *The Other Tradition*. Offering a sharp rejoinder to modernist criticism, Swenson argues that art "must be involved with the time and the world we live in, our world is too dangerous and violent for us to be anything else."[24]

Swenson soon became increasingly unable and unwilling to cope with a world inundated by cruelty. His behavior became erratic, oscillating between gentle and angry, poetic and menacing, as he became "the most controversial and talked about art writer of his generation," according to fellow critic Gregory Battcock. "He saw art and art criticism as a vehicle for improving the lot and the awareness of man," Battcock continues. "His actions first became gossip, then legend."[25]

Disintegration

In the middle of this book, things unravel and fall apart. By the mid-sixties, Swenson and Johnston had both become enmeshed in New York City's psychiatric system, resulting in harrowing experiences they wrote about publicly for underground newspapers. Both critics landed several times in the psychiatric ward at Bellevue Hospital—a legendary, imposing structure along the East River, which Johnston would later describe as "a charnel house for the living dead."[26] Johnston's diagnoses included "bizarre behavior, paranoid ideation, homosexuality," as she recounts in her memoir, quoting from her psychiatric record and noting how the close linking of paranoia with homosexuality made "the latter so explicitly criminal."[27] Swenson never publicly disclosed his official diagnoses—and perhaps he did not have access to them during his lifetime. In a newspaper column from 1968 he proclaims: "I have never been told what particular incident led to my arrest, if any did"—despite having requested information from Bellevue Hospital and the state's investigating commission.[28]

Swenson's and Johnston's paths converged in 1968 when they met and became friends. Together in Johnston's loft they reimagined their trips as expansive journeys into the recesses of outer space. "Sometime during '67 Gene cracked up and went to Bellevue," Johnston recalls. "I believe that event radicalized him. Unlike myself, he found an immediate target for his rage. . . . But I saw Gene in quiescent moods also," Johnston continues, "withdrawn, fragile, transparent, recovering from one collision or another with the hospitals or the police. I had a welter of feelings about him, none of them very consciously connected with the aspect of my life that mirrored his."[29] Regarding her own collisions with hospitals and police, Johnston explains,

> I had come apparently to the very end of my possibilities of going on existing in contradiction to myself and in august of 1965 on my own behalf I went totally mad. In 1966 I went mad again and in january 1969 I did it again and in that condition having escaped the clutches of the psychiatric profession and its penal colonies I was travelling about the union in style convinced at last that it was the world who was fucked up and not me and that if I didn't do something about the world it would continue to mess with me and all the other mes like me wherever they were who didn't know yet that it was the world making us all such nor-

mal neurotic people but I didn't have a real strategy as I said and how could I when I was still a solo case attempting to make myself a political group of two.[30]

Chapter 2 describes what happened as Swenson and Johnston both endeavored to "do something about the world" when their crises felt urgent in 1968 and '69 but their goals unclear and their positions felt fragile and confusing. They refused to acquiesce to the psychiatric establishment's demands that they integrate into bourgeois American family life. Inspired by antipsychiatry and the psychedelic counterculture swirling around them, they both came to embrace an aesthetics and politics of disintegration: in February 1968, Swenson picketed alone outside the Museum of Modern Art wielding only a giant question mark, and in the spring of 1969 Johnston organized a panel discussion at New York University titled "The Disintegration of a Critic: An Analysis of Jill Johnston." From their standpoints as white, homosexual, "failed bourgeois" Americans (as Johnston put it) living and working downtown in the late sixties, Swenson and Johnston developed ways of being and doing that were raw and flawed but also creative, earnest, and ambitious.

Swenson's life ended abruptly and tragically. He died alongside his mother in a car crash in Kansas in August 1969. His work never finished.

Slouching Toward Consciousness

After Swenson's death, Johnston continued breathlessly, assembling a new public persona as a radical, rowdy lesbian feminist—a reintegration, of sorts, into something like a whole, but not like any preexisting or sanctioned whole. "The organism as totally illegal," Johnston writes.[31]

In 1971, Johnston published her first anthology of criticism as a Dutton paperback titled *Marmalade Me* (fig. I.5), a compilation of her *Village Voice* columns from the sixties. *Marmalade Me* is both retrospective and anticipatory: Johnston selects and sequences her old columns in ways that anticipate her burgeoning lesbian feminist life. She highlights continuities between old and new, positing disintegration and reintegration as messy processes that do not conform to a linear timeline. The title itself comprises an awkward lesbian wordplay combining sea (*mar*), mistress or mother (*marm*), illness (*malady*), and having sex (*laid*)—producing a slippery, punning series of associations involving being at sea, getting wet or seasick, and getting laid by a woman or a mother. "What does it mean to name something?" Johnston asks in a 1968 column titled "Untitled," which opens *Marmalade Me* and introduces the whole book. "Where do we come off giving everything a legal identity?"[32]

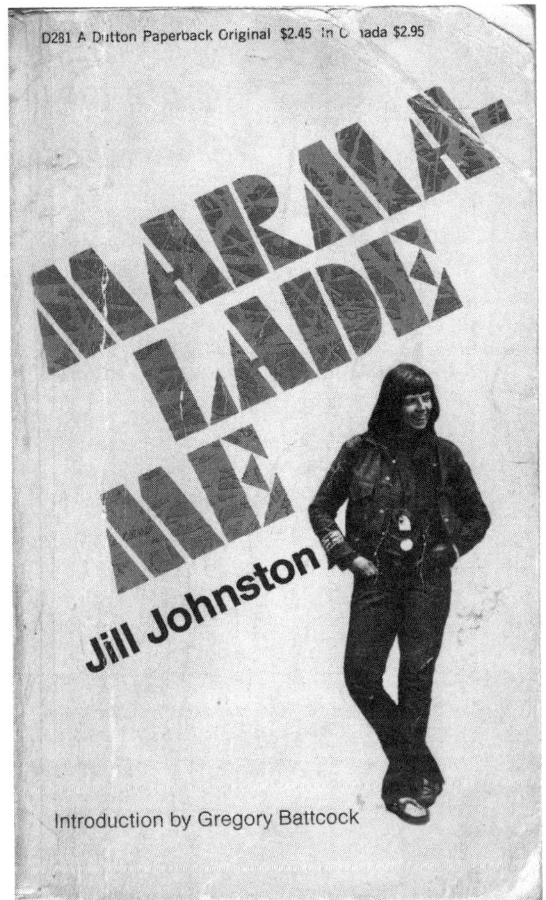

Figure I.5 Cover of *Marmalade Me* by Jill Johnston, 1971.

Around the same time that *Marmalade Me* came out in 1971, Johnston participated in a high-profile panel discussion moderated by Norman Mailer at New York City's Town Hall titled "A Dialogue on Women's Liberation." Johnston read aloud a text titled "On a Clear Day You Can See Your Mother," unleashing a rambunctious performance that culminated with two women joining her onstage for a romp on the floor.

Following on the heels of *Marmalade Me*, in 1973 Johnston published her second anthology of criticism, *Lesbian Nation: The Feminist Solution*, with the text of her Town Hall performance reprinted as the concluding section (fig. I.6). On the first page of *Lesbian Nation*, Johnston instructs: "This book should be read like an interlocking web of personal experience and history and events of the world forming a picture of an evolving political revolu-

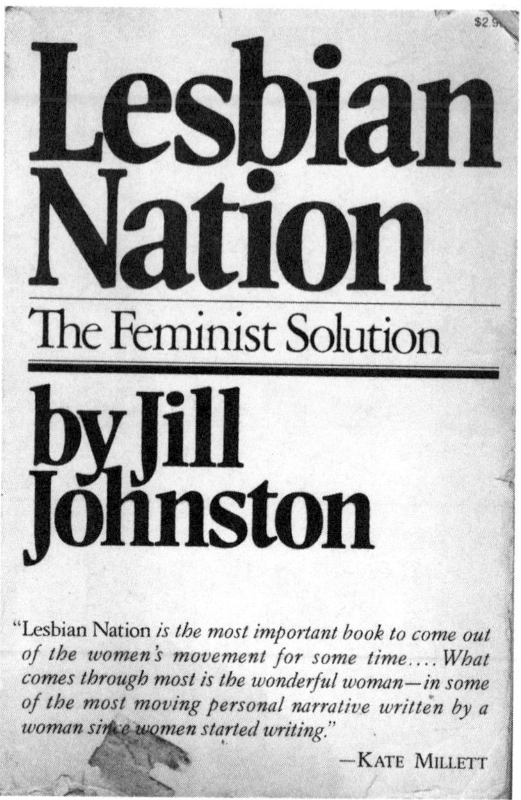

Figure I.6 Cover of *Lesbian Nation: The Feminist Solution* by Jill Johnston, 1973.

tionary consciousness of one who was female who emerged from straight middle unconscious postwar amerika"[33]—a process she dubs "slouching toward consciousness," cribbing Joan Didion's reference to W. B. Yeats in *Slouching Towards Bethlehem*.[34]

Chapter 3 traces how Johnston assembled one feminist solution after another, culminating in her grand proclamation that lesbianism is *the* feminist solution in the early seventies. From the outset, Johnston's feminist solutions involved letting the stuff of life seep into her work. Throughout the decade, she assembled brilliant methods and linguistic strategies to compel others to endure, week after week, the most awful, embarrassing, and visionary parts of her public and private worlds. Rather than cast Johnston's lesbian feminism as a political stance separate from her earlier work as a critic, I argue that *all* of Johnston's feminist solutions, including *Lesbian Nation*, belong to the history of art and performance. I insist on Johnston's importance for both art history and the history of feminism, even when that importance feels troubling and difficult to countenance.[35]

Ten years after Swenson first asked, "What do you say about homosexuals?" in 1963, Johnston replies in a sense: "Say it over and over again" until it "means nothing," or until it "becomes meaningless by becoming so much itself."[36] This book's conclusion addresses the stakes of Swenson's and Johnston's short-lived queer interventions. Their work did not succeed in normal ways. It did not accrue value or prestige or argue coherent, influential worldviews. It endures as fragmented, angry, and partial. The conclusion asks what Swenson's and Johnston's queer practices made possible, and what they might make possible still.

An Impure Situation

In May 1966, Lucy Lippard published a column in the magazine *Art International* titled "An Impure Situation"—an important analysis of contemporary art and criticism in the form of a long review of Gene Swenson's exhibition and essay *The* Other *Tradition*.[37] Extolling the impurity of Swenson's project as a virtue, Lippard defends his critical practice and, at the same time, rebukes arguments for art's "purity" coming from within modernist criticism. But more than that, Lippard underscores how significant it is that Swenson rejects the demand that criticism itself be a "pure" endeavor. "Rambling, obscure, studded with provocative extra-art quotations, everything he says is open to discussion and dispute," Lippard writes, "but it is also a flying wedge into the heart of the matter."[38]

Gregory Battcock lauds Jill Johnston's achievements from that era in related terms. "So Johnston introduced, by her writings, a new vision for criticism *without apology*, and for criticism claiming its own identification in the world of artistic expressions," Battcock writes. "It is a vision of enormous scope and one that offers considerable potential. . . . It is to Johnston's credit that her work is several things all at once. It is poetry. It is criticism. It is history. It is self-revelation."[39]

The words *impure* and *situation* were both loaded terms in art criticism in the United States in the mid-sixties. Critics including Clement Greenberg and Michael Fried used them to shore up modernist criticism's hegemony against incursions (Fried, for example, lauds the "antisituational character" of Anthony Caro's modernist sculpture).[40] To understand the stakes of Swenson's and Johnston's queer practices historically as specific interventions into a particular critical discourse, it is important to unpack how Greenberg and, especially, Fried invest these terms. In 1965, Greenberg revised and republished his 1960 essay "Modernist Painting," in which he argues that the arts can "save themselves" from "leveling down" and from being "assimilated to entertainment" by becoming purer—that is, by purging all extraneous conventions and effects: "The task of self-criticism became to eliminate from the specific effects of each art any and every effect that might conceivably be borrowed from or by the medium of any other art. Thus would each art be rendered 'pure,' and in its 'purity' find the guarantee of its standards of quality as well as of its independence. 'Purity' meant self-definition, and the enterprise of self-criticism in the arts became one of self-definition with a vengeance."[41]

Around the same time Fried began launching an impassioned defense of Greenberg's formalism. In his essay "Modernist Painting and Formal Criticism," published in *The American Scholar* in 1964, Fried not only defends Greenberg's account of how modernism works but also casts formal criticism as a moral project.[42] In concert with Greenberg, Fried argues that modernist painting has "increasingly divorced itself from the concerns of the society in which it precariously flourishes."[43] And this divorce, according to Fried, is an ethical imperative—in fact, the only ethical possibility available to a serious artist. As art turns inward and away from the concerns of society, the artist takes on "more and more of the denseness, structure, and complexity of moral experience," Fried writes, "that is, of life itself, but life lived as few are inclined to live it: in a state of continuous intellectual and moral alertness." Importantly, Fried extends this moral imperative to the critic. "In this sense," Fried continues, "the formal critic of modernist painting is also a moral critic."[44] The critic's morality, then, according to Fried, inheres in his constant vigilance to purify his aesthetic experience: "to objectify his intuitions with all the intellectual rigor at his command, and to be on his guard against enlisting a formalist rhetoric in the defense of merely private enthusiasms."[45]

Several years later, by the time Fried published "Art and Objecthood" in 1967 in the magazine *Artforum*, this defense of Greenbergian formalism had ossified into dogma. With "Art and Objecthood," Fried inveighs against minimal art, which he calls "literalist art," because, as he writes, "the experience of literalist art is of an object *in a situation*" (emphasis original)—a "situation" that is, by definition, impure. Fried explains, "It is, I think, worth remarking that 'the entire situation' means exactly that: *all* of it—including, it seems, the beholder's *body*. There is nothing within his field of vision—nothing that he takes note of in any way—that, as it were, declares its irrelevance to the situation, and therefore to the experience, in question. On the contrary, for something to be perceived at all is for it to be perceived as part of that situation."[46] For Fried, the minimal art of Donald Judd, Robert Morris, and Tony Smith is particularly pernicious because it masquerades as the real thing, occupying a position "in relation both to modernist painting and to modernist sculpture."[47] Which is to say: it looks and seems like serious modernist art, but, instead of engendering pure aesthetic experience—which Fried calls "presentness" and (even more hyperbolically) "grace"—it engenders an "entire situation" including the "beholder's *body.*" And this, according to Fried, is "antithetical to art."[48] And while the ostensible target of Fried's polemic in "Art and Objecthood" is minimal art, another target lurks just beneath the surface of the text—a target that Fried names explicitly as "faggot sensibility" in a private letter to *Artforum*'s editor Philip Leider dated March 16, 1967. "I keep toying with the idea, crazy as it sounds," Fried writes to Leider, "of having a section in this sculpture-theater essay on how corrupt sensibility is *par excellence* faggot sensibility."[49] So when Fried claims, as he does twice in "Art and Objecthood," that literalist sensibility is "corrupted or perverted by theater,"[50] that claim is—as it turns out—just as homophobic as it sounds. As Christa Noel Robbins argues in her 2018 essay "The Sensibility of Michael Fried": "With the archival evidence of Fried's characterization of minimalist sensibility as 'faggot sensibility' in view, his use, in the published essay, of terms such as 'perverted' and 'corrupt' in order to describe minimalist relations can't help but evoke a similar policing of sexuality through the language of aesthetics."[51]

In an important sense, the fact that Fried names "faggot sensibility" as the antithesis of art and states (jokes?) that "the faggots . . . ought to be kicked out of the arts" in his correspondence with the editor of *Artforum* at the height of that magazine's influence over critical discourse in the United States provides just one more piece of archival evidence (albeit a significant one) for what many scholars and critics have long argued: "Namely, that the history of modernist art in the US is a history of exclusions," as Robbins writes.[52] And not just queer exclusions. In her 2023 book *Deadpan: The Aesthetic of Black Inexpression,* Tina Post elucidates the racist effects of Fried's denigration of literalist art as "dumbly inexhaustible" and merely present. "The charges Fried levels against minimalism bear a great resemblance to discourses that surround the black subject," Post writes. "The aesthetics of minimalist art as Fried sees them are consistent with ways that black subjects have been, and continue to be, described—obstinate, aggressive, secretive, untranscendent, inexpressive, and above all, stubbornly, uncomfortably, theatrically *present.*"[53] Analyzing how artists Adrian Piper, Martin Puryear, David Hammons, and Robert Morris pose "rejoinders to the paradigm of black threat," Post tells a different, vital story of how minimalism matters.[54]

So if, at this point, art history is nonetheless still invested in the story about how "art criticism became a 'serious discipline' in the US only at this time [the 1960s and 1970s], and primarily through the medium of *Artforum*,"[55] as Hal Foster characterizes the situation, then it's time we tell different stories. Which is to say: it is not just a coincidence or accidental oversight that Swenson's and Johnston's queer practices are absent from our mainstream, dominant art historical narratives about the progress of art in the United States in the sixties. Rather, it is a consequence of our continued investment (knowingly and unknowingly) in some of the foundational, and explicitly homophobic, exclusions upon which modernist criticism established its coherence and superiority.

In the sixties, critics including Lippard and Battcock were *already* telling other stories about how Swenson's and Johnston's queer interventions matter. In lauding Swenson's project as an "impure situation" in 1966, Lippard makes a very specific claim about how it cracks the hegemony of modernist criticism in the United States at the very moment when that hegemony was anxiously being shored up and defended against queer incursions. Swenson's practice indeed becomes "a flying wedge into the heart of the matter," as Lippard puts it.

Following Lippard's lead, this book argues that criticism without authority, as both Swenson and Johnston practice it, becomes an impure situation. Impure in the sense of an alternative to modernist criticism, and impure in the sense of a "faggot sensibility" or, let's say instead, a *queer* sensibility—with everything that implies. And "situation" in the exact sense that Fried lambasts: "the entire situation . . . *all* of it," including bodies, sex, messy lives, and perverse desires.

• • •

In their 2011 book *Cruel Optimism*, theorist Lauren Berlant defines "the situation" as "a genre of the emerging event."[56] Berlant explains: "The situation is therefore a genre of social time and practice in which a relation of persons and worlds is sensed to be changing but the rules for habitation and the genres of storytelling about it are unstable, in chaos."[57] When we're in a situation, we often do a thing Berlant calls "genre flailing" in which "we improvise like crazy, where 'like crazy' is a little too non-metaphorical." This might feel like "wobbling" on "freshly uneven ground" or "groping for counter-power wedges in the angry dark," or it might feel like failing—"but even in failure," Berlant writes, "we are the future of the event."[58] Embracing Berlant's sense of the term *situation*, this book traces how Swenson and Johnston flail, wobble, and grope their way through a stretched-out present in which boundaries are unclear and everything feels "unstable, in chaos." The goal of this book is to tell an unfinished story about how Swenson's and Johnston's queer practices become the future of the event—our future.

1

What Do You Say About Homosexuals?

Gene Swenson's *Other* Tradition

He suggested the existence of a "public emotion" already fully identified with the "thing," an idea that turns the interpretive function inside
out. It may be that Gene, whose mental "health" was often in question,
and who was hospitalized at various times during his New York career,
could make these leaps away from the traditionally lineal way of thinking
and therefore understand the basic irrationale of art-making more easily.
LUCY LIPPARD, 1971[1]

In the early sixties, Gene Swenson developed queer alternatives to modernist art and criticism. The art world was hostile to overt displays of homosexuality. New York City was cracking down on queer life, with police raids
on underground film screenings and shrill denunciations of homosexuality
in the media. In a front-page story for *The New York Times* published December 17, 1963, titled "Growth of Overt Homosexuality in City Provokes
Wide Concern," reporter Robert C. Doty proclaims: "The city's most sensitive open secret—the presence of what is probably the greatest homosexual population in the world and its increasing openness—has become
the subject of growing concern of psychiatrists, religious leaders and the
police." Alerting readers that "the city's homosexual community acts as a
lodestar, attracting others from all over the country," Doty cautions against
social acceptance of homosexuality, declaring that it is an illness that "can
be both prevented and cured."[2] A few months later, *Life* magazine followed
suit with a long exposé titled "Homosexuality in America." Warning that the
so-called "gay world" is "actually a sad and often sordid world," reporter
Paul Welch exhorts the nation to quell this "immoral and disruptive force"
before it is too late.[3] In this difficult environment, Swenson worked in a
state of constant negotiation between all the queer things he could do and
say among friends and the need to redact, code, and compromise in public

among art-world institutions—a tense balancing act that he did not sustain for very long.

By the end of 1966, Swenson found himself locked out of the establishment as he took up ranting and raving outside institutions, disrupting parties and panel discussions, sending menacing letters, and picketing alone. Ultimately, he was banned from even entering the Museum of Modern Art. "In his last years, Gene was the 'innocent criminal' of the art world, a role Jill Johnston may have inherited," Lucy Lippard recalls. "He saw the situation with the accuracy 'madness' can painfully exact and 'sanity' rejects out of instinctive self-preservation."[4]

In chapter 2, I analyze how Swenson and Johnston both came to embrace modes of madness and disintegration in the late sixties in response to an untenable situation in which neither the art world nor national politics had caught up to their queer experiences, leaving them at sea. But in this chapter I trace how, for just a few years, Swenson managed to maintain a foothold inside institutional spaces and produce queer work that intersected with mainstream avant-garde artistic practice in the United States, changing it from within. I focus on two key episodes: Swenson's 1963 interview with Andy Warhol and his exhibition and essay *The* Other *Tradition*, which opened at the Institute of Contemporary Art in Philadelphia in January 1966.

Swenson conducted his interview with Warhol as part of a defining series published in *ARTnews* in 1963–64 titled "What Is Pop Art? Answers from 8 Painters."[5] In March 2016, I discovered an unknown cassette-tape recording of Swenson's interview with Warhol in Venice, Italy, where Swenson's friend Henry Martin had been quietly holding on to Swenson's papers, keeping them relatively safe but out of sight with the intention of publishing a posthumous anthology that never came to fruition.[6] On tape, Swenson begins by jokingly asking Warhol, "What do you say about homosexuals?"—to which Warhol replies, "Oh, you have to ask me a leading question." Playing with the genre of interviewing by conducting a forbidden conversation, Swenson records a whole interview with Warhol on the topic of homosexuality. None of that, of course, made it into final transcript published in *ARTnews*, where every mention of homosexuality was excised.

Here I treat the recorded interview as a collaborative work in Swenson's queer oeuvre. I write out portions of the conversation as embellished dialogue (rather than in the more conventional form of a transcript) to extend and slow the reading process and to convey the tone, pace, and tenor of the conversation. Recorded in private but intended for publication in *ARTnews*, the interview provides a vivid demonstration of how queer work in the early sixties was forged through a complicated process of intimate disclosure and witty banter, followed by redaction and encryption. The version of the interview published in 1963 quickly defined Warhol's public persona as "the great idiot savant of our time,"[7] as Hal Foster memorably put it, by introducing pithy, disaffected witticisms like "I want to be a machine" and "I think everybody should like everybody." By contrast, the recorded conversation attests to the collaborative, slow, uneven work of queer world-building. We hear Swenson, Warhol, and their friends reclaim homophobic epithets, test out new ideas, laugh, roughhouse, experiment with drugs, and brag about adventurous sex escapades—all in a tenuous space and time wrested apart from the straight world outside, overshadowed by a perhaps melancholic awareness that everything will have to be coded and erased before it can enter that world.

Like the published version of the interview in *ARTnews*, Swenson's exhibition and essay *The* Other *Tradition* represents a fraught compromise with the establishment. It is the only major project Swenson pulled off inside an art institution. With his exhibition, Swenson argues that formalist critical standards had infected everyone's vision, engendering such widespread myopia that it was hardly possible for critics and curators to see certain works of art at all. The result: an entire *other* tradition of art emerging from Dada and Surrealism occluded from view, completely "overlooked or neglected by art historians" who focus only on the "abstract-formal-Cubist tradition in modern art" to the exclusion of everything else.[8] With *The* Other *Tradition*, Swenson not only rewrites the history of modern art but also proposes new ways to understand subjectivity and sexuality in the present.

However, throughout the essay, Swenson insists that it is a partial version of an unrealized project. He stresses that the text was "written with the 'ideal' exhibition in mind, clearly not possible."[9] But Swenson never wrote a more complete version of the essay, nor did he actually plan an "ideal" exhibition. Nonetheless, *The* Other *Tradition* paved the way for subsequent critical reevaluations of Surrealism, subjectivity, and sexuality in art of the sixties. "Gene Swenson introduced Surrealism into the discourse of avant-garde art in a show titled 'The *Other* Tradition,'" critic Irving Sandler recalls, attesting to the importance of Swenson's offbeat intervention. "He even anticipated Lucy Lippard's 'Eccentric Abstraction' show of 1966."[10]

•   •   •

In this chapter, I reorient the story of what happened to art in New York City in the early sixties around Swenson's queer practices by lingering on just a few archival objects: a scratchy cassette-tape recording, damaged contact sheets, hand-annotated drafts, and a piecemeal essay. In so doing, I argue for a different understanding of what constitutes an artistic practice—an understanding that focuses on provisional and ancillary things. If, by necessity, queer work intended for public institutions in the early sixties was compromised, coded, and redacted, then it is necessary to look elsewhere for evidence of the most ardent and poignant queer practices and to develop new ways of valuing objects that may seem rough, incoherent, or incomplete. This chapter thus makes a specific argument about the importance of Swenson's particular queer intervention. At the same time, it is also an argument for what it means to do queer art history. It is an argument for scouring archives to piece together a queer story from fragile objects that are not authored, intentional, or finished in any conventional sense of those terms. It is an argument for lingering with such objects and for valuing them differently.[11]

Do You Think Pop Art's Queer?

Fall 1963

Swenson and Warhol, along with Gerard Malanga (Warhol's new studio assistant) and another friend named John, gather around a tape recorder.[12] They are likely at Warhol's studio in an old firehouse on East 87th Street, a few months before Warhol's move in January 1964 to the space that would become his famous, foil-encrusted Factory. The interview gets off to a clumsy start, as Swenson begins by saying "Now we have to start talking again"— apparently the machine was not recording when they started talking the first time.

Swenson likely recorded this interview on a reel-to-reel machine, a year before Philips introduced the Norelco Carry-Corder—the first mass-produced portable, compact cassette-tape recorder—to the American market. So at the time of this interview, Warhol had not yet acquired his first tape recorder, a machine he would become so intimately attached to that he called it his "wife." Nor had Warhol invented the breathless, error-prone, type-up-everything transcription methods that came to define later projects like *a: A Novel* (1968). By the mid-sixties, Warhol would master the art of exploiting how the tape recorder "doesn't make many choices about what is more and less important as it listens"—as scholar Gustavus Stadler writes in an essay elaborating Warhol's non-hierarchical, "queer ways of listening."[13] But here, Swenson guides Warhol through the possibilities of an emergent medium. Their performance for the tape recorder is tentative and uneven, as he and Warhol, along with Malanga and John, feel their way through how to talk to each other in the machine's presence and how self-consciously (or not) to perform the roles of interviewer and interviewee.

• • •

The tape machine clicks on, initiating a din of humming static. Swenson's voice comes on first.

"Now we have to start talking again," he says. "What do you say about homosexuals?"

"Oh, you have to ask me a leading question," Warhol replies softly, with a demure reticence that would soon become a signature trait of his interviewing style.

"Do you know a lot of closet queens who are homosexuals who are Abstract Expressionists?" Swenson asks, struggling to finish the question through barely suppressed laughter.

"Yes," Warhol says while Swenson laughs, "uhhhhh . . ."

"Who are they? Who are these girls?" Malanga asks loudly in a thick Bronx accent. "Michelle Goldberg?" he suggests cheekily, punning on the name of Abstract Expressionist painter Michael Goldberg.

"Oh really! How fantastic," Warhol says. "Who else?"

"Norma Bluhm," Malanga proposes, making fun of the butch Abstract Expressionist painter Norman Bluhm.[14]

"Ivan Karp!" Swenson adds, while everyone cracks up.

"Eva Karp, that is," Malanga playfully corrects him. "Eva Karp. How 'bout, uh . . . no . . . uh . . . think . . ."

"You'd have hours of content," Swenson jokes.

"Yeah," Warhol replies.

"Is that what Abstract Expressionism is all about?" Swenson asks with a chuckle. Then he turns serious. "They're moralists, you know, they really are," he says. "It's inconceivable to me that somebody would say about a painter that he's a homosexual, you know, as if it were a kind of criticism. You know, just inconceivable, as . . . as . . ."

At which point Warhol interjects: "I think the whole interview on me should be just on homosexuality."

•   •   •

That, of course, is not how things turned out. When the edited transcript of the interview appeared in the November 1963 edition of *ARTnews*, every mention of homosexuality had been expunged. Swenson's petty joke about which macho, second-generation Abstract Expressionist painters are actually "closet queens who are homosexuals," followed by his dismay that these same painters have real power to denigrate gay artists like Swenson and Warhol simply by calling them "homosexual" in public, sets the tone for the interview—as campy snark segues to sadness and serious insight. By redeploying the terms "homosexual" and "closet queens" in private to mock those who wield these words against them in public, Swenson, Warhol, and their friends lay claim to these epithets and use them subversively.

Writing in 1993 for the inaugural issue of the academic journal *Gay and Lesbian Quarterly*, thirty years after this interview, Judith Butler argues for the importance of claiming terms like "queer," "gay," and "lesbian" as an oppositional strategy that does not rid these words of their shaming stigma but rather redeploys that stigma as a site of collective defiance. Butler explains, "Sometimes the very term that would annihilate us becomes the site of resistance. . . . Paradoxically, but also with great promise, the subject who is 'queered' into public discourse through homophobic interpellations of various kinds *takes up* or *cites* that very term as the discursive basis for an opposition."[15] On tape, we hear this process unfold organically, in real time in 1963, as Warhol responds to Swenson's provocations by insisting that his whole interview should be "just on homosexuality"—taking up the term in order to articulate an oppositional account of how his art is, in fact, about homosexuality. Remarkably, this occurs more than two decades before scholars would begin to reclaim words like "queer" in institutional spaces and six years before the Stonewall Riots of June 1969 would launch the Gay Liberation Movement into wider visibility. Which is to say, before a social, political, academic, or artistic framework existed for queers to band together *publicly* in New York City to claim terms like "homosexual" as their own in the streets or in newspapers and magazines, Swenson, Warhol, and their friends did it in private—in the context of a recording that, as we will hear, Swenson never intended to publish unredacted (though, notably, he did preserve the recording for posterity, even transferring it to a compact cassette tape sometime in the mid- or late sixties).

The recording thus presents an opportunity to witness how Swenson, Warhol, and their friends redeploy homophobic epithets behind closed doors to articulate queer ways of making art in opposition to a repressive straight world. And, moreover, it presents a rare opportunity to trace exactly which words had to get redacted and coded to create a very different— laconic, shy, disaffected, and mysterious—Warholian persona for public consumption. As art historian Gavin Butt argues: "It is Warhol's experience of being subjected to malicious art-world gossip about his 'private' life, and in particular his homosexuality which pave the way for the construction of the now familiar Warholian persona of postmodern lore." Around 1963, Warhol made "a decidedly *queer* move," as Butt puts it, "by embracing and renegotiating his alienated and effete image as a defining strategy of his postmodern persona building."[16] The tape recording thus furnishes revelatory evidence for how this process of "postmodern persona building" transpired in and out of public view. It reveals how, in private, Warhol and Swenson redeploy the shaming interpellations "homosexual" and "queen" (and, later in the interview, "queer") and then how, in public, all of those words were sublimated in order to present a palatable version of Warhol—which is to say, the familiar effete, impassive "Warholian persona of postmodern lore."

But the recording does more than that: It also attests to Swenson's importance at this pivotal moment in establishing the critical discourse for postmodern artistic practice in the sixties. The recording reveals the queer origins of that discourse and Swenson's role in orchestrating the to-and-fro process at its heart: a process of eliciting queer disclosures, redacting them, and replacing them with a public discourse full of gaps and distancing irony. The recording also reveals a complicated, perhaps fraught, joy at the core of all this, with its laughter and joking banter—a certain thrill involved in redeploying homophobic epithets to imagine a queer world and then a certain satisfaction in pulling one over on a straight public.

Lippard notes that Swenson "was the first person I heard talk intelligently about Warhol, who was a great influence on him. His interviews on Pop Art in *ARTnews* are *the* source material for the movement. The artists trusted him."[17] So it is worth asking why the artists trusted Swenson. And it is *not* because they trusted he would transcribe every word faithfully—indeed, Swenson often explains on tape that he's not going to "copy it all down" (as we'll see from this recording). Rather, I think it is more accurate to say they trusted Swenson knew how to play the game: that he knew how to conduct a free-flowing interview on tape and construct from it a "postmodern persona" for public consumption. That trust is particularly important in the case of Warhol, as it was premised on queer comradery: a shared sense that they were in it, and in on it, together. Warhol reflects this sense of queer intimacy in a series of sensuous line drawings he made around the time of the interview of Swenson seated at his typewriter, in elegant profile, and zoomed in on his lips (fig. 1.1).

• • •

After Warhol proclaims on tape that his "whole interview" should be "just on homosexuality," John and Malanga jump in to imagine, on the fly, what form a whole interview on homosexuality could take.

"Okay, well then let's start," John says. "What do you know about homosexuals?" he asks sarcastically, adopting the tone of a talk show host. "Andy, have you ever met a homosexual?"

"Does your can represent a penis?" Malanga follows up, laughing.

"No it can't be like that," Warhol responds. Then he demurs, "No, it has to be on a different, a kind of different . . . no, it should be a different . . . it should be a different, differently than you know just sort of like, you know, sorta . . ."

"Different than direct?" Swenson interjects.

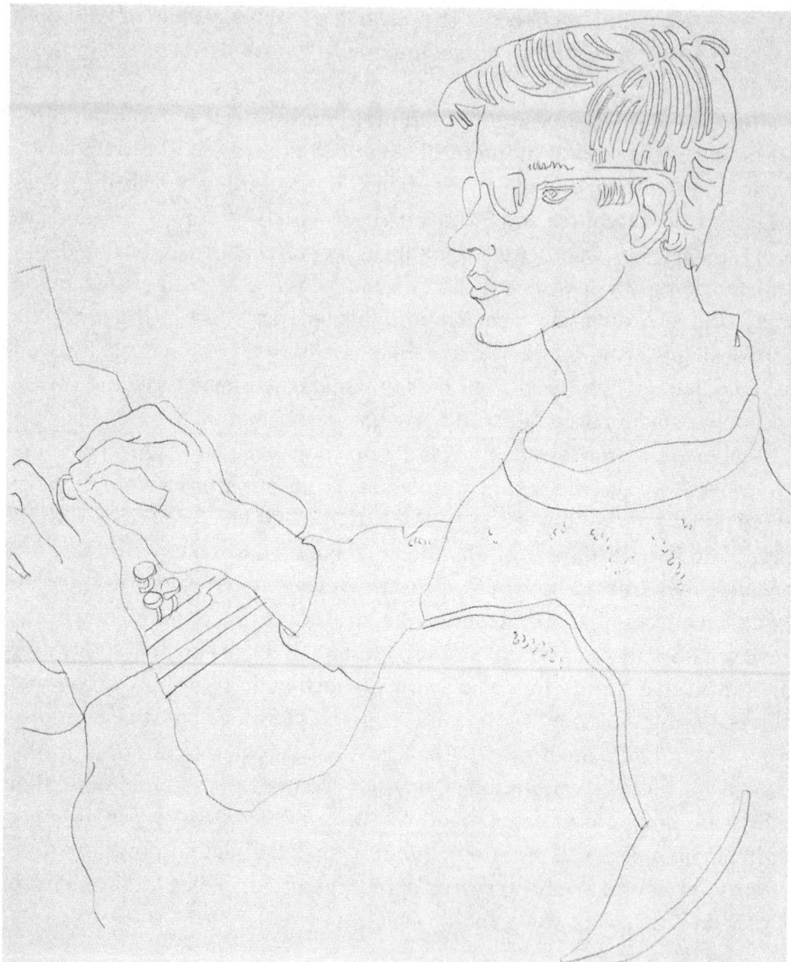

Figure 1.1 Andy Warhol, drawings of Gene Swenson, c. 1962. Ballpoint pen, wove paper, 16¹⁵⁄₁₆ × 13⅞ in. Spencer Museum of Art, University of Kansas (1970.0151.a, 1970.0151.b, 1970.0151.c). Gift from the Gene Swenson Collection. © 2025 The Andy Warhol Foundation for the Visual Arts, Inc. / Licensed by Artists Rights Society (ARS), New York.

"Yeah," Warhol responds.

"Like, uh, when you were drawing shoes, did you want to draw women's shoes?" Swenson asks, also jokingly adopting the faux-serious tone of a reporter.

"Yes," Warhol says, playing along.

"Why did you like to draw women's shoes?" Swenson follows up, laughing. "Did you see yourself being put under the heel of one of them?"

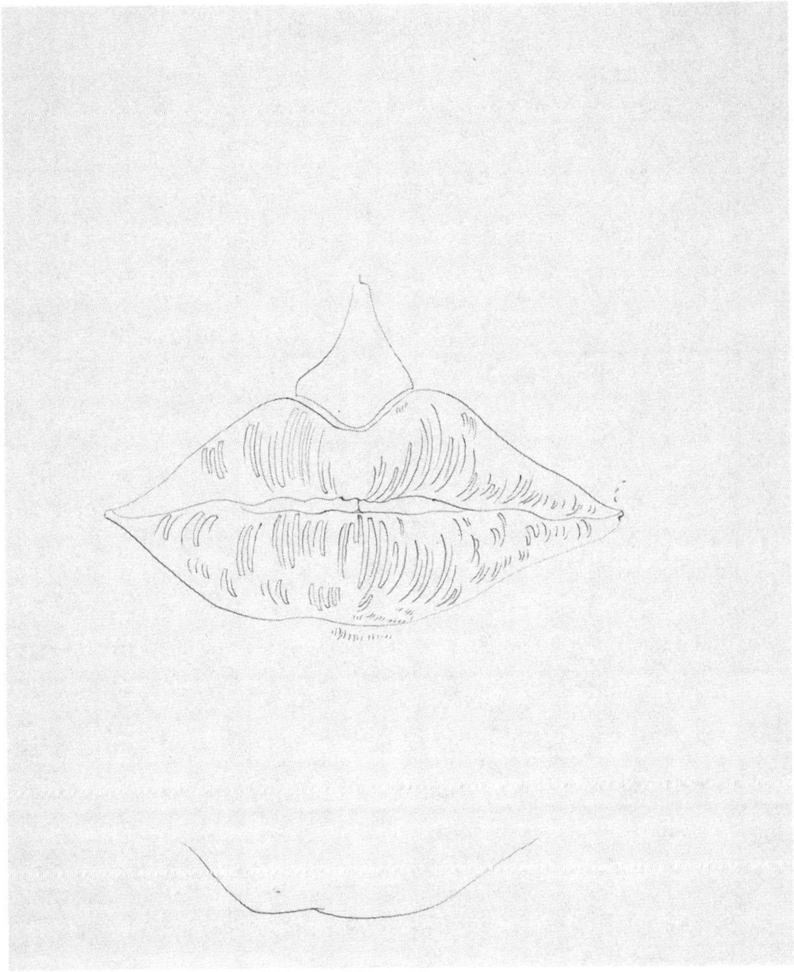

Figure 1.1 (*continued*)

"Oh, yes!" Warhol responds. As they continue to joke around, Warhol pauses and then turns earnest. "No it can't be like that, can it?" he asks. "Well it has to be something like the idea that, uh, uh . . ." Warhol pauses, thinking as he speaks. ". . . That all Pop artists aren't homosexual. And it really doesn't . . . you know . . . and everybody should be a machine, and everybody should be, uh, like . . ."

"I don't understand the business about . . ." Swenson cuts in, "if all Pop artists are not homosexual, what does this have to do with being a machine?"

"Well, I think everybody should like everybody," Warhol answers.

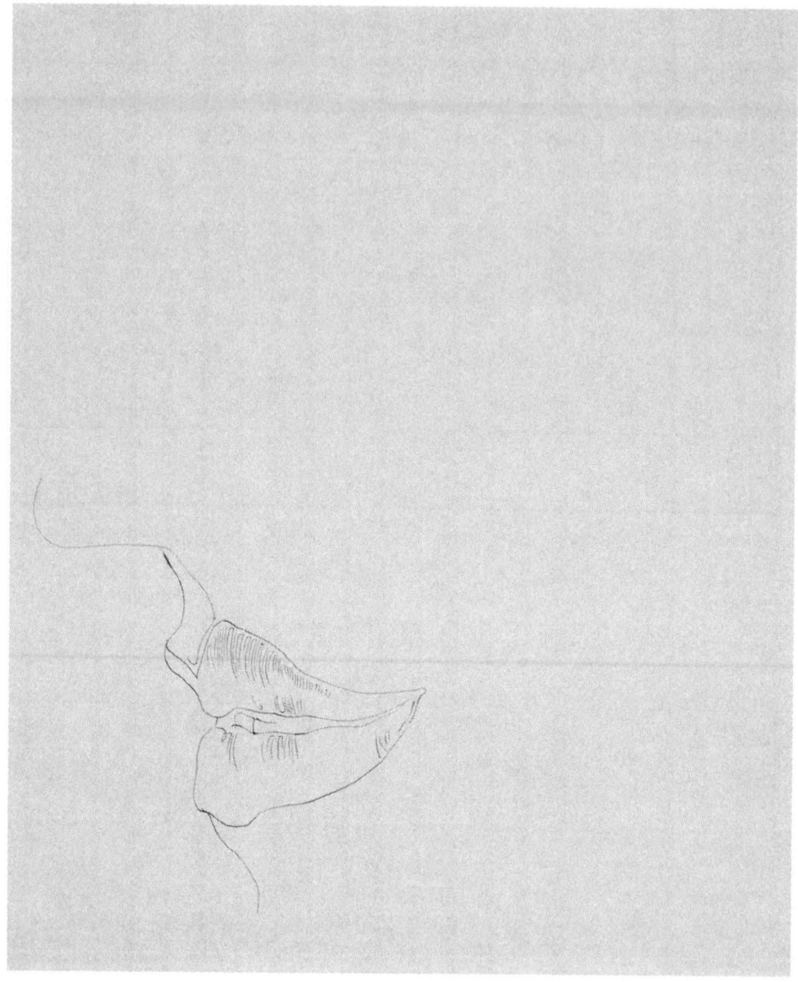

Figure 1.1 (*continued*)

"You mean you should like both men and women?" Swenson asks.

"Yeah," Warhol says.

"Yeah? Sexually and in every other way?"

"Yeah," Warhol says.

"And that's what Pop Art's about?"

"Yeah, it's liking things," Warhol says.

"And liking things is being like a machine?"

"Yeah," Warhol says. "Well, because you do the same thing every time. You do the same thing over and over again. And you do the same . . ."

"You mean sex?" Swenson interrupts.

"Yeah, and everything you do," Warhol responds.

"Without any discrimination?" John chimes in to ask.

"Yeah," Warhol says again. "And you use things up, like, you use people up."

"And you approve of it?" Swenson asks.

"Yes," Warhol responds with a pause and then trails off. "Because it's all a fantasy . . ."

. . .

As it was printed in the November 1963 edition of *ARTnews*, and in every subsequent anthology and textbook, the exchange above is cut up so it reads:

I think everybody should be a machine.

I think everybody should like everybody.

Is that what Pop Art is all about?

Yes. It's liking things.

And liking things is like being a machine?

Yes, because you do the same thing every time. You do it over and over again.

And you approve of that?

Yes, because it's all fantasy.[18]

. . .

When Warhol says on tape "because it's all a fantasy," the word "it" points back to the idea that he approves of "us[ing] people up" in the context of a fantasy about a world where everybody can "like both men and women," as Swenson says, "sexually and in every other way." Warhol thus approves of consuming people and things until they are used up—men, women, and commodities alike—via "sex" (as Swenson says) and "everything you do" (as Warhol adds)—because "it's all a fantasy." And *this* fantasy of erotic, promiscuous queer consumption—with its dark undercurrent of using people up—is, as Warhol affirms, "what Pop Art's about." Pop Art is about *everybody*'s dark queer fantasies as expressed everywhere in the culture. If you want proof, Warhol suggests with his art, just look around at all the things *you* like and consume over and over again: men *and* women, shiny fetishy things, disasters, and grisly death. All at the same time, without any apparent contradiction. In the months leading up to and following this interview, Warhol produced hundreds of silk-screened repetitions of sex icons, both men and women, including Troy Donahue, Elvis Presley, Marilyn Monroe, and Liz Taylor; commodities including cars, shoes, Coca-Cola bottles, and Campbell's soup cans; and the harrowing aftermaths of people being "used up" via wrecked cars and suicides.

In the redacted version of this exchange that Swenson published in

ARTnews, all of the queer content is stripped away. Rather than Pop Art being about a dark, erotic *queer* fantasy of liking men and women, in the published interview Swenson construes Warhol as saying, more simply: Pop Art is about a fantasy of liking everybody and everything like a machine, over and over again. In their banter on tape, Swenson says it all explicitly: the culture is full of repressed queer desire (as Swenson jokes, just among the Abstract Expressionists there are enough "closet queens who are homosexuals" to provide "hours of content"), and Warhol's Pop Art is about the explicit, often dark, manifestation of all that closeted, repressed queer desire everywhere in the culture, via the queer things everyone consumes over and over—that is, "men and women . . . sexually and in every other way." In the published interview, all that text becomes seemingly unstated (though, as we now know, actually redacted) subtext. The public Warhol who says, flatly, "I think everybody should be a machine. I think everybody should like everybody," becomes a blank screen or mirror in which everybody can see their own (perhaps secret, perhaps unacknowledged) queer desires reflected back to them. And for the rest of his life and career after this interview, Warhol adopts this strategic, blank "postmodern persona" as the hallmark of everything he would do, say, and make. After the publication of Swenson's redacted 1963 interview, Warhol never looked back: he leaned into his role as a blank mirror and quickly mastered the form of the interview as his own strategy of postmodern persona building. As Roland Barthes would put it in 1980, in reference to Warhol's influence: "The Pop artist does not stand *behind* his work, and he himself has no depth: he is merely the surface of his pictures."[19] Which is right. And what we learn from the recording is just how explicitly this Warholian postmodern strategy grew out of a queer necessity to redact and code homosexual things, under Swenson's guiding influence.

•   •   •

No paper trail survives to answer the question of how exactly the editorial decision-making transpired at *ARTnews*.[20] In a later recorded conversation with artist Joe Raffaele from 1966, Swenson explains (somewhat elliptically) that Thomas Hess, executive editor at *ARTnews*, insisted upon certain redactions.[21]

"I asked Tom Hess if we couldn't, I mean, you know, like . . . you see, in the interview I did with Andy, he cut out all those words," Swenson says on tape to Raffaele.

"And is he going to do it again?" Raffaele asks.

"Well I don't know," Swenson replies. "But I'll fight for it this time."[22]

In the sixties, Hess had a troublesome reputation among artists and critics for his interventionist editorial tactics. For example, in an unpublished transcript of a 1968 interview, Lippard says to artist Donald Judd: "I don't understand how people can write for them [*ARTnews*] when that's what they do. I mean Scott Burton said Gene Swenson—of course you don't mess with Gene Swenson, but in those days you could mess with him a little more—they said that Hess would completely change the meaning of a thing."[23] But even if it was the case that Swenson left to Hess some of the dirty work of censoring homosexual content, it seems that Swenson knew what he was doing and worked strategically within the limitations imposed upon him (the published interview is, in a sense, just too good to be the product of a haphazard bowdlerization). And more to the point, Swenson never publicly corrected the record, even though he had ample opportunity to do so. For example, in an unpublished draft of a 1965 lecture Swenson explains: "Warhol's statement that 'I want to be a machine' has misled many people. Either they do not know or do not understand history, let alone Warhol's context."[24] But, tellingly, Swenson does not provide that context, nor does he fill in the redacted queer content. In fact, while conducting the interview, Swenson tells Warhol explicitly that he does *not* intend to transcribe their discussion of homosexuality, even joking that he could use the tape as blackmail.

• • •

About twelve minutes into the conversation, Warhol pauses to ask, "Is this still going on?"

"Yeah," Swenson says.

"We didn't say anything, Gene, did we?" Warhol asks.

"Well, I'm not going to copy it all down," Swenson replies. "But I'll keep the tape," he says with a cackle, "and use it against all of ya!"

"But, I think it's, uh . . ." Warhol says tentatively. "I think you could really . . . I, I would want that on my interview, you know that. You know what we were talking about . . ."

"What?" Swenson asks.

"You know, the homosexuality, and . . . and . . ."

"You want it in your interview?" Swenson asks.

"Yeah," Warhol says. "But it should be on somebody else's too, just to, uh . . ."

"Oldenburg," Swenson suggests. "Who would be the best one?"

"Uh, Rosenquist," Warhol responds.

"He's too gentle!" Malanga interjects.

"Yeah, he's so gentle," Warhol agrees. "No, no, he's just . . . no, I mean, he's sweet."

"Do you think Pop Art's queer?" Swenson interrupts, while cracking up. "I'll ask Rosenquist that."

"Yesssssss," Warhol says, drawing out the word. "That would be fantastic! Oh, that's really marvelous," he adds. "And Jim Dine too, just to get his reaction."

"No, Bob Indiana!" Malanga interjects. "Awww, are you kidding me!"

"No, well you can't do it on everyone's," Warhol says.

"No, but Bob Indiana should have that question asked to him," Malanga replies, as everyone else laughs, "because he'd go, 'Ooooh, no . . . that doesn't make sense' . . ."

"Is he like that?" Swenson asks.

"Yeah," Malanga replies. "He came to my poetry reading wearing a knit t-shirt, a net t-shirt, a t-shirt, but it's a net."

"Oh I like Bob," Warhol interjects.

"He went into this big thing about how coooool it was to wear it," Malanga continues, drawing out the word "cool" to make fun of Robert Indiana's (very gay but apparently not very cool) fashion sense.

• • •

It is startling to hear the question "Do you think Pop Art's queer?" asked in 1963 with such terse clarity. Startling because that question was never posed in any published criticism or writing from the early sixties. And that, of course, is why it makes for a funny, if biting, inside joke. These friends share knowledge that Warhol's Pop Art really *is* about queer desire, and they also know that it implicates "everybody," as Warhol says—including the other Pop artists, even though (or, especially if) they would be freaked out by the question. As Warhol put it a few minutes earlier in the conversation: "Well it has to be something like the idea that, uh, uh . . . all Pop artists aren't homosexual. And it really doesn't . . . you know . . ." Which is to say (and to fill in the missing word): it really doesn't *matter*. Like a funhouse mirror, Warhol's Pop Art reflects *everybody*'s (perhaps repressed) queer fantasies via distorted, garishly colored, nightmarishly repeated versions of the things and people everybody consumes over and over again all the time via "sex" and "everything you do." It doesn't matter, then, whether a person will ever get hailed in public by the shaming interpellation "homosexual" or whether a person will ever take up that term as an oppositional strategy to use it as their own. It therefore makes sense that a "sweet" artist like Rosenquist *and* a straight artist like Dine *and* a perhaps charmingly naïve gay artist like Indiana (with his "cool" fishnet shirt) *all* have the capacity to be riled or even repulsed by the question "Do you think Pop Art's queer?," because they all have the potential to see themselves and their art reflected in it—whether they like it or not. As Jonathan Flatley theorizes: "Warhol's liking is queer, and queer as distinct from gay," because it does *not* rely on a "homo/hetero opposition."[25] And, as Flatley notes, "the indispensable starting point for thinking about Warhol's liking is his well-known 1963 interview with Gene Swenson."[26]

What we learn from the recording, then, is just how central Swenson was to the endeavor of developing the discourse about Pop Art as a postmodern practice with, as we have seen, queer fantasy, redaction, and distancing irony at its core. If, as Lippard notes, Warhol was "a great influence" on Swenson, then I argue that Swenson was also a great influence on Warhol—which we hear very clearly on tape as Warhol and Swenson switch roles, and Warhol begins peppering Swenson with questions about his involvement with sadomasochism.

Feelings Are Things

About half an hour into the interview, Swenson, Warhol, Malanga, and John get off topic and begin trading stories about smoking marijuana, doing poppers, and having all sorts of edgy sex.

• • •

"I thought poppers were amphetamine," Warhol says, a bit confused.

"No, amyl nitrate is poppers," Malanga explains.

"You've had it during sex?" Swenson asks.

"Near climax, I'd break one open," Malanga boasts, while the others hoot and laugh. "You come twice as much, I think."

"Well, if you're a masochist, it's wild," Swenson says, adding, "you know, I've been all tied up."

"What do you get beat up for?" Warhol asks. "And it doesn't hurt?"

"I mean, it's like beau-ti-ful!" Swenson responds, exaggerating each syllable in the word.

"Oh, but doesn't it hurt afterwards?" Warhol asks.

"Oh, I don't know," Swenson says.

"Huh? No?" Warhol replies. "But I mean, uh, being a sadist and being beaten and stuff, if you can really do it well, it really doesn't hurt, does it? I mean, it's just the idea that, you know . . ."

"It hurts," Swenson says.

"It does, really? Oh. I thought it really wouldn't hurt," Warhol says. "It really hurts?"

"It really hurts," Swenson affirms.

"But how long can you take it for?" Warhol asks. "Five minutes? Two seconds?"

"Well, if you're tied up there's nothing you can do," Swenson replies.

"And it goes on for hours?"

"It can," Swenson says, with a chuckle.

"Are you serious, Gene?" Warhol asks.

"Andy, why are you asking such questions?" Malanga interrupts. "You know you'll never become a sadist."

"I'm asking for my new paintings," Warhol replies.

Continuing on, Swenson claims that he's quit S&M recently (though evidence from his journals suggests that didn't last very long). "I got involved in London in a way that was almost, that was heading toward it going all the way," Swenson says. "And I didn't like it, I didn't like it."

"What was going all the way?" Warhol asks.

"I mean, I mean like, it might not have ended in, you know, in sort of, I don't know whether you'd call it murder or suicide," Swenson explains slowly. "But, but there was someone who wanted to do it, I mean, who wanted to push it as far as it would go. And I sort of, except that I saw something happening, and, you know, something happened inside of me. One time I went to this one session where things were going really violent. And I suddenly realized that my face was all twisted up. And my insides were all twisted up. And everything about me was twisted up. And it was so ugly. I mean, you know, just so ugly."

"Was it just, uh, a scene?" Warhol asks. "Or was it, you know, somebody doing it to somebody else?"

"Somebody doing it to somebody else," Swenson replies. "But it was like those horrible pictures in the newspapers," he continues haltingly, "because they don't really . . . they don't . . . they're not as effective, it seems to me, as . . . I mean, you know, the pictures you use are not ugly in the same . . . the subject matter may be ugly but the pictures are not ugly. Why don't you use ugly pictures?"

"Well, uh, will you find me some?" Warhol responds.

"They're in the newspapers all the time," Swenson says.

"Well, I use some of those."

"But you wouldn't use ones like the ones that are in *This Week*, would you, of that burned baby?" Swenson asks.

"Oh yeah, yeah, I plan to use all those," Warhol says tentatively. "But they don't, you know, they don't come out that way. They just don't . . ."

"They just don't really have any effect, because they're so horrible, it seems to me," Swenson suggests.

"Yeah," Warhol says. "That's why I feel these paintings that I do . . . you do them over so many times, there really is no effect."

• • •

In the context of the published interview, this entire exchange is truncated into a sentence uttered by Warhol: "But when you see a gruesome picture over and over again, it doesn't really have any effect."[27]

. . .

Why is Warhol so curious about Swenson's desire to get "beat up" during sex and to watch others suffer? In the end, what does Swenson's sadomasochistic sex experience have to do with Warhol's Death in America silk screen paintings (as he refers to them later in the interview)? When Warhol says to Malanga, "I'm asking for my new paintings," he lays his cards on the table. Adopting the role of interviewer, Warhol seeks information about Swenson's sadomasochism ostensibly because he is curious about how Swenson's avowed desire to get off on witnessing and experiencing suffering might relate to everybody's everyday desires to witness "horrible" pictures of death and suicide over and over again in tabloids and on TV. Following up on Warhol's curiosity, Swenson makes this connection explicit. "Why don't you use ugly pictures?" he asks Warhol, right after disclosing how "ugly" it was to witness a "really violent" S&M session on the brink of murder or suicide. Warhol responds by asking Swenson to find "ugly pictures" for him—which points to the key difference between Warhol and Swenson. This exchange sets them up as foils for one another, throwing into sharp relief differences between their respective queer commitments and ways of being in the world.

Warhol analyzes things from a distanced remove. Attracted to "the open sores of American political life," as art historian Thomas Crow memorably put it, Warhol holds a mirror up to everybody's desires.[28] But Warhol's art is not prescriptive. Nor is he in the business of explaining to anybody how their desire to look at horrible pictures in tabloids might not actually be so different from, say, Swenson's avowed sadistic queer desire to watch other men get beat up during sex. He's just interested in how it *might* be and then leaves the rest up to you. In his art and (as we've just seen) on tape, Warhol opens space for other people to fill in the blanks by projecting their own responses and, oftentimes, to sit with their discomfort in doing so. As Flatley theorizes: "Warhol's work sought not to produce a *specific* affective response so much as to clear the space for *any* affect to occur"—a strategy that "is also not unlike the one employed by a psychoanalyst."[29] And throughout his career, Warhol adopted various tools and accoutrements to maintain this (psycho)analytic distance, including silk screens, film cameras, and, perhaps most significantly, his "wife": the Norelco cassette-tape recorder he acquired in 1964.

Swenson, on the other hand, analyzes things from inside the fray, without analytic distance. In response to Warhol's incredulity that "being a sadist and being beaten and stuff" really hurts, Swenson describes how intense it feels to be in the thick of it—which, perhaps unexpectedly, engenders a state of confusion about *what* he's actually feeling. "My face was all twisted up," Swenson shares. "And my insides were all twisted up. And everything about me was twisted up. And it was so ugly. I mean, you know, just so ugly." It is unclear whether the "it" of Swenson's sentence refers to the violent S&M session he witnessed or rather his tangled confusion as he "saw something happening, and, you know, something happened inside of me." Which is the point. Swenson uses the word "ugly" to describe how witnessing something horrible causes an unsettling feeling of being "all twisted up" inside and outside. "Ugly" points to the confusing space between "I saw something happening" and "something happened inside of me." And for several years after the interview, this question of confusion over a feeling's subjective or objective status (whether a feeling occurs inside or outside the so-called individual) becomes a central preoccupation not just of Swenson's sex life but also of his critical practice.[30] From 1963 through 1966, Swenson devotes much of his critical attention to analyzing how feelings are not simply internal responses to external conditions. Rather, as Swenson puts it over and over: "Feelings are things."[31]

A few months after his interview with Warhol, Swenson authored a cryptic, provocative flyer (fig. 1.2) to advertise Warhol's second solo exhibition in April 1964 at the Stable Gallery, where Warhol filled the gallery with wooden replicas of Brillo, Heinz, and Campbell's boxes. On the flyer, a full-bleed, diaphanous photo of an impassive, tuxedo-clad Warhol looms above a short but dense essay by Swenson titled "The Personality of the Artist"—an ironic title to convey how the artist's "personality" is something assembled in public, rather than something innate that emanates from within. Swenson writes: "'I want to be a machine,' the painter has said, misleading many; his work does suppress those symptoms of modern art—personality and creativity—which have been sanctified to the point of blasphemy." Swenson then proclaims that "the paintings and boxes of Warhol *are* feelings."[32]

Swenson elaborates this point in a lecture also titled "The Personality of the Artist," delivered on the occasion of Warhol's first solo museum exhibition, which opened on October 8, 1965, at the Institute of Contemporary Art (ICA) in Philadelphia. A hand-annotated draft of the lecture is preserved among Swenson's papers (fig. 1.3). In it, Swenson explains how Warhol's art points to a new "post-Freudian" sensibility: "The possibility of a kind of new psychology based on public attitudes and even cliches," Swenson proclaims, "with a different definition of objectivity as well."[33] Older but still ingrained modernist notions of creativity and originality—those "sanctified to the point of blasphemy"—presume a model of selfhood based on a separation between inside and outside: a model where an individual artist feels

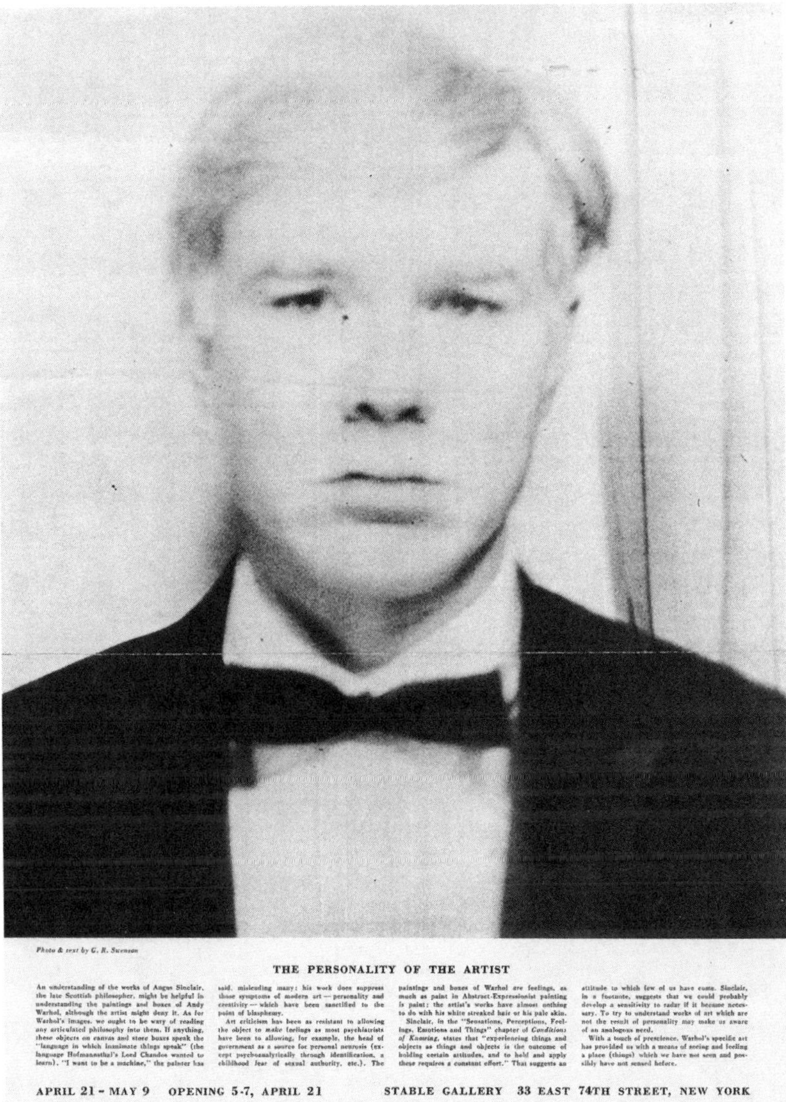

Figure 1.2 *The Personality of the Artist*, flyer advertising Andy Warhol's Stable Gallery exhibition, April 21–May 9, 1964. Photo and text by G. R. (Gene) Swenson. Smithsonian Library and Archives, Washington, DC.

things internally and then projects his emotions outward onto the canvas as a kind of cathartic release. As Swenson explains, by way of critiquing such beliefs: "It is said that the abstract patterns of the inner life of the artist are the only things that are important. . . . [A]bstract art tries to be an object which we can equate with the private feelings of the artist, the canvas being

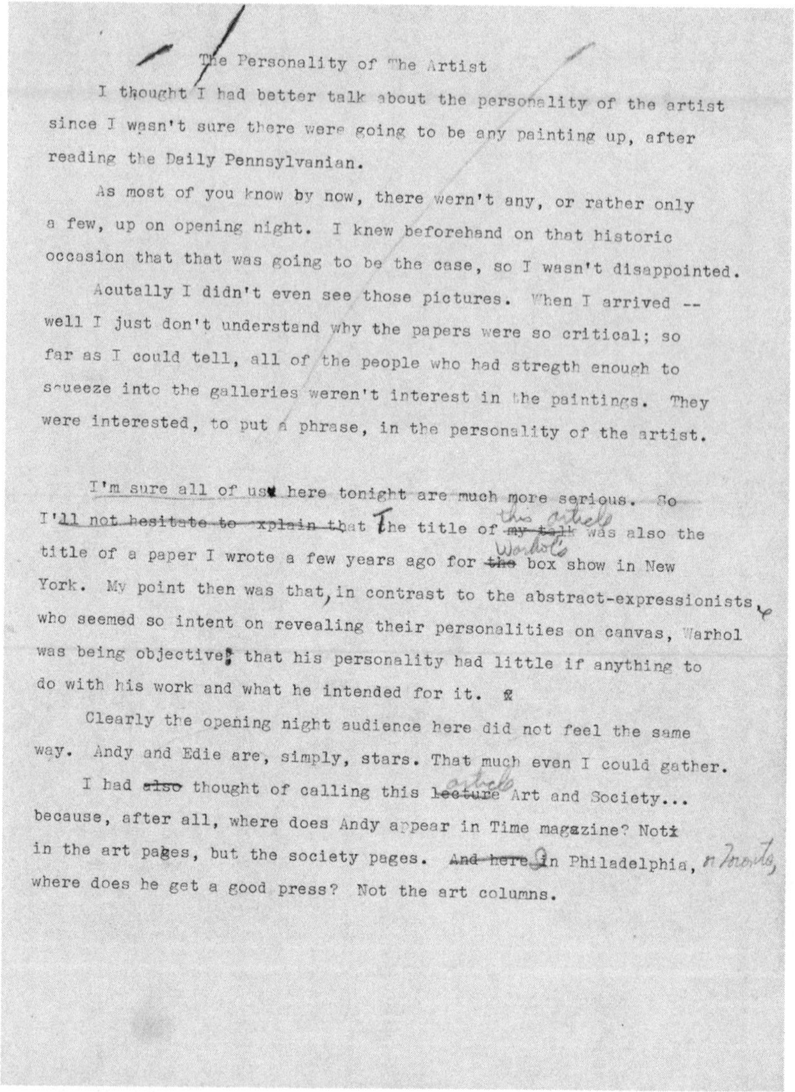

The Personality of The Artist

I thought I had better talk about the personality of the artist since I wasn't sure there were going to be any painting up, after reading the Daily Pennsylvanian.

As most of you know by now, there wern't any, or rather only a few, up on opening night. I knew beforehand on that historic occasion that that was going to be the case, so I wasn't disappointed.

Acutally I didn't even see those pictures. When I arrived -- well I just don't understand why the papers were so critical; so far as I could tell, all of the people who had stregth enough to squeeze into the galleries weren't interest in the paintings. They were interested, to put a phrase, in the personality of the artist.

I'm sure all of us here tonight are much more serious. So I'll not hesitate to xplain that the title of my talk was also the title of a paper I wrote a few years ago for the box show in New York. My point then was that, in contrast to the abstract-expressionists, who seemed so intent on revealing their personalities on canvas, Warhol was being objective; that his personality had little if anything to do with his work and what he intended for it.

Clearly the opening night audience here did not feel the same way. Andy and Edie are, simply, stars. That much even I could gather.

I had also thought of calling this lecture Art and Society... because, after all, where does Andy appear in Time magazine? Not in the art pages, but the society pages. And here in Philadelphia, where does he get a good press? Not the art columns.

Figure 1.3 Gene Swenson, "The Personality of the Artist," 1965. Unpublished manuscript draft. Gene Swenson papers, 1950–1969, Archives of American Art, Smithsonian Institution, Washington, DC.

the arena on which these private feelings are acted out." Warhol's art, by stark contrast, points toward an entirely different model of subjectivity—or, really, "objectivity," as Swenson calls it—appropriate to life in the sixties, where feelings are things that are *already* external, public, and shared. "Warhol presents objects which, in a sense, we can equate with public, communal feelings," Swenson declares. Warhol's paintings "are mirrors of what happens to us without our knowing or realizing it," he continues. "In a way they might be said to objectify experience, turn feelings into things."[34] And, for Swenson, this amounts to a huge paradigm shift that opens exciting possibilities for reimaging the intimacy of everyday life.

A Post-Freudian Situation

January 27, 1966

Swenson's exhibition *The* Other *Tradition* opens at the ICA Philadelphia, following on the heels of Warhol's solo show there, building on its success and notoriety. Photos from the opening document a fashionable soiree, full of cocktails and chitchat (fig. 1.4). We glimpse Roy Lichtenstein, Paul Thek, and a clean-cut, bespeckled, suit-clad Swenson conversing with a woman in lavish fur, which conveys a sense of integration into a well-heeled art world that would prove fleeting for Swenson.

With *The* Other *Tradition*, Swenson expands his argument about Warhol to produce an entire treatise about how artists of the late sixties should deal with this new "post-Freudian" situation, identifying historical precedents from the early twentieth century. "The paintings of the *other* tradition are not mirrors of society," Swenson proclaims, repeating verbatim his claim about Warhol's work. "They are mirrors of what happens to us without our knowing or realizing it. In a way they might be said to objectify experience, to turn feelings into things so that we can deal with them."[35] To accompany the exhibition, Swenson published a forty-page essay as a stark black paperback pamphlet that got passed around New York's art world like "radioactive material," in the words of critic Peter Schjeldahl (fig. 1.5).[36] "There was also an exhibition called 'The *Other* Tradition,' which took place in Philadelphia at the ICA—hardly The Museum of Modern Art," recalls fellow critic Robert Pincus-Witten. "The catalogue was kind of manuscript, kind of typed. It was *so* alternative, it was *so samizdat*, that it didn't even merit the nobility of glossy paper and real type."[37] Mounted as an explicit rejoinder to arguments for modernist art's autonomy and purity, *The* Other *Tradition* put forth new aesthetic criteria and an alternative modernist genealogy rooted in Dada and Surrealism.[38]

Swenson's "samizdat" essay-cum-catalogue is somewhat piecemeal, with old writings sliced apart, reconfigured, fit back together, and then framed as a polemical injunction against the paucity of the prevailing "formal criticism" that sees only "the abstract-formal-Cubist tradition in modern art."[39] Swenson acknowledges the fragmentary and partial form of his essay, as well as "the rash decision," as he calls it (writing in the third person), "to make public his opinions on so complicated and rich a theme as the *other*

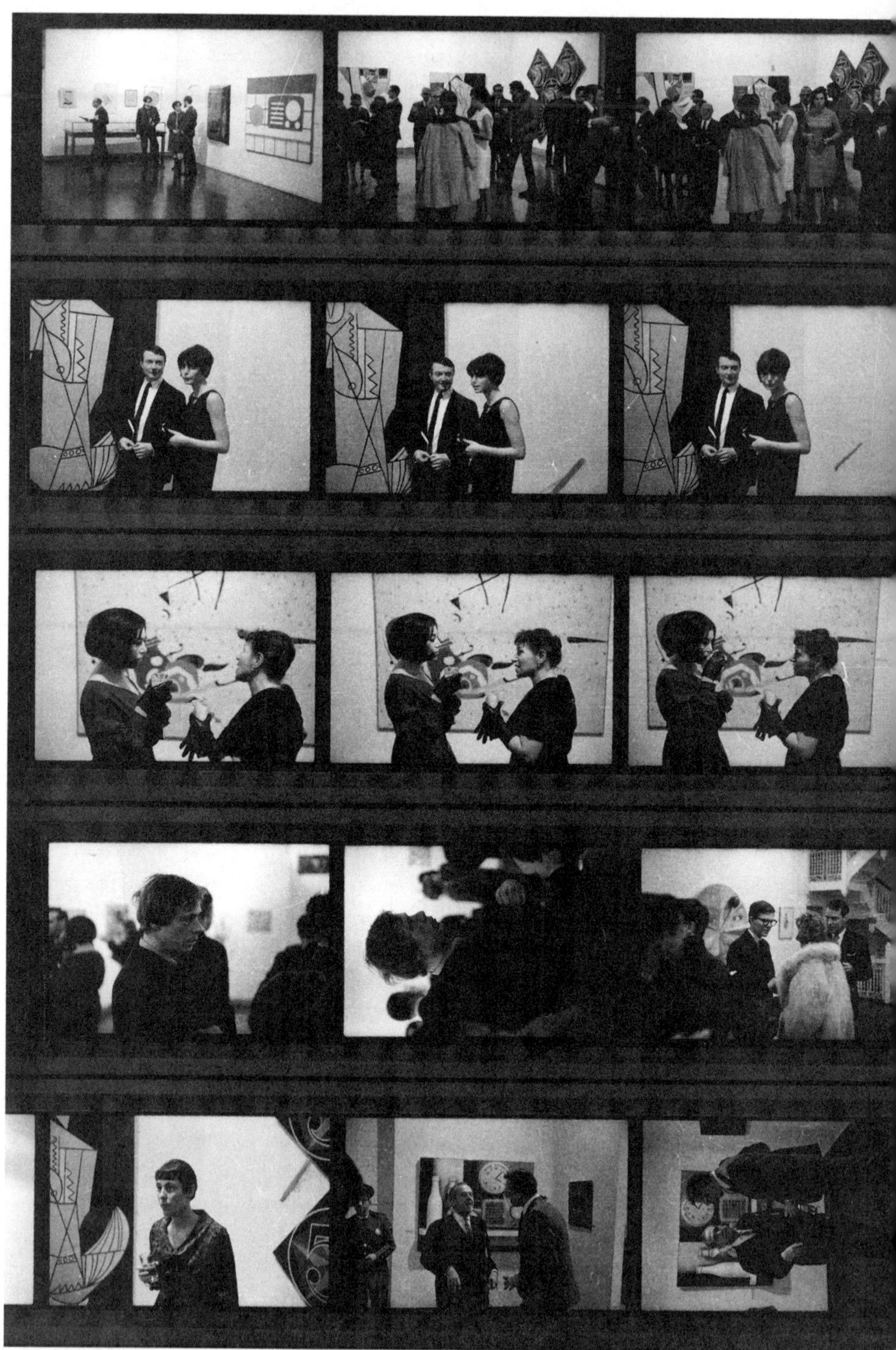

Figure 1.4 Opening reception of *The* Other *Tradition*, January 1966. Contact sheet.
Image courtesy of Institute of Contemporary Art, University of Pennsylvania.

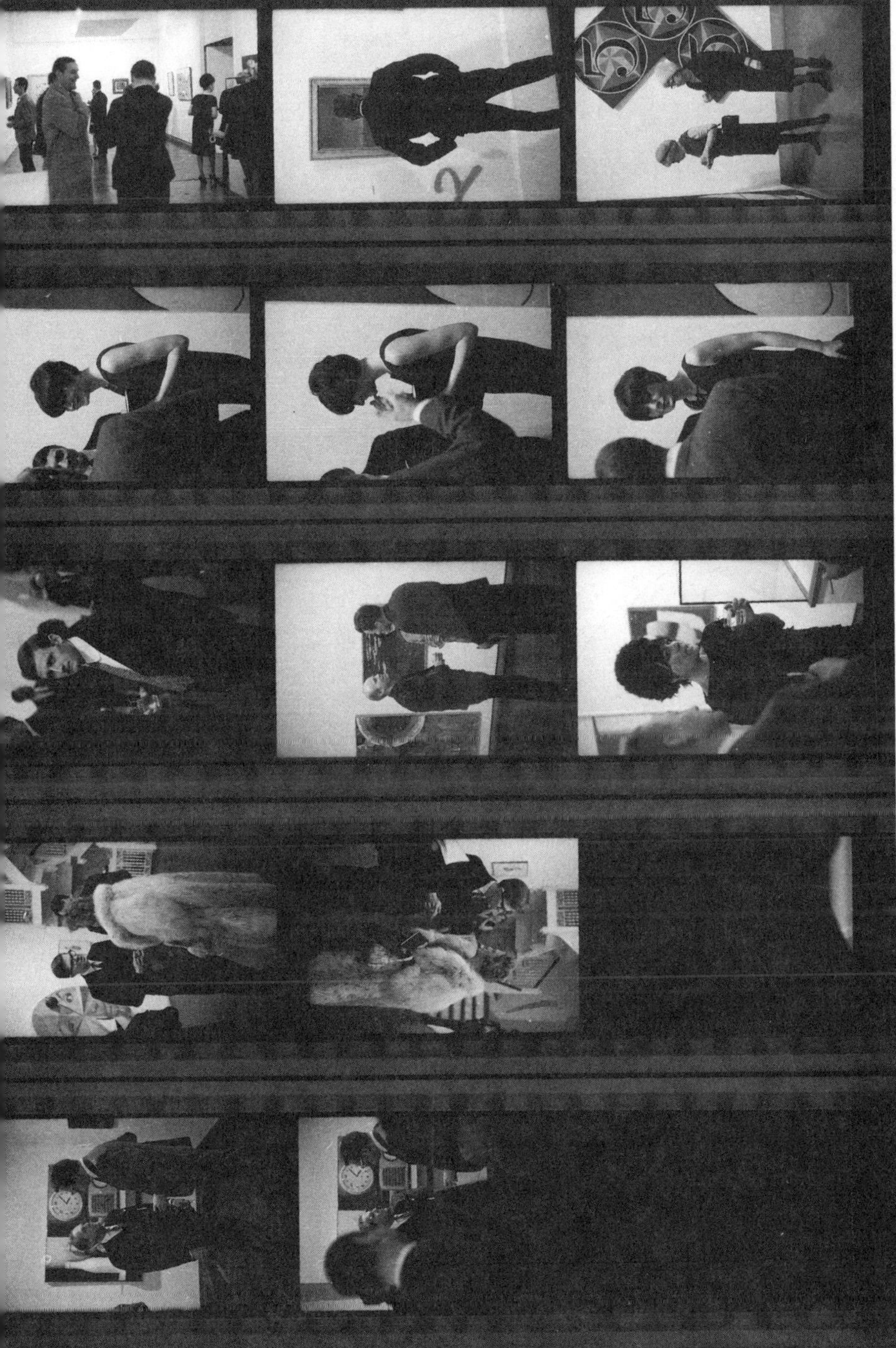

Figure 1.5 Cover of *The* Other *Tradition* by Gene Swenson, 1966.

tradition at this time." He continues: "This is an essay—a try. Only the uniformity of contradictory opinions has emboldened me to make public these views at this time, without waiting to develop them more completely."[40]

Swenson devotes the first half of his essay to decrying formal criticism. Which means at the same moment Michael Fried was proclaiming that "the formal critic of modernist painting is also a moral critic" because he uses "all the intellectual rigor at his command" to purify his aesthetic experience, Swenson, in a sense (and to put it crassly), called bullshit.[41] According to Swenson, Fried's claim that "the history of painting from Manet through Synthetic Cubism and Henri Matisse may be characterized in terms of the gradual withdrawal of painting from the task of representing reality in favor of an increasing preoccupation with problems of painting itself"[42] just ignores everything that does not fit into that story. "The deficiencies of the exclusively formal approach, particularly in these late manifestations, grow increasingly obvious even as received opinion grows monolithic," Swenson writes. "It is hard for me to muster more than boredom in greeting that humorously ubiquitous subject, the picture plane." Swenson's essay is full of zingers and one-line takedowns. "Why bother with 'modernist' originality if it is so easily defined?"—Swenson snaps back at Clement Greenberg's denigration of Pop Art as merely amounting "to a new episode in the history of taste, but not to an authentically new episode in the evolution of contemporary art."[43]

"How much longer will we rest content with our defective and infectious critical tools and our academic standards?" Swenson asks rhetorically, with acerbic wit. "How many more times can we see the words 'picture plane,' 'modernism,' 'crisis,' 'new,' and 'literary' without flushing?"[44]

In the second half of his essay, Swenson assembles the contours of the *other* tradition, producing what art historian Anne M. Wagner lauds as "one of the first—if not the first—pieces of writing to propose an alternative to modernist criticism."[45] Explaining that "images of the *other* tradition possess artistic qualities beyond those which formalist critics have found in them—percipient and psychical qualities,"[46] Swenson emphasizes the importance of content and subject matter over purely formal concerns. Rather than a story about art's gradual withdrawal from the task of representing reality over the course of the twentieth century (as Fried would have it), Swenson is invested in telling a very different story about how art forces us to "reactivate our sense of the world around us"[47] by reflecting the world back to us. But Swenson's story has no easy upshot. It is not a straightforward narrative of art's progress or development. Instead, I think it is more productive to read the second half of *The* Other *Tradition* as Swenson's unfinished, meandering effort to make sense of why certain artworks compel his conviction in the present—most prominently, works by Andy Warhol, James Rosenquist, Jean-Luc Godard, and Paul Thek, among others, that include straightforward, often hyperrealistic, representations of things in the world.

Swenson's goals are twofold: to find historical precedents for these works and to explain how they engender new understandings of subjectivity and sexuality appropriate to life in the sixties. According to Swenson, one thing we learn from Godard's film *Vivre sa vie* (1962) is that people in the sixties are "already more likely to know why they are doing something than what they are doing," which means that "we are not dealing with a 'psychological' situation in its usual sense at all: it is, in a way, the reverse—as if one probed the psyche through the present rather than the past, through politics and business and culture rather than sexuality."[48] Throughout the second half of his essay, Swenson asks over and over: What could it mean to live in a society no longer defined by a Freudian model of repression? How would this undermine normative distinctions between inside and outside, subjectivity and objectivity, or feelings and things? What historical precedents exist for this changed awareness? And what new possibilities are available to us in what he once called this "brave but not altogether hopeless new world"?[49]

In terms of the historical roots of the *other* tradition, Swenson focuses on Dada explorations of "man as machine" and Surrealist attempts "to make dreams 'concrete' so that it would be possible to deal with them," as he explains in the exhibition's press release.[50] In both cases, he is interested in how early twentieth-century artists engaged the world around them by imagining the conflation of subjective and objective reality. According to Swenson, by picturing man as "a partially receptive receiver of light, sound, heat and other kinds of mass-energy wave lengths," Dada artists were among the first to expose the objective, material basis of our supposedly subjective, inner psychic life. Likewise (though in some ways reversed), Surrealist artists were among the first "to galvanize men against the unconscious"[51] by hardening dreams and emotions into concrete things— a counterintuitive take on the legacy of Surrealism.

In the hanging of the show, Swenson stages connections between early twentieth-century experiments in Dada and Surrealism and contemporary art of the *other* tradition. Three contact sheets preserved among Swenson's papers, marred by water damage, document the installation (figs. 1.6–1.8). Surrealist works in gilded frames segue to large Pop Art paintings and assemblages. While some formal resonances echo across walls, there is no distinct throughline.

"Unlike most 'theme shows,' the Other Tradition did not demonstrate a single theory cut, dried, and laid out for the spectator's second-hand delectation," Lippard notes in her review of the exhibition. And delivering a devilish backhanded compliment, she writes: "The hanging was not so handsome that the paintings were visible first as attractive groups and secondly as individual works, which is so often the case."[52] But rather than being a detriment, for Lippard this inelegance disrupts standard viewing protocols in productive ways. The exhibition becomes an open-ended situation where feelings reverberate among works in unexpected directions. Indulging comparison after comparison, skipping backward and forward in time, Lippard's analysis of the installation unfurls almost breathlessly:

> In one room, Magritte's *L'Appel de choses par leur nom* and Johns's *Periscope (Hart Crane)* immediately set up a dialogue, joined by Rosenquist's *Marilyn II* and echoed by the Dine, Lichtenstein, Oldenberg, two Wesselmanns, and glass cases of Dada, Surrealist and contemporary periodicals, literature and graphics. The Johns demonstrated how far artists of the last decade have gone beyond Magritte's paradox. I doubt, for instance, if it would have occurred to the Surrealist to use color and

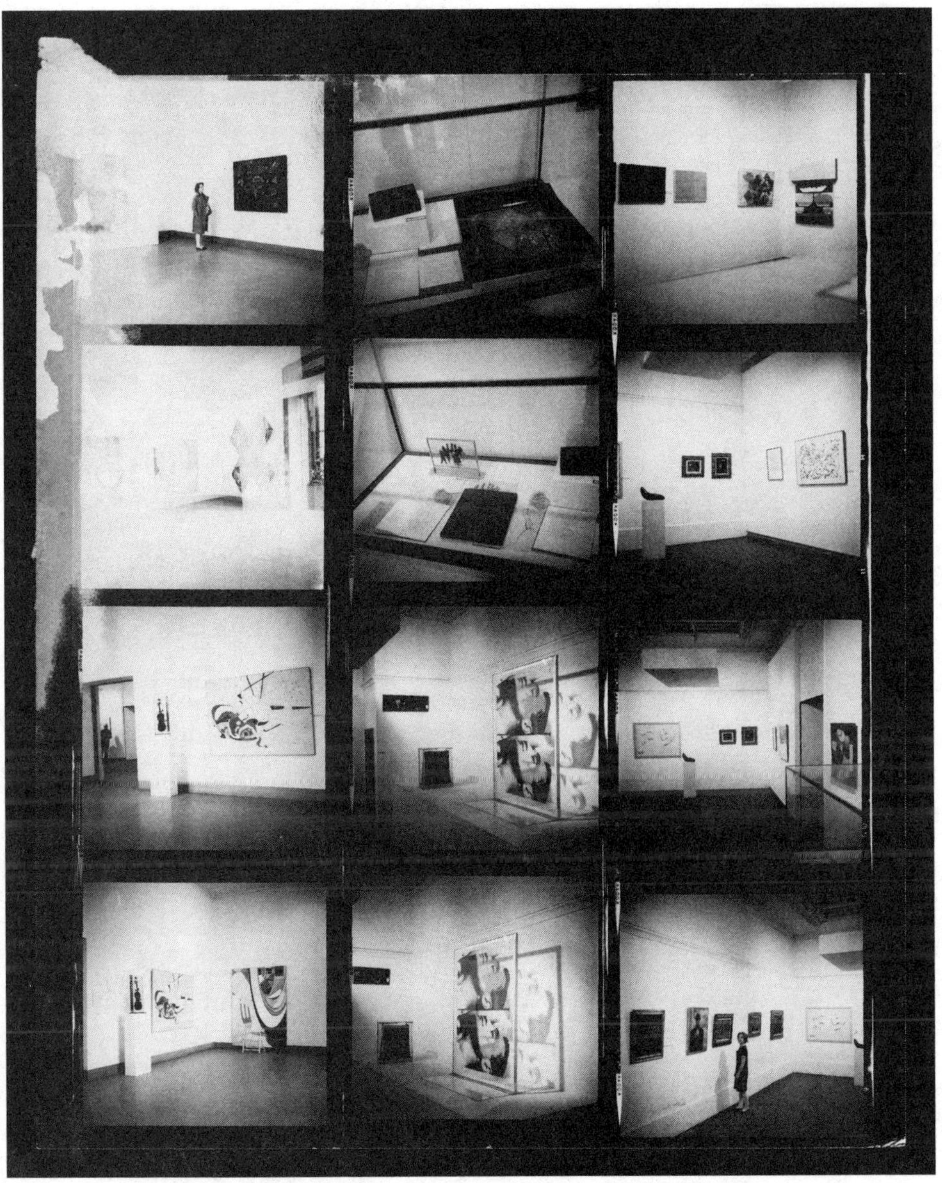

Figure 1.6 Installation photos of *The* Other *Tradition*, Institute of Contemporary Art, University of Pennsylvania, January 27–March 7, 1966. Contact sheet. Gene Swenson papers, 1950–1969, Archives of American Art, Smithsonian Institution, Washington, DC.

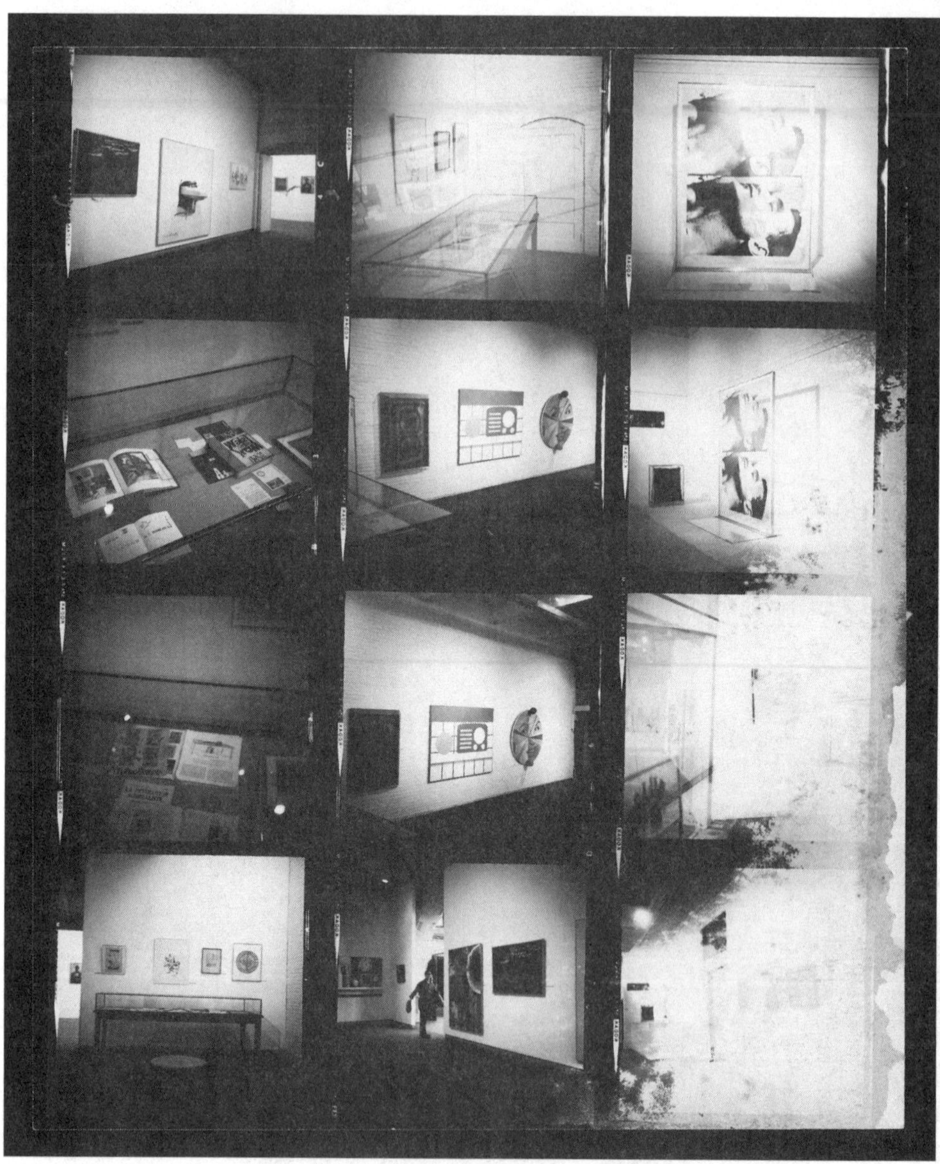

Figure 1.7 Installation photos of *The* Other *Tradition*, Institute of Contemporary Art, University of Pennsylvania, January 27–March 7, 1966. Contact sheet. Gene Swenson papers, 1950–1969, Archives of American Art, Smithsonian Institution, Washington, DC.

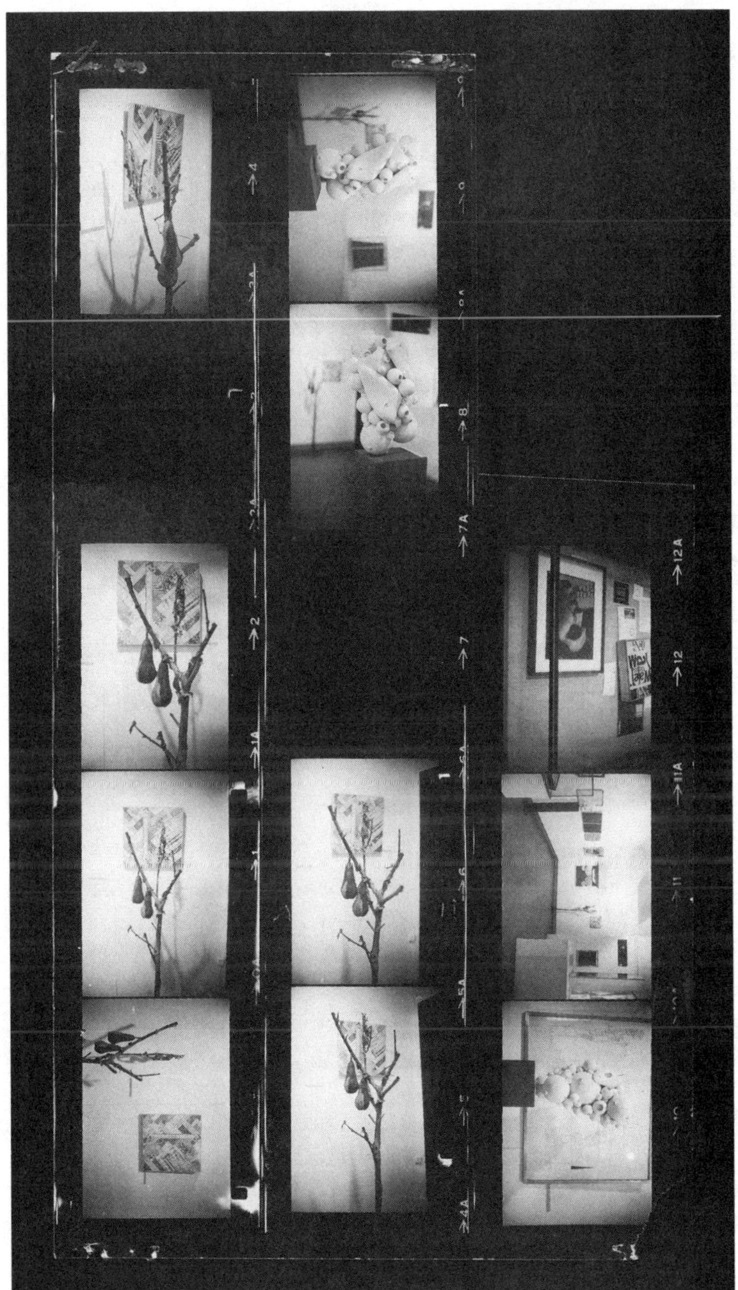

Figure 1.8 Installation photos of *The* Other *Tradition*, Institute of Contemporary Art, University of Pennsylvania, January 27–March 7, 1966. Contact sheet. Gene Swenson papers, 1950–1969, Archives of American Art, Smithsonian Institution, Washington, DC.

brushstroke as ironic tools. Yet the Magritte and the Johns in question did communicate a similar *feeling*, partly because the Magritte—brushy "clouds" on a dark ground, labeled "cannon" and "miroir"—is atypically free, recalling Tanguy's early *Storm* more than the usual precise Chiricoesque alignment. The Johns is a "grey" one of 1963 . . . at the upper right is a semicircular "device" made by scraping the paint surface from a central point: the module by which it was drawn ends in a handprint. This could refer to Leonardo's outstretched arms as a human measure of art, to Reinhardt's standard of 5 feet by 5 as a similar unit of human scale, or, as Rosalind Krauss has noted in reference to other instances of this motif, to the handprint in Pollock's *Autumn Rhythm*—or, for that matter, to the whole "hand of the artist" syndrome.[53]

In a different corner of the exhibition, Swenson places a freestanding plexiglass work by Warhol titled *Large Sleep* (1965) across from a vitrine containing works by Marcel Duchamp: a miniature replica of his freestanding glass painting-sculpture *Nine Malic Moulds* (1914–15) and *The Bride Stripped Bare by Her Bachelors, Even (The Green Box)* (1934), a collection of documents, notes, and miniatures relating to his major work, *The Large Glass* (fig. 1.9). Warhol's *Large Sleep* contains two silk screen prints of nearly identical, consecutive frames from his 1963 film *Sleep*, a five-hour and twenty-one-minute film composed of multiple shots of his then-boyfriend John Giorno sleeping. Warhol reproduces the frames one above the other so Giorno appears twice with head tilted back and eyes closed, enlarged to fill the 5½′ × 3′ piece of plexiglass that, like Duchamp's *Large Glass*, is mounted upright away from the wall so that it projects large shadows around it, creating an amorphous environment that confuses boundaries between inside and outside.[54] Warhol thus transforms Duchamp's narrative allegory of heterosexual sex, in which the "bride" and her "bachelors" are rendered as strange sex machines with orgasms externalized as plumes of smoke, into an ethereal erotic queer fantasy of blurred boundaries between inside and outside, where dreams become the stuff of objective reality and men become explicit objects of desire.[55]

Swenson pairs *Large Sleep* with another freestanding work in plexiglass: Paul Thek's *Hippopotamus Poison* (1965), part of his Technological Reliquaries series (fig. 1.10). Thek places a bloody fragment of butchered hippopotamus flesh, realistically rendered in wax, inside a plexiglass vitrine inscribed with a paranoid message that begins: "I SYLVIA KRAUS, BEFORE GOD, DO HEREBY ALLEGE, THAT A PROTRACTED DESOLATING WEAPON HIPPOPOTAMUS POISON IS BEING USED TO INSIDIOUSLY ANNIHILATE MEN, WOMEN AND CHILDREN." According to Swenson, this message is an excerpt from an actual mimeographed broadside that Kraus distributed on the

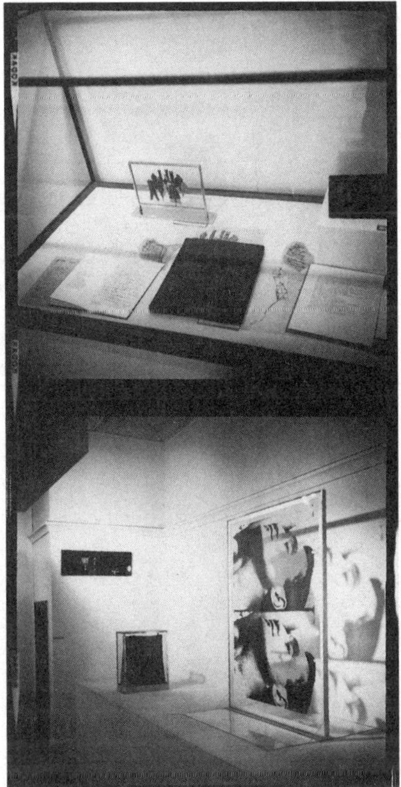

Figure 1.9 Installation photos of *The* Other *Tradition* (detail of fig. 1.6). Works pictured include: Marcel Duchamp, *The Bride Stripped Bare by Her Bachelors, Even (The Green Box)*, 1934; Andy Warhol, *Large Sleep*, 1965; Paul Thek, *Hippopotamus Poison*, 1965; and Robert Morris, *Untitled (Cloud)*, 1962.

streets of New York, claiming to be a messenger of God.[56] In the context of *The* Other *Tradition*, Thek's *Hippopotamus Poison* evokes Dalí's "paranoiac-critical method" by making the paranoiac's delusion into a concrete, fleshy thing. "Dali's meaning is related to common usage, because the paranoiac is able to find concrete proof of persecution in the world of so-called reality," Swenson explains. "An object corresponds, becomes an alternate state of mind."[57] But Thek's work also pushes beyond Dalí's "paranoiac-critical method," or beyond the individual's effort to reshape his psyche. Instead, it points to paranoia as a defining condition of so-called objective reality in the mid-sixties. With *Hippopotamus Poison*, Thek suggests that Sylvia Kraus's paranoia is perhaps not so different from the cruel paranoia of a whole society that would rather be dead than Red. Or, as R. D. Laing famously put it in 1965: "The statesmen of the world who boast and threaten

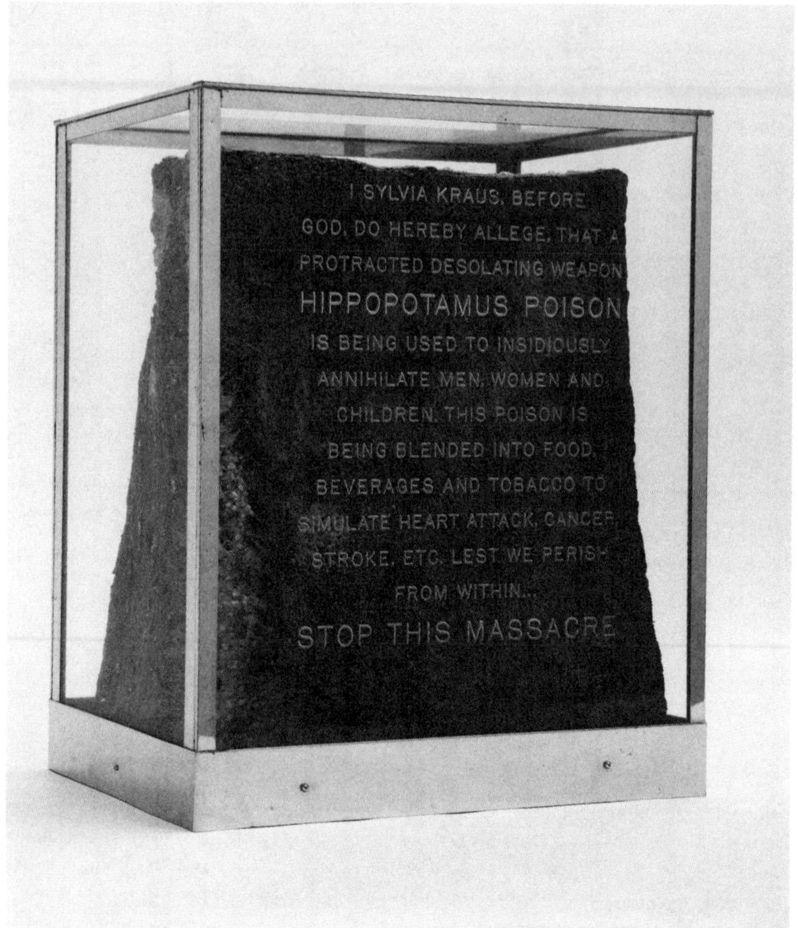

Figure 1.10 Paul Thek, *Hippopotamus Poison*, 1965. Wax, stainless steel, and plexiglass, 25¼ × 19¼ × 11⅜ in. The Museum of Modern Art, New York (375.1991). Gift of Neil Jenney in honor of Ann Wilson. © The Estate of Paul Thek. Digital image © The Museum of Modern Art / Licensed by SCALA / Art Resource, NY.

that they have Doomsday weapons are far more dangerous, and far more estranged from 'reality' than many of the people on whom the label 'psychotic' is affixed."[58]

• • •

"Another vital problem which artists have begun investigating in a new light is sex," Swenson proclaims in the essay's final section, "Art as Exploration."[59] He argues that desires and drives are no longer repressed in the subconscious but rather explicit and conscious. As a result, according to Swenson, "traditional Freudian psychological motivations" are simply not "very interesting or applicable in telling stories of *later* twentieth century people."[60] We are dealing instead with a "post-Freudian" situation, as Swenson calls it, or with the end of a Freudian model of repression. This gives way to a new model of subjectivity in which feelings are things that are already public and shared. Moreover, it engenders a whole new model of sexuality premised on explicit embrace of Freudian "perversions," including fetishism, sadomasochism, and homosexuality, without moralism or shame. "We still psychoanalyze ourselves in a Freudian manner although we may not be the least bit suppressed with Victorian 'secrets,'" Swenson quips, accusing other critics and scholars of harboring "a cold and Victorian prissiness hidden beneath assurances of jaundiced boredom."[61] But Swenson also tempers his own claims in *The* Other *Tradition*. Without mentioning the words "homosexuality" or "queer" at all, he leaves much to inference and innuendo.

Swenson puts forth three young artists—Paul Thek, Joseph Raffaele, and Michael Todd—as key exponents of the new post-Freudian sensibility. These artists embrace fetishism, sadomasochism, and same-sex eroticism as the explicit content of their work. As Lippard notes: "Swenson's comments on the new objectivity of a post-Freudian sexuality are thought-provoking. Since sexuality, Freudian sexuality, is the prime mover of all Surrealist art, this provides both a connection to and a breakaway from the earlier movement."[62] When Swenson prods Joseph Raffaele in an interview to answer the question: "Are your paintings a Surrealistic investigation of the subconscious?" Raffaele responds, "No, not really." He explains, "Everybody knows that fingers can be penises, mouths and ears are vaginas, nostrils are assholes."[63] Raffaele's hyperrealistic paintings of cut-up pictures of things like lipstick protruding from its tube, glossy fingernails, sharp dental tools, breasts, and penises present fetishistic attachment as fact—as something conscious on the surface and not at all repressed (fig. 1.11). Michael Todd likewise draws from Surrealism while subverting its emphasis. According to Swenson, Todd's white biomorphic sculptures make "some of the disturbing but abstract qualities of fetishism and sexuality in Yves Tanguy's work explicit" (see fig. 1.8).[64]

Thek places hunks of butchered flesh, realistically rendered in wax, inside sleek plexiglass boxes, revealing the sadomasochism that undergirds pleasures of space-age consumerism as a matter of fact. In an interview, Swenson asks Thek, "Are your works sado-masochistic?" To which he replies, "Yes. It's one—*one*—of the components." Thek forces the viewer to linger up close: "The dare of simply being able to look at it with a solid stomach," as Thek explains.[65] All three artists picture sex and desire untethered from norms of heterosexual reproduction, spinning away from the so-called

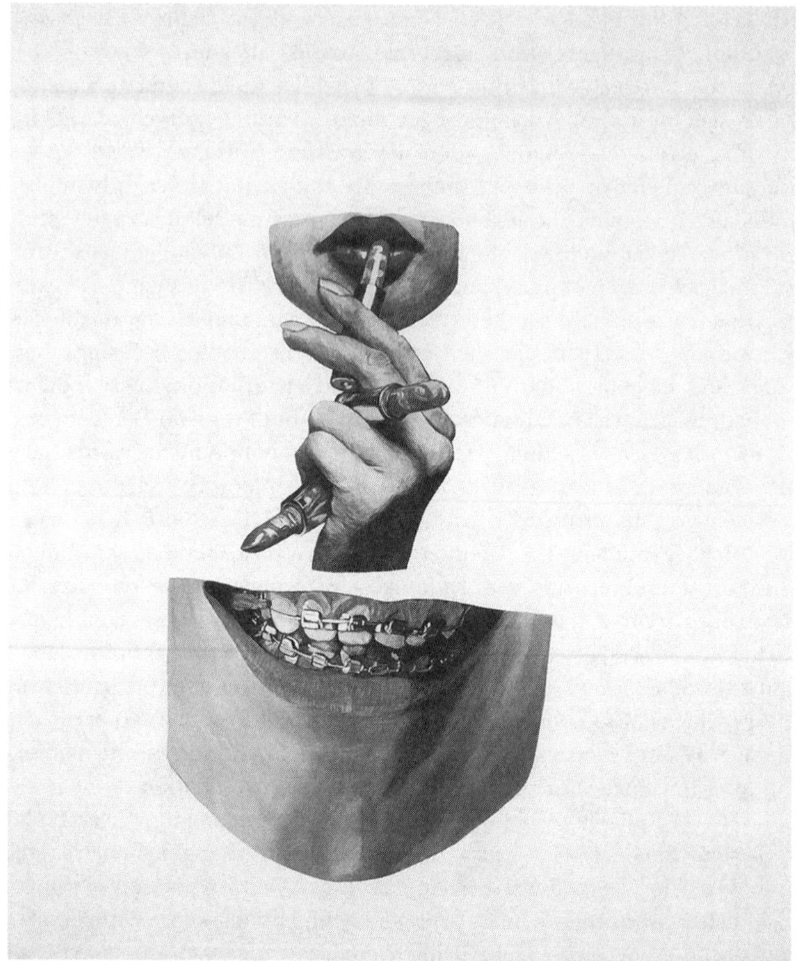

Figure 1.11 Joseph Raffael, *Lipstick, Braces*, c. 1966. Oil on canvas, 55¾ × 45¾ in. © Joseph Raffael Estate, courtesy Nancy Hoffman Gallery.

proper object-choice and congealing instead in body parts, bulbous forms, and sharp implements. But none of it is repressed. It's all explicit.

In her review, Lippard notes that "Swenson scoffs at the irrelevancy of applying formal criteria" to post-Freudian artists "but offers no alternative." And for her part, Lippard remains unconvinced by Thek, Raffaele, and Todd's "warmed over and updated Surrealism," as she puts it (ouch!). In response to Swenson's provocations—the "curiously withdrawn, objectified subjectivity of 'Swenson's new sexuality,'" as she calls it—Lippard proposes an alternative roster of contemporary artists including Frank Lincoln Viner, Robert Breer, and Eva Hesse who "share certain attitudes with the more conceptual branches of current art as well as with the Other

Tradition." Lippard proclaims, "This kind of art could be called Eccentric Abstraction"—a moniker she then uses as the title for her epoch-defining 1966 exhibition and essay.[66] Lippard thus emerges as another important foil for Swenson—a fellow critic invested in understanding and engaging his ideas as an interlocutor, and even as a collaborator. Lippard succeeded, though, in ways Swenson could not—as she found a home in the art world, albeit tenuous and always provisional. She managed to use the spaces of art magazines, galleries, and museums, as well as spaces of solidarity in collectives and coalitions, to develop brilliant arguments and projects capable of speaking back to the art world's entrenched authority in ways it could understand and sometimes would even be willing to hear.[67]

Comfortless Tears

The Other *Tradition* endures as a bold curatorial gambit and a tragically unfinished project. Swenson's roster of artists—all white men, with the lone exception of Ann Wilson—never quite caught up to the radical potential of his ideas. Swenson did not turn his critical attention to the many women artists or Black artists who were also drawing on legacies of Dada and Surrealism in the sixties. He did not collaborate with others to explore how the pursuit of a post-Freudian world might also subvert norms that undergird so much sexism and racism.

Reflecting on Swenson's work with nearly fifty years' hindsight, critic William S. Wilson recalls "the feeling of permissiveness, the oceanic feelings, which Gene was encouraging." He explains, "Gene had a theory expressed to me that everyone was sadomasochist, they just didn't always know it yet."[68] Which is basically right. Across all of his work, Swenson imagines the end of Freudian repression. He imagines a world where everyone can embrace and pursue so-called perversions explicitly, without moralism or shame—including fetishism, sadomasochism, and same-sex eroticism. And Swenson theorizes how this world would obviate traditional notions of creativity, originality, and individuality that subtend modernism.

We witness this imagined world flicker to life on the scratchy audio recording of Swenson's 1963 interview with Warhol—an all-too-rare chronicle of what could transpire between queer friends in the relative security, or obscurity, of a private room. And we catch fleeting glimpses of this world in *The* Other *Tradition*, although tempered by the hard limitations of what words and ideas an art-world institution would be willing to print. In his essay, Swenson proclaims: "The erotic is turned toward a wider range of human possibilities"[69]—but he does not (or perhaps cannot) elucidate what these possibilities are and how they would engender a better, queerer, more ethical world.

Along with the end of Freudian repression, Swenson imagines a whole new model of subjectivity—or "objectivity," as he calls it—no longer premised on separation between the subconscious and the conscious or between the psyche and the world outside. "The relationship between object and emotion in the *other* tradition is not traditional," as Swenson explains, over and over. "'Emotions' have been objectified," he continues, "perhaps some would say they have been mechanized. The author sees nothing necessarily sinister in this; in fact he finds in it an exciting variety of possibilities of human awareness."[70] He reiterates: "To put our case another way, there are tears in things." And then he elaborates: "There is, in other words, a possible correspondence between feelings and things, and of a new psychology based on public attitudes and even cliches, a new definition of objectivity."[71] Swenson, of course, does *not* want to revive any kind of traditional notion of artistic expression imagined as a moment of cathartic release. He is not interested in rescuing the idea of an artist's psyche as an internal reservoir of feelings to be projected outward as a gesture or cry. But crucially, for Swenson, this post-Freudian breakdown between the psyche and the world in which feelings become objectified does *not* result in impassivity or in feeling things less intensely. Instead, the opposite is true. Uncontained, feelings become more intense.

Writing fifteen years after Swenson, Fredric Jameson theorizes that a "radical break or *coupure*" occurred in the early sixties that inaugurated postmodernism as "the cultural logic of late capitalism."[72] In terms remarkably redolent with Swenson's, Jameson argues that postmodernism signals "the end of the bourgeois ego" and with it the end of "the Freudian model of latent and manifest, or of repression," and "the waning of affect."[73] Jameson argues that "feelings . . . are now free-floating and impersonal"[74] because there is no stable self present to hold everything together. But in Jameson's account, the fragmented postmodern subject (who replaces the alienated but integrated modernist subject) also becomes a euphoric subject. Unable "to organize its past and future into coherent experience," the fragmented postmodern subject experiences—and, in turn, imagines and then produces—the world of late capitalism as a euphoric array of depthless, intensely present signifiers.[75] But this is not Swenson's story.

Swenson did not embrace blank parody as a primary mode of cultural production or hallucinogenic euphoria as a strategy to cope with the world of late capitalism as a fragmented subject. Rather, for Swenson, experiencing breakdown between inside and outside—that amorphous, confusing feeling of being "all twisted up," as he put it to Warhol back in 1963—seems to have mired him even more intensely in a world that he kept trying, and kept failing, to change. It seems to have produced in Swenson an overabundance of commitment that he could neither figure out how to deal with nor extricate himself from. As Lippard would later describe Swenson's situation in heartbreaking detail: "His hyper-critical sensitivity to and responsibility for remedying the ills of the world he lived in amounted to obsession; he left himself raw and open to a world all too ready to devour him and he was, consequently, hurt by it as a more 'normal' person would not be."[76]

After *The* Other *Tradition* concluded its run in March 1966, things in the art world never really worked out again for Swenson. He curated a show at the Museum of Modern Art titled *Art in the Mirror* later that year but could not complete it due to an attack of appendicitis. "The show opened," artist James Rosenquist recalls, "but naturally it didn't have Gene's touch."[77] Swenson wrote an essay for a major Rosenquist retrospective exhibition at the National Gallery of Canada in 1967, but the museum refused to publish it. Which is heartbreaking, as Swenson sent drafts of his essay to the museum with notecards that proclaim: "I almost can't believe that it is as good as I think it is" and "Here is the end of my piece and, after a few corrections, the beginning of a new era in criticism and possibly even in art. I can never again thank you as I can now for making this possible."[78] In that essay (published posthumously by the Spencer Museum of Art at the University of Kansas), Swenson lays bare the despair he began to feel earlier in the decade, following the assassination of John F. Kennedy—despair that would not relent. "Suddenly the optimism of the Kennedy years was gone with the crack of a rifle, never to be recaptured," Swenson writes.

> In my memory I cannot separate a half-belief that the television would deny the reports—that sense of life with which he lighted that box could not possibly be snuffed out—and the hope that the television would make me believe that there was a fragment of hope and, in truth, reality left in my world. I wept comfortless tears. "I suffered death but could not die." I weep now as I recall the terror, the disbelief, the utter confusion I felt as the day wore on, and my inconsolable grief as night fell around my heart.[79]

Confused, inconsolable, angry, and searching for fragments of hope and reality in his world, Swenson proceeded unsteadily into the late sixties. And around this time, he met and befriended Jill Johnston, who published a fractured account of his disintegration strewn together with fragments of her own life.

2
The Disintegration of a Critic

Gene Swenson's and Jill Johnston's Protests and Panels

April 25, 1968

Pick up *The Village Voice* and turn to page thirty. Jill Johnston's weekly column Dance Journal is more disjointed than usual.

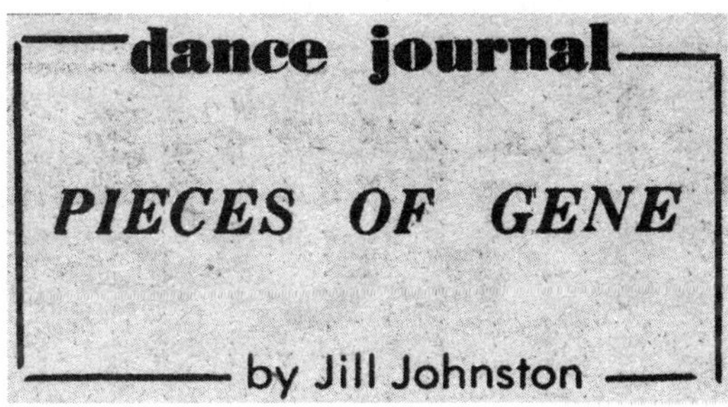

The lavender angels return from one white house to another. Gene Swenson has been banned from the Dada Surrealism show. The constant shape of the cube held in the mind, but which the viewer never literally experiences, is an actuality against which the literally changing perspective views are related. (Morris) But I ask you, how much arms can you smuggle in a canoe? Gene is waging a one man happening against the art world. Doesn't the night always belong to the day before and early in the morning is a new day again? He went to the UN to give himself up as an international citizen. The state, Trudeau declared, has no business in the bedrooms of the nation. An intruding pig throws the family in an uproar and forces the girl to hide behind the piano. . . . Cage said he knew when she was going out of her mind because she would begin to speak the truth. Alan Watts told me there's no place to go in this country if you're enduring an expansion of consciousness. Gene was thrown out of the UN by the way.[1]

Try to make sense of the facets by picturing the whole shape in your mind, but they all fall apart again. The center does not really hold. Johnston surrounds news of Swenson's recent exploits—protesting and getting banned from the Museum of Modern Art's exhibition *Dada, Surrealism, and Their Heritage*, then attempting to relinquish his citizenship at the United Nations building—with non sequiturs. She imagines pieces of Gene scattered on the sidewalks outside these institutions. There's a nightmarish quality to these fragments of a world spinning out of control: hiding from an intruding pig, smuggling arms in a canoe. The article goes on like that for five more paragraphs. To construct the column, Johnston collages together sentences from disparate sources including *Artforum, Life* magazine, Melanie Klein's essay "The Development of a Child," and Erik Erikson's book *Childhood and Society*. But it's a ruse. There is no secret code to be deciphered, no comfort in finally figuring "it" out. Instead, what you see is what you get: a fractured account of Swenson's actions strewn together with fragments of Johnston's own life, strange snippets of psychoanalysis, exaltations of madness, quotes from magazines, and art-world gossip.

Gene is waging a one man happening against the art world.

• • •

One month after Johnston published "Pieces of Gene," on May 30, 1968, Swenson published a column titled "The Thought Police" in the underground newspaper *The New York Free Press* (fig. 2.1). Swenson decries psychiatrists as brutal enforcers of capitalist conformism in cahoots with the actual police and the psychiatric ward as a penitentiary for the unruly. He narrates the disturbing tale of being hauled out of his apartment by police a year earlier and then forcibly confined in the psychiatric ward at Bellevue Hospital, where he was "fed drugs," as he writes, "a practice which I most vocally protested." Swenson continues,

> If a citizen disagrees, he is swept into a "mental hospital" where the thought police have complete control. . . . At Bellevue I asked every official I met for a lawyer. The police were taunting a young man with a bleeding hand in the waiting room, and I reprimanded the officer—effectively. I was at least in charge of my manners. After a perfunctory examination involving several minor humiliations, I was relieved of my clothing and given the "blue coolie" uniform—as I called it—which I was to wear during my confinement.[2]

In the sixties, conditions in the psychiatric ward at Bellevue Hospital were deplorable, with patients confined to overcrowded rooms and hallways

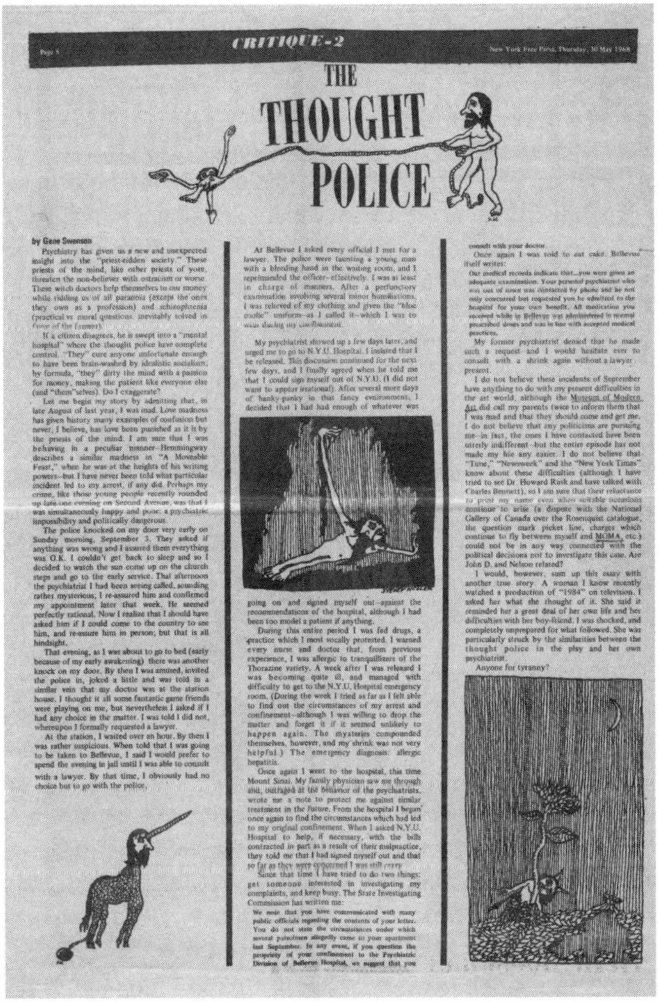

Figure 2.1 Gene Swenson, "The Thought Police," *The New York Free Press*, May 30, 1968. Newspaper clipping. Museum of Modern Art Archives, New York, NY. Digital image © The Museum of Modern Art / Licensed by SCALA / Art Resource, NY.

for up to two weeks after only a fifteen-minute evaluation, according to a front-page exposé in *The New York Times*, published in 1966. Titled "Bedlam for City Mental Patients," the article quotes the outgoing hospitals commissioner as saying: "We take people with a tenuous hold on reality and then remove all traces of reality by placing them in a stark, barren environment—it's inhumane."[3]

Johnston befriended Swenson in 1968. Like Swenson, she too had been in and out of the psychiatric ward at Bellevue twice by then. Both critics expressed ire at a world that would sooner lock them up than accommodate them. But I want to be clear from the outset of this chapter: My point is not to romanticize psychosis as a special creative power. Nor, of course, is it to dismiss Swenson's or Johnston's queer practices as mere bouts of insanity. I do not attempt to adjudicate whether Swenson or Johnston was really psychotic, as the reality of psychosis is inseparable from the reality of, say, Bellevue's "inhumane" environment (which is enough to drive anyone so-called crazy, one might be thinking). Moreover, Johnston would later discover that "my medical abstracts from Bellevue, Mt. Sinai, and St. Vincent's all included 'homosexuality' as a factor in my condition," as she writes in her 1985 memoir *Paper Daughter: Autobiography in Search of a Father*. "The St. Vincent's report ('66) went so far as to say that I was 'transferred here after spending one month in Bellevue because of bizarre behavior, paranoid ideation, homosexuality'"[4]—a reminder that homosexuality itself was still a certifiable condition during the sixties.[5]

Swenson and Johnston both publicly rejected the psychiatric establishment's demands to integrate into bourgeois American family life. Furious, determined to change the world, and striving in complicated ways to transcend their circumstances, they both did and wrote a whole lot of things that were flawed, troubling, raw, messy, and embarrassing. But they were also creative, earnest, new, and ambitious. And to dismiss these things as simply outside of art history or as an anathema to the progressive thrust of movement-based politics is to erase the difficult parts. Striving does not always amount to success. Doing and saying things to stave off the pressure of a world that is not working can look, sound, and feel a whole lot of ways: a jab, a tender word, an awkward silence, an outburst, an accusation, a protest, a riot. Lauren Berlant calls this "genre flailing," and it can be both "anchoring *and* transformative." But, as Berlant reminds us, no matter what happens, "the story's form will have to pass through our struggles to create it."[6] And in this chapter, I linger on Swenson's and Johnston's struggles. Refusing to play it cool or to develop ironic or analytic strategies to cope with conditions of erasure and repression, Swenson and Johnston both developed ways of being, doing, and writing fueled by anger and marked by disintegration.

Here I focus on the tense year between the spring of 1968 and the spring of 1969, just before New York's art world would erupt into organized coalition-based protests, and just before the Stonewall Riots of June 1969 would inaugurate gay liberation protests. Swenson did not witness any of that come to fruition—he was in the psychiatric ward at Bellevue during the spring of 1969 and back at his childhood home in Kansas that summer where he died in a car crash in August. Tragically, he never made it back to New York City after Stonewall. He spoke at the first Open Hearing of the

Art Workers' Coalition in April 1969 but never attended another one. His life ended in the midst of waging his "one man happening against the art world," making people around him uneasy, and protesting alone.

Johnston survived. By 1969 she had wrested tenuous control of her means and assembled a queer practice durable enough to endure into the seventies. She transformed her weekly *Village Voice* column into a space to experiment with new, autobiographical forms of writing capable of accounting for still improbable ways of being. In May 1969, she organized a panel discussion event titled "The Disintegration of a Critic: An Analysis of Jill Johnston" to herald her artistic achievements. After that, she accelerates into the seventies, writing constantly about what happened at the end of the sixties with the kind of retrospective vision that Swenson did not live long enough to achieve.

• • •

This chapter is an elegy for Swenson's tragically unfinished project. It is an argument for the significance of Swenson's and Johnston's queer practices. And it is a testament to Johnston's creative endurance.

An Uninvited Bully

At the end of May 1968, the same week Swenson's column "The Thought Police" appeared in *The New York Free Press*, he showed up to a panel discussion featuring Johnston and disrupted the proceedings by shouting from the audience. Unexpectedly finding herself on the authoritative side of the panel table and charged with upholding proper art-world protocols, Johnston analyzed her discomfort with the situation in her *Village Voice* column published a week later. "Gene is basically a harmless democrat with excellent vocal projection," Johnston explains about Swenson's interruption. "He could improve his style but what he's doing is actively creating the kind of impossible situation that reduces all that talking to zero."[7] The panel, titled "Dance and Its Alternatives," featured Johnston alongside dancers Yvonne Rainer, Simone Forti, and Meredith Monk, moderated by Robert Morris. Morris's idea for the panel was to discuss the cleavage between traditional dance based on studio techniques and the newer dance "reconsidered as a response to tasks, rule-games, objects, and the like," as Johnston writes — a premise that would not have been new or particularly controversial in New York's art world by May 1968. On the panel, Johnston pushed Morris's idea a little further by proposing "a broader sense of an 'alternative' being an attitude about dance as a constant activity in the world whether it's framed in a box or wandering on the streets." According to Johnston, this engendered a bit of disagreement among the panelists but not too much. "My panel companions have a greater vested interest in dance framed by a box to be viewed by invitation only," Johnston writes, "but they're completely hip to the nonsense of both the box thing and the street thing and I feel confident that as artists they'll continue to provoke controversy in their funambulism over the confusion of streets and boxes."[8]

Given that all the panelists already agreed on the importance of blurring life and art (or "streets and boxes") in their own work, and given that Swenson's interruption temporarily reduced "all talking to zero," for Johnston, the real question becomes: What is the point of a panel discussion anyway? "Not that lovers don't quarrel on occasion," Johnston muses, "but when the lovers meet in public they present a united front and it comes over quite cozy. I'm still mystified by the function of a panel discussion. Perhaps it's just another community get-together. That sounds vague enough to make it seem both essential and unnecessary. If the idea is to be instructive I don't believe in it. Nobody wants to be instructed."[9] By disrupting the flow of business as usual, Swenson suspended everyone in the auditorium— panelists and audience members alike—in a state of being unnerved. Johnston writes, "That Gene was ejected finally was the power of the law. Since I'm a minor criminal myself I felt uncomfortable being on the side of the law. . . . When Gene was up there on the balcony screaming quotes from Mao or Ho Chi shortly before ejection Yvonne [Rainer] was sputtering to me to do something because I'd promised I could 'handle it' but I thought it was handling itself. Assuming authority is one kind of occupational hazard and Gene knows the price he can pay for being an uninvited bully."[10] If the panel was premised on a tacit agreement among the panelists that blurring life and art is a radical and liberatory gesture, Swenson exposed the thin limits of that consensus. Simply by behaving outside the protocol of the panel, Swenson forced the panelists into an uncomfortable position of policing boundaries they strived usually, in their own work, to break down: boundaries between art and life, performer and audience, acceptable and unacceptable behavior. However, there is nothing particularly liberatory about Swenson's menacing, rude gesture. If he intended his disruption as a statement against the Vietnam War or against capitalism, then the fact that Johnston could not even tell if he was quoting "Mao or Ho Chi" demonstrates the ineffectiveness of his message.[11]

A few months after Swenson provoked his crisis of authority by screaming from the balcony, Johnston staged a second panel in October 1968 intended to amplify this kind of crisis by intentionally causing the whole thing to devolve into chaos. "The key word became 'disintegration,'" Johnston writes. "Traditionally a panel is a serious affair. . . . So I suppose the idea of our panel was to undermine its seriousness (in terms of settling any issues) by exposing the emotional roots of any authoritative situation." By encouraging the whole audience "to express its hostility" through "an agony of extreme confusion," Johnston took up Swenson's mantel and pushed it even further.[12]

· · ·

Swenson's interruption of May 1968 was part of series of troubling actions that he performed that spring aimed at disrupting art-world proceedings by knocking things off course and making people around him feel uneasy, even sometimes unsafe. In a letter to the Museum of Modern Art (MoMA) dated "March, 1968," Swenson threatened to "embarrass the top brass of this museum and the speakers at the symposium by a surprise event, an act of high melodrama,"[13] which turned out only to involve Swenson showing up alone with a tin cup, wearing hand-scrawled brown paper signs that read "Virtue is its own reward" and "Have a heart"—tender objects still preserved among Swenson's papers (figs. 2.2–2.3).

Later that month, on the opening night of MoMA's exhibition *Dada*,

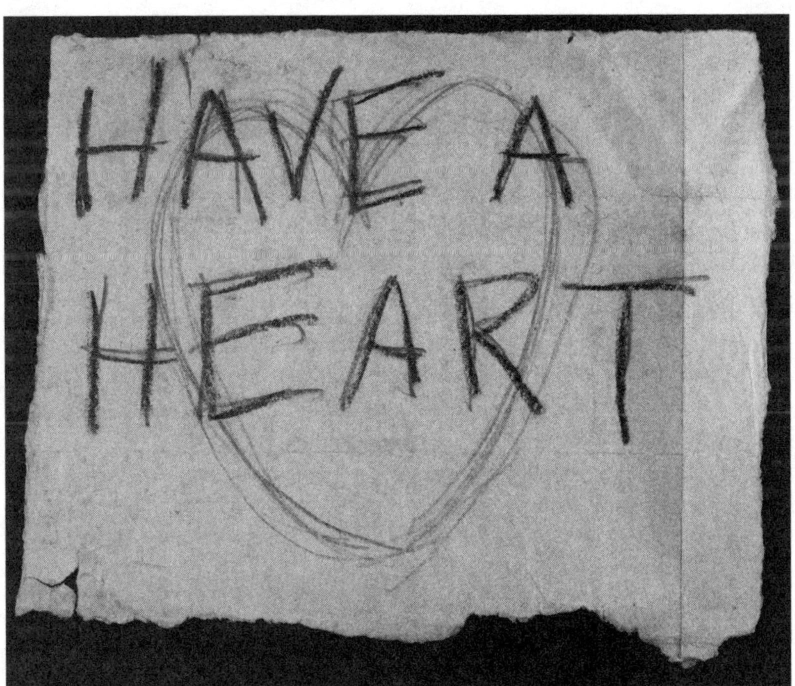

Figure 2.2 Gene Swenson, "Have a Heart," 1968. Handmade sign on brown packing paper. Gene Swenson papers, 1950–1969, Archives of American Art, Smithsonian Institution, Washington, DC.

Figure 2.3 Gene Swenson, "Virtue Is Its Own Reward," 1968. Handmade sign on brown packing paper. Gene Swenson papers, 1950–1969, Archives of American Art, Smithsonian Institution, Washington, DC.

Surrealism, and Their Heritage on March 25, Swenson organized a protest "dedicated to the lost but not forgotten spirit of Dada and Surrealism" whose "historical bodies are now embalmed at the Museum of Modern Art," as he put it in a *Village Voice* advertisement, proclaiming: "Freud is Dead. So, too, is Marx. And Modern Art . . . ? . . ." (fig. 2.4).[14] Adopting the moniker "The Transformation," Swenson crafted a broadside with hand-drawn doodles issuing "A CALL TO CULTURAL REVELATION" (fig. 2.5). "We call on all groups to join us on the steps of the Museum of Modern Art from 7–11 P.M.," the flyer announces. "This evening will be dedicated to the ritual dis-establishment of Dada and Surrealism. MOMA IS DEAD. DADA IS DEAD."[15] But for all of his bombast, Swenson's protest "turned out to be a remarkably gentle demonstration outside the museum," according to a report in *The New York Times* published the next day, despite the overzealous presence of "a sawhorse barricade to contain the demonstrators" and "helmeted members of the Tactical Patrol Force." In the end, about "300 subdued demon-

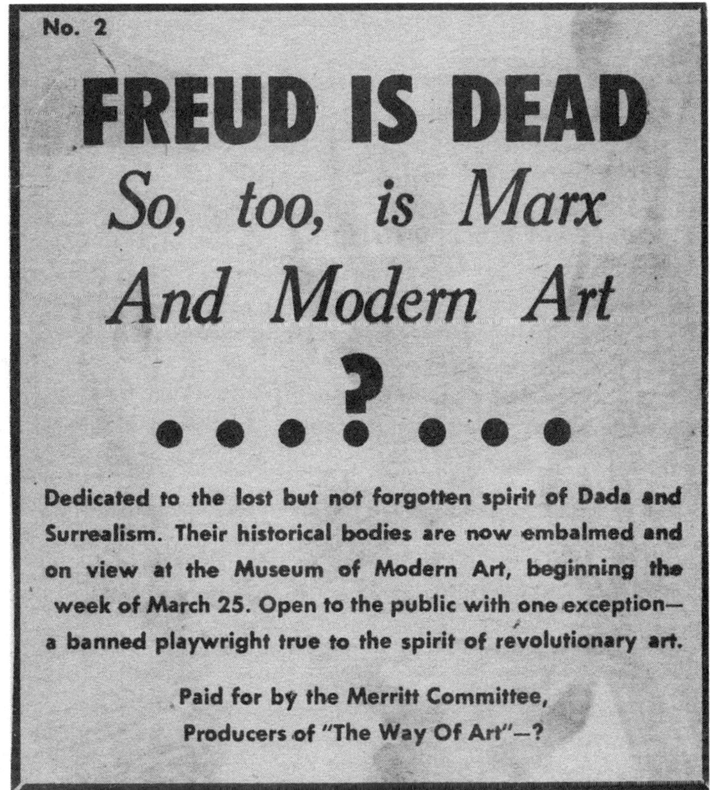

Figure 2.4 Advertisement in *The Village Voice*, March 21, 1968. Newspaper clipping.

strators" showed up. "Clad in quilts and waving gaily painted banners they marched and danced behind the barricade" (fig. 2.6).[16]

A few months prior, Swenson had sent a lavish funeral wreath to the Metropolitan Museum of Art bearing the name "Henry" (as in Geldzahler) to be delivered to "the foot of the great Roman statue in the south end of the Great Hall," according to a write-up in *The New York Times*.[17] "Gene didn't take this lightly and neither did Henry," recalls James Rosenquist, who was a close friend of Swenson's. "Henry was afraid, and Gene became more and more angry that his ideas were not getting across and he could not get a real platform to speak from."[18]

On April 25, 1968, Swenson published a scathing indictment of the art world in *The New York Free Press* titled "The Corporate Structure of the American Art World" (fig. 2.7). He decries "that handful of vile money-changers to whom *Time* and *Life* listen before they look," proclaiming: "The chief villain is a word—Capitalism." Swenson calls out by name Henry

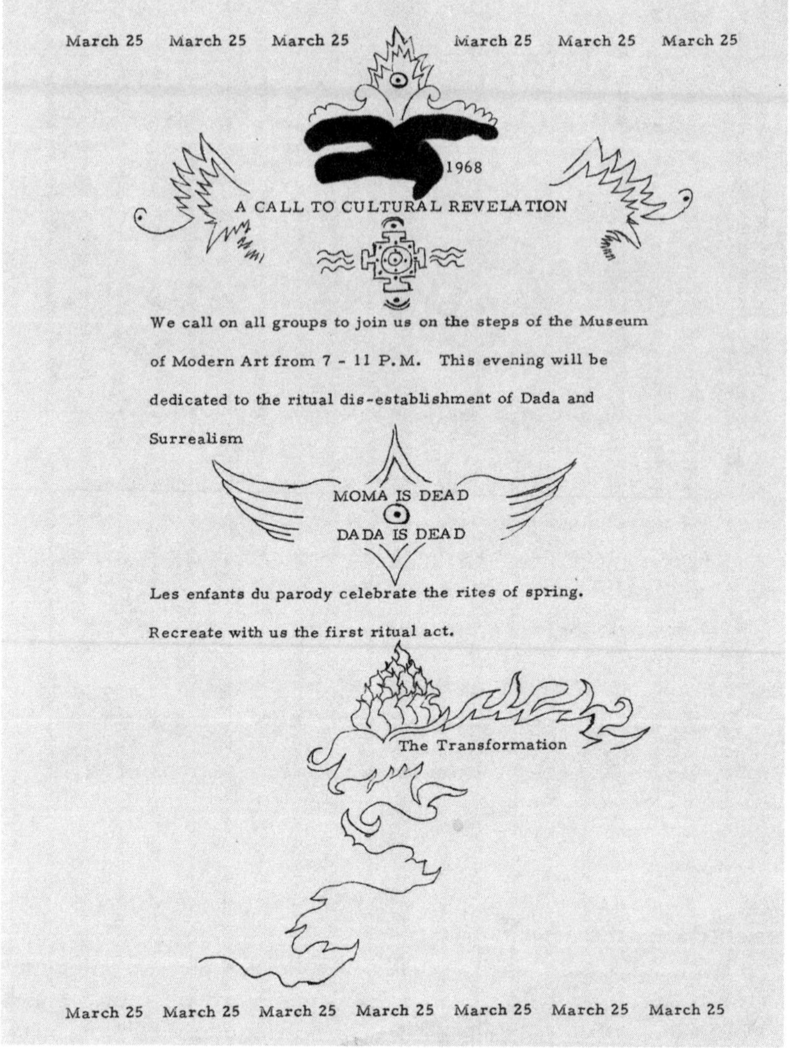

Figure 2.5 "A Call to Cultural Revelation," 1968. Broadside. Gene Swenson papers, 1950–1969, Archives of American Art, Smithsonian Institution, Washington, DC.

Geldzahler along with "that powerful if squabbling former triumvirate—Greenberg, Rosenberg and Hess" for having "succeeded," as he puts it, "in rooting out what they formerly called the 'homosexual and drug addict conspiracy' which, they said, would produce fagged art."[19] Swenson makes no secret of the fact that he perceived blatant suppression of homosexuality, or "fagged art" (as he says it got called), from the highest levels of the art

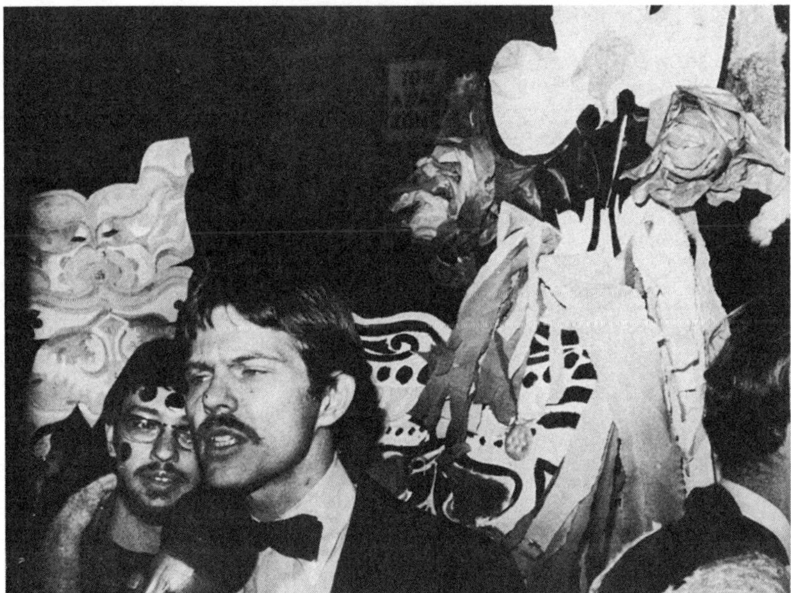

Figure 2.6 Gene Swenson protesting outside during the opening of *Dada Surrealism and Their Heritages* at the Museum of Modern Art on March 25, 1968. Photograph by Fred W. McDarrah. © Fred W. McDarrah / MUUS Collection.

world on down—suppression he links explicitly to the capitalist greed of the art world. "I have attacked them all," Swenson writes, "and, for my pains, I have been told to eat cake."[20] However, a dark current of antisemitism permeates Swenson's public attack decrying Jewish critics and curators as "vile money-changers" who control the art world. Swenson acknowledges this antisemitism and grapples with it explicitly, albeit problematically, in an unpublished essay titled "Favoritism," dated May 1968. Proclaiming his affinity with and admiration for Jews ("My life would be easier if my name were Swenberg," he claims to have joked with a Jewish friend), Swenson nonetheless frames his essay as "an attack on a particular Jewish-American elite in the fine arts" whom he accuses of "favoritism," deploying a whole lot of antisemitic tropes in the process.[21]

Reflecting back on Swenson's writings in her 1985 memoir *Paper Daughter*, Johnston asks: "So what did Gene Swenson, midwestern descendant of Scandinavian immigrants, do? We don't know," she continues, "because his writings have not yet been popularly published. By reputation, they were daring and original. Some of them, we know, were flawed by rage."[22] Certainly "flawed by rage" is one way to describe Swenson's antisemitic vitriol, but I have no interest in excusing it here. It juts out like a sharp edge. And,

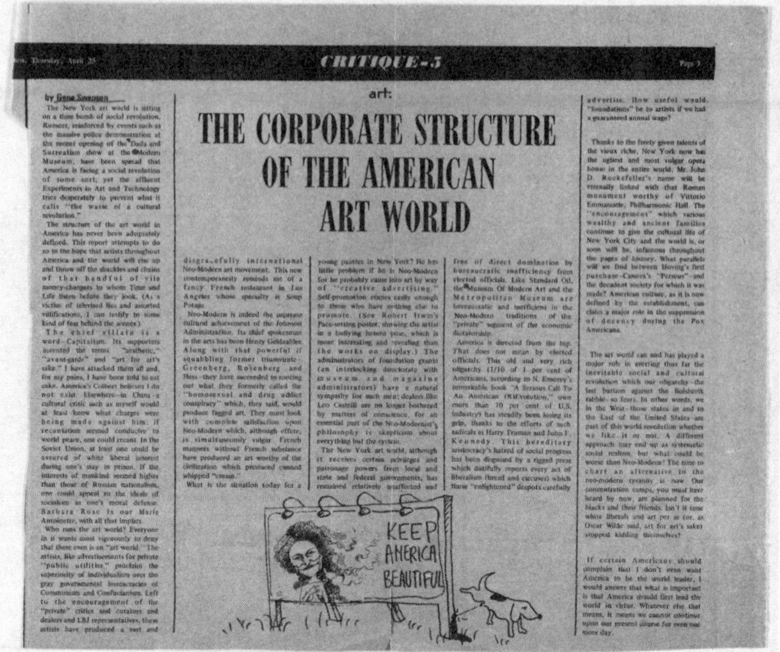

Figure 2.7 Gene Swenson, "The Corporate Structure of the American Art World," *The New York Free Press*, April 25, 1968. Newspaper clipping. Museum of Modern Art Archives, New York, NY. Digital image © The Museum of Modern Art / Licensed by SCALA / Art Resource, NY.

importantly, it points to significant stresses and fractures within New York City's politics at the end of the sixties.

"This short essay does not answer the growing Black vs. Jew controversy," Swenson writes in his unpublished text. "I cannot answer the line 'My father was lynched,' with the line 'My mother was gassed,'" as Swenson puts it, crudely. "I cannot say that I understand the problem of the blacks because I understand the problems of the minority group to which I belong—for I am a white Scandinavian Protestant."[23] Tensions between Black and Jewish New Yorkers were particularly high in May 1968, and they would come to a head during a teachers' strike a few months later.[24] In 1969, during the months leading up to and following Swenson's death, these tensions would explode publicly in the art world during the Metropolitan Museum of Art's exhibition *Harlem on My Mind: Cultural Capital of Black America*. Curated by Jewish curator Allon Schoener, the exhibition was modeled on Schoener's successful 1966 exhibition *The Lower East Side: Portal to American Life* at the Jewish Museum, which featured photographs and documents to tell a triumphal story of how the Lower East Side became a portal for many Eastern European Jewish immigrants to integrate successfully into bourgeois American family life. "The Lower East Side symbolizes the epic of Jewish adaptation to America," Schoener writes in the catalogue. "There is pride that so much came out of it."[25] When the Met hired Schoener to apply the same formula to tell the story of how Harlem became the "Cultural Capital of Black America," it did not work. *Harlem on My Mind* failed in part due to Schoener's arrogance, as he neglected to meaningfully consult Black scholars and opted for an entirely documentary show, neglecting Black artists. He further fanned the flames by deliberately including antisemitic statements in the exhibition catalogue that were attributed to a Black high school student (but, as it turns out, decontextualized and misquoted by Schoener to make them seem more authentic). However, as Susan E. Cahan argues, Schoener also failed more fundamentally to grasp that "the immigrant analogy was not applicable to the experience of African Americans" because of entrenched anti-Black racism long encoded into law.[26]

Swenson's take on the "growing Black vs. Jew controversy," as he put it, is both troubling and telling. Indignant at the art world's homophobia and irate that he was not being taken seriously, Swenson accused the "Jewish-American elite" of consolidating power and closing ranks. An ugly accusation. Searching for a place for his revolutionary socialist ideals— a place for his anger, for his rejection of bourgeois American family values, and for his embrace of rage and disintegration—Swenson wrote about seeking affinity with Black radical politics, where activists were calling for an embrace of madness (in both senses of the word) as a strategy of Black resistance against the insidious psychosocial effects of racism.[27] Noting with a bit of false modesty that his own "rather feeble list of contributions to 'brotherhood'" include several "one man crusades" to integrate the prom at his own high school in Kansas in the fifties, to form a socialist club at Yale while he was a student there, and to "antagonize almost all my friends with Maoist slogans in 1968," Swenson confesses: "But my list of excuses is much longer."[28] And it should be noted that both times he had the chance, Swenson did not actually include any Black artists in his museum exhibitions: neither in his 1966 exhibition *The* Other *Tradition* at the Institute of Contemporary Art in Philadelphia nor in his 1968 exhibition *Art in the Mirror* at MoMA.

In an unpublished essay titled "We Are All Nationalists—in Our Art," dated April–May 1968, Swenson proclaims: "One of the great contributions which the artists of our time can make is in the understanding of black history"—but he focuses the essay only on his own incomplete attempts to do so. "What can I, as a white writer, do?" Swenson asks rhetorically.

"I could expend my efforts toward the feeling that black is beautiful. That is a little imaginative effort I have been making tentative strives to get to."[29] Seeking affinity with Black radical politics, Swenson mostly failed to achieve it during his tragically truncated lifetime. If Swenson had lived just a little bit longer, if he had stayed out of Bellevue during the spring of 1969, if he hadn't gone home to Kansas that summer, his story could have perhaps ended differently. The formation of the Black Emergency Cultural Coalition to protest *Harlem on My Mind* precipitated, according to art historian Darby English, "the art world's first significant collision with black cultural nationalism," which came to a head in 1970 and 1971.[30] The Stonewall Riots of June 1969 launched gay liberation protests. If Swenson had made it back to New York after the summer of 1969, he could have found affinity by participating alongside other activists, or he might not have. "I wish he were around today," Lucy Lippard would lament in 1971, "to lend his fire to exposure of censorship at the Guggenheim, private exploitation of the Metropolitan's expansion, discrimination in the art world against women and blacks. . . ."[31] At the end of his life, Swenson flailed angrily in the impasse.

But, as Berlant reminds us, "flail isn't fail, though. It's just a big suck of our best creative energy toward holding off the pressure pushing at the survival wall." Flailing involves "making statements to keep the event open," Berlant writes. "Many of them feel clotted, a groping for counterpower wedges in the angry dark. But even in failure we are the future of the event."[32] At the end of his life, Swenson jabbed with sharp elbows, flailing and railing indiscriminately and with increasing ferocity at friends and foes alike. In an editorial published June 20, 1968, titled "Why Have None of My Fellow Artists Spoken a Word in Behalf of the Revolution?" (fig. 2.8), Swenson declares: "We of the art world have been wearing our responsibilities too lightly these days. This frivolity will live in the pages of history as The Shame of the Artists. Unfortunately I must include myself in my roles as critic, poet, prophet, and revolutionary. None of us in any of our capacities—except the Rev. Dr. Martin Luther King—has done enough."[33] Swenson wanted more commitment from art, and more from art criticism, than he was ever able to glean or to produce at the end of his life. He stayed irate, raw, and open—and throughout it all, he nurtured faith that art might provide spiritual transcendence. On April 10, 1969, just four months before his death, Swenson professed this faith unironically in front of everybody at the first Open Hearing of the Art Workers' Coalition.[34] "We wish to learn from the art which our spiritual ancestors have left us . . . those rituals which liberate the soul, those lessons which turn a collective past into the free man, which turn individuality into supreme fiction," Swenson proclaimed, according to a draft of his speech preserved in his archive. "We begin. We sound the tocsin, and its cry already rises above the jangling voices of

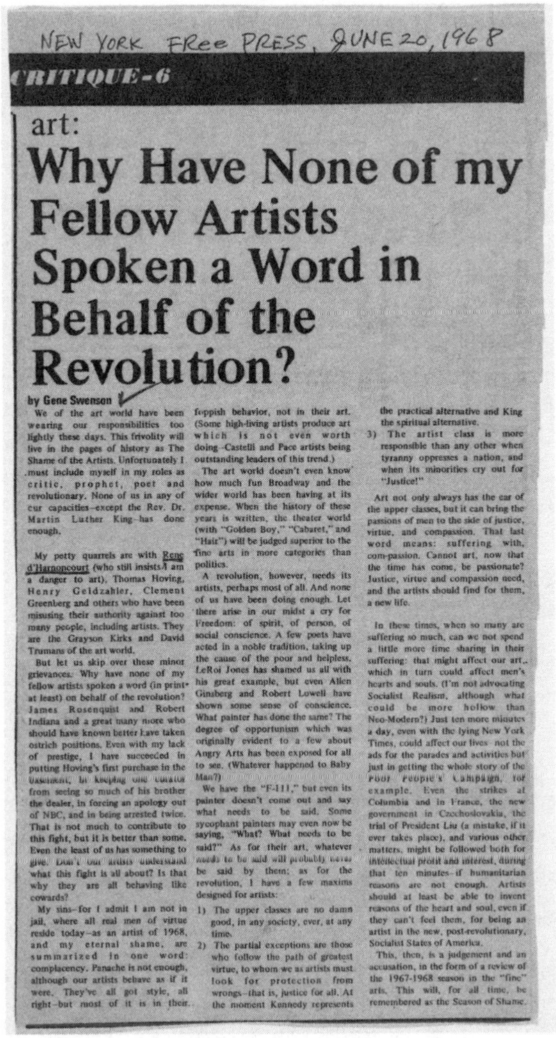

NEW YORK FREE PRESS, JUNE 20, 1968

CRITIQUE-6

art:

Why Have None of my Fellow Artists Spoken a Word in Behalf of the Revolution?

by Gene Swenson

We of the art world have been wearing our responsibilities too lightly these days. This frivolity will live in the pages of history as The Shame of the Artists. Unfortunately I must include myself in my roles as critic, prophet, poet and revolutionary. None of us in any of our capacities—except the Rev. Dr. Martin Luther King—has done enough.

My petty quarrels are with Rene d'Harnoncourt (who still insists I am a danger to art), Thomas Hoving, Henry Geldzahler, Clement Greenberg and others who have been misusing their authority against too many people, including artists. They are the Grayson Kirks and David Trumans of the art world.

But let us skip over these minor grievances. Why have none of my fellow artists spoken a word (in print-at least) on behalf of the revolution? James Rosenquist and Robert Indiana and a great many more who should have known better have taken ostrich positions. Even with my lack of prestige, I have succeeded in putting Hoving's first purchase in the basement, in keeping one curator from seeing so much of his brother the dealer, in forcing an apology out of NBC, and in being arrested twice. That is not much to contribute to this fight, but it is better than some. Even the least of us has something to give. Don't our artists understand what this fight is all about? Is that why they are all behaving like cowards?

My sins—for I admit I am not in jail, where all real men of virtue reside today—as an artist of 1968, and my eternal shame, are summarized in one word: complacency. Panache is not enough, although our artists behave as if it were. They've all got style, all right—but most of it is in their foppish behavior, not in their art. (Some high-living artists produce art which is not even worth doing—Castelli and Pace artists being outstanding leaders of this trend.)

The art world doesn't even know how much fun Broadway and the wider world has been having at its expense. When the history of these years is written, the theater world (with "Golden Boy," "Cabaret," and "Hair") will be judged superior to the fine arts in more categories than politics.

A revolution, however, needs its artists, perhaps most of all. And none of us have been doing enough. Let there arise in our midst a cry for Freedom: of spirit, of person, of social conscience. A few poets have acted in a noble tradition, taking up the cause of the poor and helpless. LeRoi Jones has shamed us all with his great example, but even Allen Ginsberg and Robert Lowell have shown some sense of conscience. What painter has done the same? The degree of opportunism which was originally evident to a few about Angry Arts has been exposed for all to see. (Whatever happened to Baby Man?)

We have the "F-111," but even its painter doesn't come out and say what needs to be said. Some sycophant painters may even now be saying, "What? What needs to be said?" As for their art, whatever needs to be said will probably never be said by them; as for the revolution, I have a few maxims designed for artists:

1) The upper classes are no damn good, in any society, ever, at any time.

2) The partial exceptions are those who follow the path of greatest virtue, to whom we as artists must look for protection from wrongs—that is, justice for all. At the moment Kennedy represents the practical alternative and King the spiritual alternative.

3) The artist class is more responsible than any other when tyranny oppresses a nation, and when its minorities cry out for "Justice!"

Art not only always has the ear of the upper classes, but it can bring the passions of men to the side of justice, virtue, and compassion. That last word means: suffering with, com-passion. Cannot art, now that the time has come, be passionate? Justice, virtue and compassion need, and the artists should find for them, a new life.

In these times, when so many are suffering so much, can we not spend a little more time sharing in their suffering: that might affect our art, which in turn could affect men's hearts and souls. (I'm not advocating Socialist Realism, although what could be more hollow than Neo-Modern?) Just ten more minutes a day, even with the lying New York Times, could affect our lives—not the ads for the parades and activities but just in getting the whole story of the Poor People's Campaign, for example. Even the strikes at Columbia and in France, the new government in Czechoslovakia, the trial of President Liu (a mistake, if it ever takes place), and various other matters, might be followed both for intellectual profit and interest, during that ten minutes—if humanitarian reasons are not enough. Artists should at least be able to invent reasons of the heart and soul, even if they can't feel them, for being an artist in the new, post-revolutionary, Socialist States of America.

This, then, is a judgement and an accusation, in the form of a review of the 1967-1968 season in the "fine" arts. This will, for all time, be remembered as the Season of Shame.

Figure 2.8 Gene Swenson, "Why Have None of My Fellow Artists Spoken a Word in Behalf of the Revolution?," *The New York Free Press*, June 20, 1968. Newspaper clipping. Museum of Modern Art Archives, New York, NY. Digital image © The Museum of Modern Art / Licensed by SCALA / Art Resource, NY.

fear. . . . We are the revolution. We will be free, because our spirit is free."[35] According to Gregory Battcock, Swenson's remarks "brought down the house."[36]

The louder and more emphatic Swenson got at the end of his life, however, the harder, it seems, he became to hear—and not only because his message was drowned out in an overabundance of angry noise spread too thin over too many issues. For a handful of Swenson's closest allies, those artists and critics most sympathetic to his plight and willing to vouch for the veracity of his condemnations, it became too taxing and painful to keep listening. So they stopped, for the most part, which became an avowed source of mournful regret after Swenson died. "I didn't see much of Gene in the last year of his life," Lippard would recollect. "He frightened and embarrassed me because he demanded of me as much commitment as he was willing to offer himself and I couldn't meet his demands."[37] Eulogizing Swenson after his death, Battcock recalls, "He had been in and out of Bellevue and many thought him crazy. But he was articulate and implacable in his efforts to remind artists and intellectuals of their social and political responsibilities. . . . Swenson's large and passionately held reformist views give his own single-handed attempts to accomplish them a degree of pathos. Yet his brief career was exemplary in its pursuit of them at any cost—and the cost in friends, stability and financial security was great. When Swenson died, many of us felt as though we had lost our conscience."[38]

•   •   •

During the month of February 1968, every weekday from 11:00 a.m. to 1:00 p.m., Swenson picketed alone outside MoMA wielding only a giant, blue plexiglass question mark as a sign (fig. 2.9). Writing about Swenson's

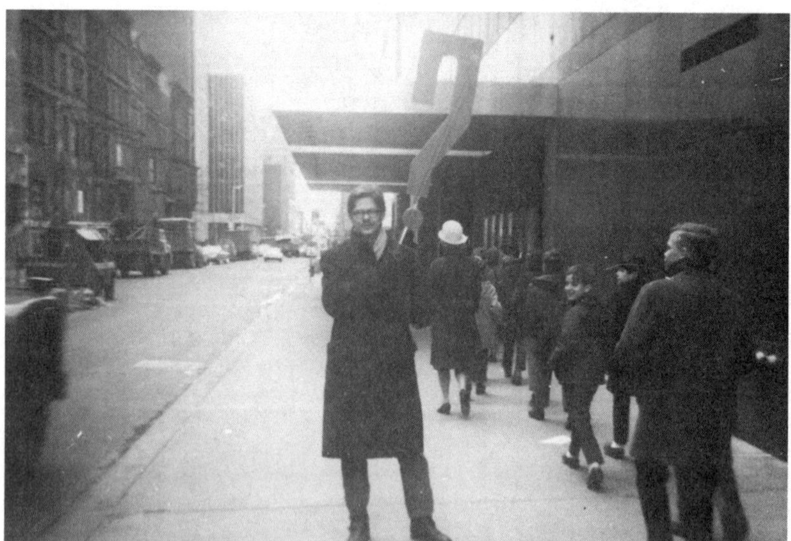

Figure 2.9 Gene Swenson picketing outside the Museum of Modern Art, 1968. Black-and-white snapshot. Photo by Ann Wilson. © The Estate of Ann Marie Wilson.

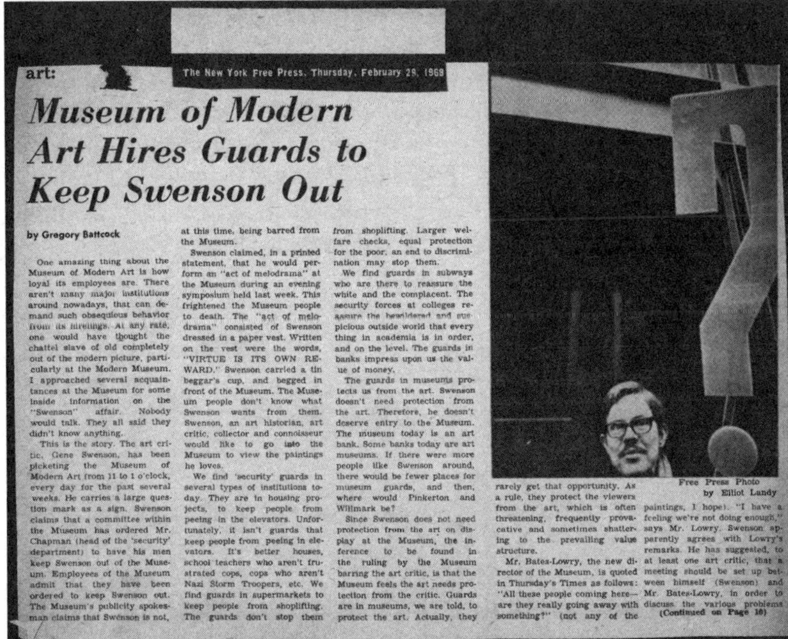

art:

The New York Free Press, Thursday, February 29, 1968

Museum of Modern Art Hires Guards to Keep Swenson Out

by Gregory Battcock

One amazing thing about the Museum of Modern Art is how loyal its employees are. There aren't many major institutions around nowadays, that can demand such obsequious behavior from its hirelings. At any rate, one would have thought the chattel slave of old completely out of the modern picture, particularly at the Modern Museum. I approached several acquaintances at the Museum for some inside information on the "Swenson" affair. Nobody would talk. They all said they didn't know anything.

This is the story. The art critic, Gene Swenson, has been picketing the Museum of Modern Art from 11 to 1 o'clock, every day for the past several weeks. He carries a large question mark as a sign. Swenson claims that a committee within the Museum has ordered Mr. Chapman (head of the 'security' department) to have his men keep Swenson out of the Museum. Employees of the Museum admit that they have been ordered to keep Swenson out. The Museum's publicity spokesman claims that Swenson is not, at this time, being barred from the Museum.

Swenson claimed, in a printed statement, that he would perform an "act of melodrama" at the Museum during an evening symposium held last week. This frightened the Museum people to death. The "act of melodrama" consisted of Swenson dressed in a paper vest. Written on the vest were the words, "VIRTUE IS ITS OWN REWARD." Swenson carried a tin beggar's cup, and begged in front of the Museum. The Museum people don't know what Swenson wants from them. Swenson, an art historian, art critic, collector and connoisseur would like to go into the Museum to view the paintings he loves.

We find 'security' guards in several types of institutions today. They are in housing projects, to keep people from peeing in the elevators. Unfortunately, it isn't guards that keep people from peeing in elevators. It's better houses, school teachers who aren't frustrated cops, cops who aren't Nazi Storm Troopers, etc. We find guards in supermarkets to keep people from shoplifting. The guards don't stop them from shoplifting. Larger welfare checks, equal protection for the poor, an end to discrimination may stop them.

We find guards in subways who are there to reassure the white and the complacent. The security forces at colleges reassure the bewildered and suspicious outside world that everything in academia is in order, and on the level. The guards in banks impress upon us the value of money.

The guards in museums protects us from the art. Swenson doesn't need protection from the art. Therefore, he doesn't deserve entry to the Museum. The museum today is an art bank. Some banks today are art museums. If there were more people like Swenson around, there would be fewer places for museum guards, and then, where would Pinkerton and Willmark be?

Since Swenson does not need protection from the art on display at the Museum, the inference to be found in the ruling by the Museum barring the art critic, is that the Museum feels the art needs protection from the critic. Guards are in museums, we are told, to protect the art. Actually, they rarely get that opportunity. As a rule, they protect the viewers from the art, which is often threatening, frequently provocative and sometimes shattering to the prevailing value structure.

Mr. Bates-Lowry, the new director of the Museum, is quoted in Thursday's Times as follows: "All these people coming here— are they really going away with something?" (not any of the paintings, I hope). "I have a feeling we're not doing enough," says Mr. Lowry. Swenson apparently agrees with Lowry's remarks. He has suggested, to at least one art critic, that a meeting should be set up between himself (Swenson) and Mr. Bates-Lowry, in order to discuss the various problems (Continued on Page 16)

Free Press Photo
by Elliot Landy

Figure 2.10 Gregory Battcock, "Museum of Modern Art Hires Guards to Keep Swenson Out," *The New York Free Press*, February 29, 1968. Newspaper clipping. Gregory Battcock papers, 1952–circa 1980, Archives of American Art, Smithsonian Institution, Washington, DC.

protest in an article for *The New York Free Press* titled "Museum of Modern Art Hires Guards to Keep Swenson Out," Battcock, who was a careful and sympathetic observer, surmises, "The museum won't let Swenson in, because they don't know what to expect from him. They don't know what he wants" (fig. 2.10). Illustrated with a photo cropped dramatically to include just Swenson's head punctuated by his giant question mark, Battcock's article presents Swenson's question mark as "the prime symbol, in writing, of existential man." Battcock proclaims, "Everything is question, and **in** question."[39] In a letter to the editor Swenson thanks *The New York Free Press* for its coverage. "Your image of me in an existential pose . . . has helped me to bear some of this pain I am feeling these days," he writes, signing the letter "Gene 'Kansas' Swenson" and adopting a deliberately folksy tone to signal his distance from an art world that, as he saw it, often dismissed his concerns in the name of cultural sophistication.[40] As Lippard would later remember the situation: "The whole Art Workers' Coalition couldn't match the courage of Gene, the year before it was founded, persistently picketing the Museum of Modern Art, alone, with a huge blue question mark on a stick."[41] Likewise, artist Howardena Pindell would recall: "In the late 1960s, Gene Swenson walked back and forth in front of the Museum of Modern Art carrying a blue question mark. His actions seem to have ushered in a brief period of dissection and examination of the art world establishment by concerned white and nonwhite artist and critics."[42] Angry, anguished, and alone, armed only with a giant existential question mark and faith in the power of art, Swenson succeeded, perhaps, in making space for other artists and critics to craft new activist commitments in his wake.

Battcock interprets Swenson's protest as a poignant gesture of surrender in the face of a nation's depravity. Near the conclusion of his article, Battcock recalls a statement from the previous week's *New York Free Press*, written by a soldier recently returned from Vietnam:

He had seen three babies, burnt to a crisp, being taken away in an ambulance. Very appropriately, and with profound existential humility, he concluded his article with:

Nor could we find out where they had been taken from.
Neither, really, matters very much.
Nor, of course, does it matter when the mother died.

Battcock then concludes: "Alone Swenson pickets, itself an existential gesture as it provides confrontation in isolation. What does he want? Who could ever know. Will he achieve his goal? In as much as there is a goal, it has already been achieved. Equally, we have already lost the war."[43] But Swenson did not declare the war lost. Picketing alone outside MoMA wielding only that giant blue question mark, Swenson withholds comforts of slogans and solidarity, of simple demands shouted in unison. With his question mark, Swenson suspends the popular protest chant uneasily at "What Do We Want?" Only in his protest, the "We" never materializes. No rallying cry rises up in response to his question mark. How could it? By dramatizing a breakdown of reciprocity and foreclosing the possibility for collective response, Swenson demands an excruciating kind of ongoing commitment: to dwell in a state of unknowing and disintegration, alert and ill at ease, unsatisfied and creative.

• • •

September 11, 1969
Pick up *The Village Voice* and turn to page seventeen. Jill Johnston's weekly column Dance Journal is a mournful lament, a eulogy for Gene Swenson.

LIKE A BOY IN A BOAT

dance
JOURNAL
by Jill Johnston

How do you report a death without sounding sorry? I could write a classical obituary but Gene isn't a proper subject. Gene Swenson is dead. I thought it would be from flying off a rooftop but it happened in Kansas in a car with his mother. The next to last time I saw Gene was before leaving for Europe in June he was yelling at me behind an extended arm and pointed finger. I don't know the content of his fury because I was making just as much noise in my own distress while cowering toward the exit. . . . The next to last time I saw Gene was the day he was released from Bellevue in June and I drove him across a bridge into some trees and he hung a hand out the window like a boy in a boat having never felt the drag of the water before. . . . The last time I saw him he was Gene the Gentle, walking down the Bowery slow motion, fragile, transparent, not really there. And scared shitless. Trapped. Didn't know what to do. Leave New York and don't go back to Kansas, that was all I ever said, I dunno what the others said. Not that anyone could keep up with his roles. The Village Priest, Poet, and Philosopher. The hippie revolutionary. The scholar and art historian. The home town boy from Kansas. And at last the reports would come in how he was barefoot on the streets with a bible and getting the number messages off the radio and he was becoming his Crazy Gene self and he was beautiful but it wouldn't be long before they'd come to get him because he'd wreck his place or something considered unsociable and thus for the third time in June he was going into the recovery phase of a cycle that included being a prisoner of state and so forth the garbage everybody knows about. Maybe he's lucky now. I have no opinion really.[44]

Signaling Through the Flames

The year 1969 was an intense one for Johnston, even before Swenson died in August. It began in January with a psychic breakdown—her third. Twice before, in 1965 and 1966, she had landed in the psychiatric ward. But in

January 1969, she managed for the first time to escape "the clutches of the psychiatric profession and its penal colonies" by leaving New York City on a cross-country road trip with her lover, an experience she would chronicle in her 1973 book *Lesbian Nation: The Feminist Solution*. "I began in fact to exploit my crazy trip," Johnston continues, "and to make a kind of career out of it by presenting the evidence in my column as a celebration as well as a defense."[45] By 1969 she was finally, by her own account, "convinced at last that it was the world who was fucked up and not me." She was also "convinced that I had to be a dyke but how."[46] The Stonewall Riots that would launch gay liberation in New York City were still many months away. And, for Johnston, there was not yet a way to be a dyke in the city. She claims to have known a few gay men in New York in the sixties but no lesbians, as she would explain in *Lesbian Nation*. "I never said I was a dyke even to a dyke because there wasn't a dyke in the land who thought she should be a dyke or even that she was a dyke so how could we talk about it."[47] Furious, determined, and still condemned by a "conspiracy of silence," Johnston hatched a vague plan at the end of the sixties, or at least what she describes in retrospect as a plan: "I was so angry that I was conducting a one woman revolution through a very slow calculated but unrelenting exposure of myself in the guise of literary code hopefully so challenging and fascinating and entertaining and difficult to read that any premature retaliation from a hostile society would be discouraged, and in this sense from the standpoint of anger I was certainly no longer capable of keeping a secret."[48] When Johnston returned to New York City after her great escape in January 1969 "unmolested by the psychiatric profession," she submitted herself to analysis. Not to a psychiatrist, but rather to a panel of her peers. She got to work planning a panel discussion titled "The Disintegration of a Critic: An Analysis of Jill Johnston" to take place May 21, 1969, placing several promotional ads in *The Village Voice* (figs. 2.11–2.12).

Johnston promoted the "Disintegration of a Critic: An Analysis of Jill Johnston" panel as a grand culminating event: her "third and last panel," as she put it in a press release that circulated around New York (fig. 2.13).[49] "My first panel at N.Y.U. in 1968 was a conventional one with Robert Morris moderating," Johnston writes. After Swenson showed up as the "uninvited bully"—provoking an impossible, sputtering situation that temporarily eroded boundaries between artist and audience—Johnston devised her second panel, intended to aggrandize the crisis of authority by transforming the whole audience into bullies.

"My second [panel] in the fall of '68 was a disintegration panel," Johnston explains in the press release for her third panel. "I moderated and the panel members and myself relinquished our places to the audience. It was a 'difficult' object lesson for everybody, us too, in the absurdity of author-

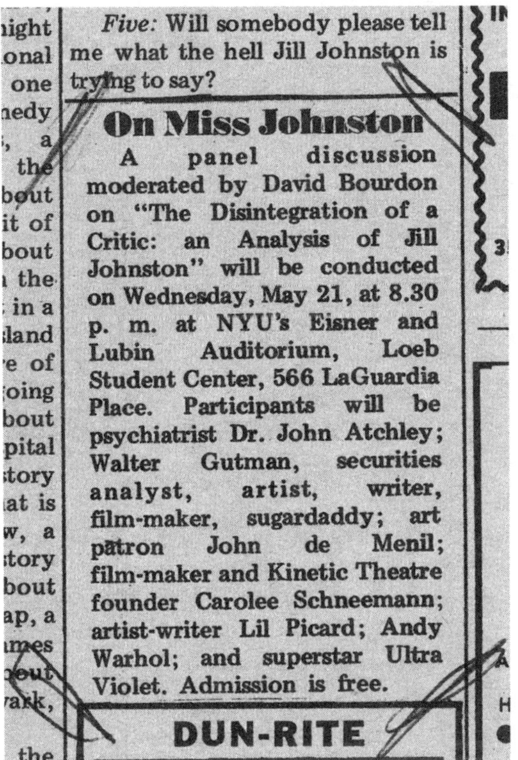

Figure 2.11 Advertisement in *The Village Voice*, April 24, 1969. Newspaper clipping. Lil Picard papers, Special Collections and Archives, University of Iowa Libraries, Iowa City, IA.

ity."[50] Johnston's second panel featured artists Les Levine, Allan Kaprow, Gordon Mumma, Barbara Lloyd, and Trisha Brown. It fell apart almost as soon as it began. Lloyd brought a live pig onstage; Mumma distorted everyone's voices with an electronic sound modification system; Levine hid behind three television sets; Brown slammed her chair down and stormed off; artist Willoughby Sharp got onstage, tackled Johnston, and got naked; audience members rushed the stage; and someone yelled fire over and over again. Then someone actually tried to start a fire. "But the fire which must have moved everyone was the unhappy desperate girl who mounted the stage at last to burn the place up in a plea for love," as Johnston reports in her *Village Voice* column titled "The Unhappy Spectator," published right after her second panel on October 17, 1968. "She was absolutely for real. She was signaling through the flames," Johnston continues, evoking Antonin Artaud's *The Theatre and Its Double*. "She was everybody's transfigured sacrifice. She was the crucible of the day. If she wasn't in fact, resurrected,

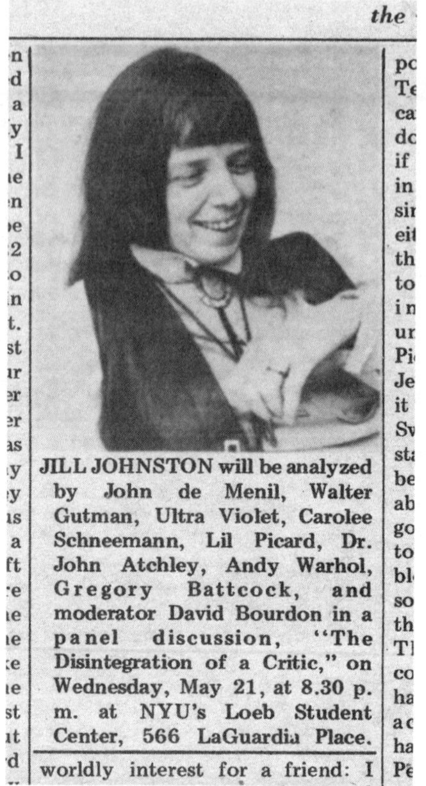

Figure 2.12 Advertisement in *The Village Voice*, May 15, 1969. Newspaper clipping.

I think we all wanted her to be, to be resurrected right there out of the center of her own catastrophe."[51]

Throughout the late sixties, Johnston frequently conjured Artaud as a model of a fractured subject who produces disintegrated art and, simultaneously, as a romantic spiritual martyr for whom art provides transcendence from a hellish world. But this apparent contradiction is, as art historian Lucy Bradnock demonstrates, entirely characteristic of the times: "The artistic production of postwar America manifested a widespread, if haphazard, mobilization of Artaud's ideas."[52] Although Artaud's "emphasis on fragmentation and the deferral of meaning . . . lend him decidedly postmodern credentials," Bradnock argues, "his mythopoetic quest for authentic expression, and the spiritual transcendence implied by the body that 'signals through the flames,' root him in the modernist cause."[53] Johnston's engagement with Artaud manifests this tension in all of its difficulty, and it demonstrates that postmodernism in New York City in the sixties was a contradictory, impure endeavor on the ground, especially among avant-

PRESS RELEASE

Re Panel Discussion May 21st at Loeb Student Center of N.Y.U. "The Disintegration of a Critic — An Analysis of Jill Johnston" with panel members David Bourdon (moderator), John de Menil, Walter Gutman, Ultra Violet, Carolee Schneemann, Lil Picard, Dr. John Atchley, Andy Warhol, Gregory Battcock.

My purpose in arranging this my third and last panel was to offer my name as a sort of sacrifice if you like for the idea(1) of a disintegration of criticism, which I view as an outmoded form of communication. Reportage may be necessary and interesting. I like it myself. Poetry and all forms of fiction, history, autobiog., etc., I accept as forms of speech and writing not coercive as to the salesmanship of immediate artistic events, i.e., reviews in the newspapers and the magazines. A critic has come to be an unpaid publicity agent. The artist expects this of the critic and privately coerces him; the critic has accepted this role and uses the artist to build his own reputation: by the game of playing off one artist against another in the "historical sequence of trends." Anybody familiar with the history of art knows also how history is made by the winners of the moment: those with the power of money, press, fame etc., to urge an old artist on a new public, to resurrect a forgotten artist, to exhume an artist completely unknown to his own time even, to relegate to the grave a whole era popular for a time and so on. I am now interested solely in autobiographical history, from the cradles as well as from the history of an (our) archetypal past. As anything else I see both immediate and more remote history as imposed upon people from without and the people who take it as unwilling to accept the responsibility for deciding what their own history is, dependent always upon the judgment the authority of one who assumes it in the historical guise of the father of the Judaic-Christian patriarchal tradition. That this dependence will continue to exist I see as fated for the present yet equally fated to terminate in the near future, as a state of affairs family, educational and cultural and finally political. Having been a so-called critic I fall into the cultural category and the panel May 21st is meant to illustrate, as an art event of the "object lesson" variety, the demise of a particular critic who both literally and figuratively (or intellectually) disintegrated. In 1965 as I was hospitalized one aspect of my vision was in the form of a command to relinquish the role of judge, a role I never dreamed I would assume in 1950 in the first place, for in 1957 I was inspired solely to find a new language a new vocabulary for dance — to make a new dance literature which I thought was historically and contemporaneously appalling. My first panel at N.Y.U. in 1968 was a conventional one with Robert Morris moderating. My second in the fall of '68 was a disintegration panel, I moderated and the panel members and myself relinquished our places to the audience. It was a "difficult" object lesson for everybody, us too, in the absurdity of authority. The panel May 21st is my final solution to a personal problem which I would hope to have some effect on all those caught in a similar trap if indeed they see it that way.

JILL JOHNSTON

Figure 2.13 "Re Panel Discussion May 21st at Loeb Student Center of N.Y.U. 'The Disintegration of a Critic—An Analysis of Jill Johnston,'" press release, 1969. Lil Picard papers, Special Collections and Archives, University of Iowa Libraries, Iowa City, IA.

garde artists. Art historical accounts of the postwar United States tend to elide this difficulty, positing instead a tidier trajectory from Abstract Expressionism to postmodern allegory and appropriation, which becomes a neat story about "the abandonment of expressionism in favor of detached and analytic irony," as Bradnock aptly characterizes it.[54] The problem, of course, is that Swenson and Johnston have no place in this story—except as naïve, embarrassing outliers—even though they were both right there in the middle of it all doing some really ambitious and earnest, angry and disquieting queer protests and panels that garnered a whole lot of art-world attention.[55]

Johnston describes Swenson as having an "air of permanently shocked naiveté, or of 'signaling through the flames' from behind his glasses, an extreme idealism contradicted by some personal knowledge of brutality."[56]And throughout the late sixties, she often describes herself too as "signaling through the flames." As Sally Banes recounts in a 1980 text titled "Jill Johnston: Signaling Through the Flames,"

> [Johnston] glories in, even mythologizes, the direct experience of "reality"—chaotic, messy, raw vitality of movement and materials unmediated by deadening forms. . . . Yet Johnston goes farther, calling for an art that "signals through the flames"—as she frequently quoted from Artaud, evoking the image of the artist as an ecstatic martyr and projecting a romantic vision of nature and reality, and of the innocent grace of artists who can make life yield its secrets. That is a view as freighted with political and social meaning—albeit an alternative meaning—as the art of the academy.[57]

For her third panel, the "Disintegration of a Critic: An Analysis of Jill Johnston" panel of May 21, 1969, Johnston offers herself up as a version of Artaud's martyr. As she proclaims in the press release:

> My purpose in arranging this my third and last panel was to offer my name as a sort of sacrifice if you like for the idea(l) of a disintegration of criticism, which I view as an outmoded form of communication. . . . Having been a so-called critic I fall into the cultural category and the panel of May 21st is meant to illustrate, as an art event of the "object lesson" variety, the demise of a particular critic who both literally and figuratively (or intellectually) disintegrated. In 1965 as I was hospitalized one aspect of my vision was in the form of a command to relinquish the role of judge, a role I never dreamed I would assume. . . . The panel May 21st is my final solution to a personal problem which I would hope to have some effect on all those caught in a similar trap if indeed they see it that way.[58]

As Johnston would make clear a few years later in *Lesbian Nation*, there was no way to be an integrated person (or critic) as a lesbian in the sixties—or at least for her there wasn't. To be a dyke was by necessity to exist as a fractured subject in contradiction to oneself: to indulge queer actions and desires that did not correspond to any way of actually living in the world.

"Dykedom was not a reality for the world nor was it real for any of us who were actually doing it," Johnston writes. "We never said it so it didn't exist."[59] For Johnston, this fractured, disintegrated existence did not resolve neatly into any kind of hallucinogenic euphoria to displace anxiety and alienation, as Fredric Jameson would later theorize, nor did it give rise to Warholian detached irony. It stayed painful, and Johnston kept striving. She kept striving to be a dyke. She also kept striving for spiritual transcendence, for something more real beneath the surface, for a mystical wholeness in the "total transcendent One," as she would put it in her 1971 preface to *Marmalade Me*, and for "affirmation of the visionary experience they call insane if not drug induced or church defined."[60]

Flailing in the impasse in the late sixties, Johnston transformed her weekly *Village Voice* column into something new: a space to shatter and disorganize language, to subvert literary codes, and to assemble experimental modes of expression capable of accounting for her still impossible existence. Her columns express a wish for wholeness and, at the same time, exult in breakdown—of language and of the self. The painful intractability of this contradiction became Johnston's creative fuel. Rather than seeking resolution in the form of a quieter, more integrated life, Johnston transformed the difficulty into an art practice. Every week in *The Village Voice* and then on the "Disintegration of a Critic" panel, she offered herself up, in all of her brilliant struggling, as a "sort of sacrifice"—a self-indulgent act to be sure, but also one of heartbreaking generosity. And, as it turns out, artists and critics in New York City were compelled by Johnston: some with embarrassment, some with a bit of disdain, but many with great excitement, especially fellow critic Gregory Battcock. Johnston's new vision for "criticism *without apology*," as Battcock calls it, invites messy contradictions without resolution.[61] She masters postmodern strategies of appropriation and pastiche, she understands selfhood as something unstable that is always constantly assembled in language, *and* she maintains a romantic striving for something more *real* underneath it all—for "life" in the Artaudian sense of a "fragile, fluctuating center which forms never reach."[62] She revels in messy, raw modes of expression as being "absolutely for real," in her words. And she means it.

With the "Disintegration of a Critic" panel on May 21, 1969, Johnston assembled a who's who of the art world to herald her artistic achievements in front of a packed audience at the Loeb Student Center at New York University. The purpose of the panel was not simply to analyze her psychic disintegration but more importantly to trumpet her artistic innovations as representing an "idea(l) of the disintegration of criticism" and its transformation into something more vital and capacious. She invited Battcock along with Andy Warhol, Ultra Violet, Brigid Berlin, Charlotte Moorman,

Walter Gutman, Lil Picard, and philanthropist John de Menil to serve as panelists, with critic David Bourdon moderating (fig. 2.14). Warhol did not say anything, but he brought his cassette-tape recorder and recorded the whole thing.

The panelists showed up late and drunk, with Johnston showing up even later and drunker. Battcock exposed his cock, Brigid Berlin exposed her tits; the panel was marked (or marred) by interruptions and cross talk. Whether the panel represents a success or a failure is beside the point. In the end, it

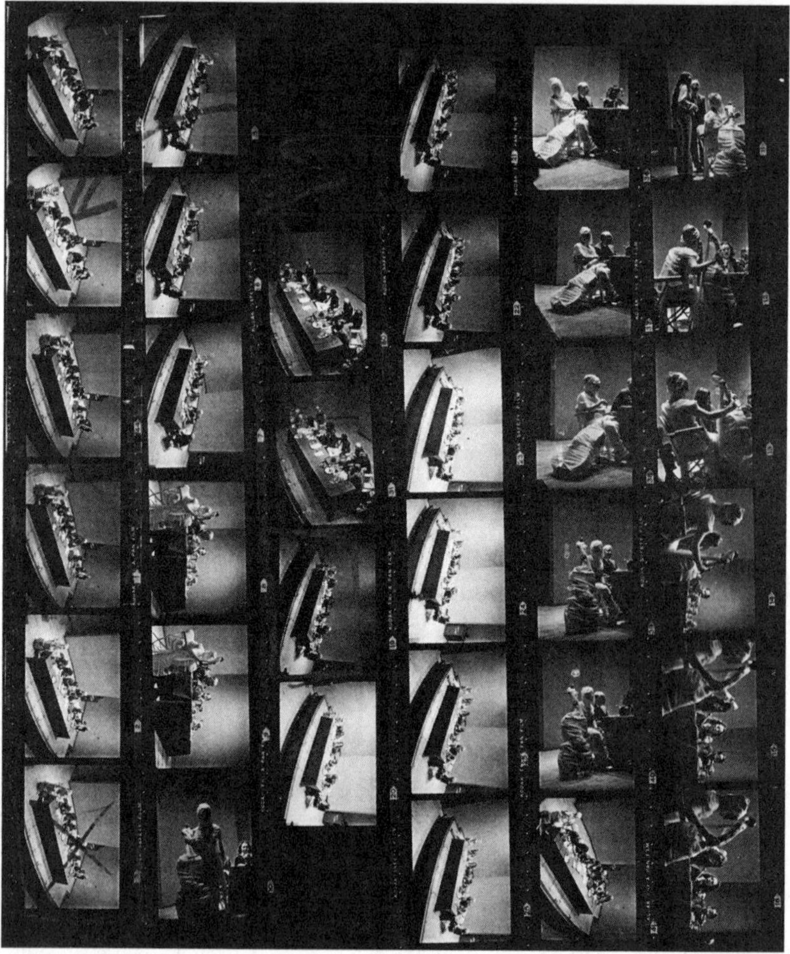

Figure 2.14 "The Disintegration of a Critic: An Analysis of Jill Johnston" panel at Loeb Student Center, New York University, May 21, 1969. Contact sheet. Photos by Fred W. McDarrah. Courtesy of Charles Deering McCormick Library of Special Collections and University Archives, Northwestern University Libraries, Evanston, IL. © Fred W. McDarrah / MUUS Collection.

aggrandizes the contradictions that gave rise to Johnston's artistic achievements, without resolution. It was messy and absurd, sincere and striving, and it was also impossible to ignore on the ground in New York City in 1969. John Perrault reported on it for *The Village Voice*, Lil Picard for *The East Village Other*, Gregory Battcock for *The New York Review of Sex & Politics*, and John Gruen for *Vogue*.

A Sort of Sacrifice

All the panelists arrived thirty minutes late except for Charlotte Moorman, who arrived on time only to sit onstage in front of the packed audience alone for thirty minutes wrapped in pink gauze with her cello. "By 9 o'clock I began to think that the bastards had really done it and that the rascals were not going to arrive at all," Perrault reports in a column titled "A Sort of Sacrifice," covering the event as part of his art beat for *The Village Voice*. "I toyed around with the idea and felt comfortable with it and felt it appropriate given the announced topic, so at 9.05, when they began filing in, I was a little disappointed."[63] Writing for *The New York Review of Sex & Politics* a month later, Battcock explains what happened:

> For ten weeks before the thing Jill is phoning every day so is David Bourdon, moderator. Nobody was sure who would show up though practically everybody did in the end. . . . The panel is at Loeb at 8:30. At 8:30 they're bringing us more Meursault at SHOEI. David is a nervous wreck. Lil Picard sends out for some scotch. Andy is taking pictures with his new Polaroid. So is Bridget but her's don't come out so good. More fantastic dishes come to the table. We can't tear ourselves away. It's nine o'clock already and still nobody is sure whether or not the panel will come off. Charlotte Moorman is missing. The hotel Paris they don't answer. Bridget orders more sake. Me too. And off we go. Everything is extremely serious, but like the good lord said, if you don't mind, be so kind and unwind which we did. So we get to Loeb and the audience is all there, thousands of them waiting for only god knows what, we certainly didn't.[64]

"Well, David started things off fine," Battcock continues, "alot of straight talk, everybody listened politely, somebody passed around a little bottle of bourbon, somebody else scotch, Charlotte had her beer, I had a little thing of sake still."[65] While it seems an exaggeration to call it "straight talk," Bourdon did kick off the panel discussion according to a fairly standard formula: introductory remarks about the significance of Johnston's critical practice followed by several questions for the panelists.

After the panel, Johnston prodded everyone to keep talking about her. A few months later, she asked everyone in New York's art world, including all the panelists, to contribute 1,500 words about her for a special issue of artist Les Levine's short-lived underground paper *Culture Hero: A Fanzine of Stars of the Superworld*, which hit newsstands in February 1970 with a run of around four thousand copies and the sensational title "Jill Johnston Exposed: A Life Dominated by Strange Arts, Consuming Desires, and Ego-Eroticism . . ."[66] For his contribution, Warhol published a transcript of his recording of the "Disintegration of a Critic" panel. Printed in italic font and extending over two and a half newspaper pages, the transcript seems to reproduce every word, including all the *ums* and *uhs*, with ellipses to indicate pauses and stutters (fig. 2.15).

"*Um,*" Bourdon begins (according to Warhol's transcript), "*in the beginning Miss Johnston restricted herself to fairly routine dance reviews. Uh, after a short time, uh, she branched out to, uh, pursue more unconventional pursuits. Um, she was one of the first to recognize and write about the new forms of the medium, was one of the earliest and most sympathetic interpreters of Happenings in the theatre. Her critical writings played an integral part in the development and flowering of the Judson Dance Theatre in the early Sixties.*"[67]

"*The reason that we do pay so much attention to her tonight—and every night—is that her past writings have proved to be so prophetic that we can't really ignore her,*" he goes on, a bit further down. "*However,*" he continues, "*during recent years her writing has become increasingly—erotic. Her writing has become increasingly congested in style, extremely subjective in content, enormously subtuitous in its logic. It would appear that she has disintegrated personally and professionally on an enormous scale.*"

By way of kicking off the discussion portion of the evening, Bourdon asks the panel, "*'How Objective Can Criticism Be, Anyway?' . . . um. . . . When Miss Johnston made this shift from third person to first person, uh, was she really in on something new. . . . um, and uh, things she doesn't want to— I forgot the vision . . . where is the vision. . . . uh, in 1965, uh, she was under intensive care for, uh, for visions. . . . she had a—*"

Responding to this initial question, John de Menil counters, "*. . . and when you said, David, that she has had 'visions,' I don't think she had 'visions'—I think that she had 'vision,' which is totally different.*"

Bourdon asks the panelists whether Johnston "*represents, uh, future criticism*" and if she provides "*a corrective to formalist criticism.*" He also asks, "*Does Miss Johnston live her column?*" which he follows by asking, "*Um, has it come a kind of substitute for her life? Uh, is it a kind of therapy that keeps her going from week to week—if she weren't able to practice her life in weekly installments, would she collapse completely, or has she some kind*

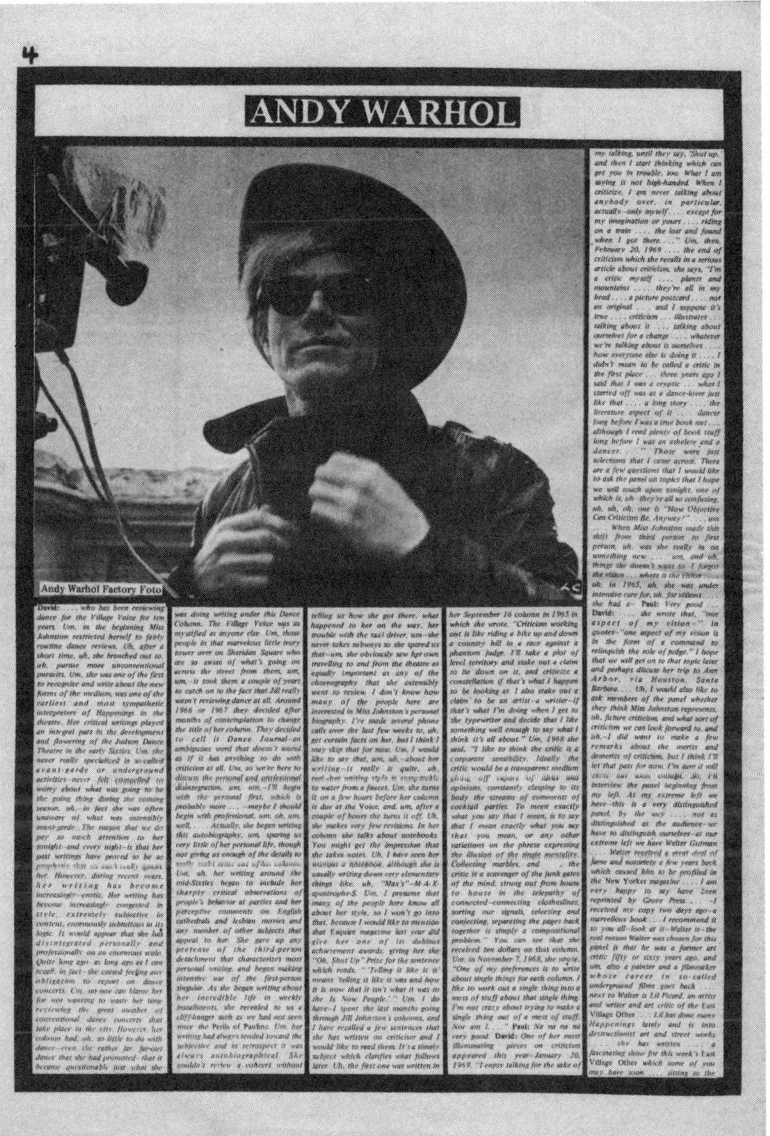

ANDY WARHOL

Andy Warhol Factory Foto

David: .... who has been reviewing dance for the Village Voice for ten years. Um, in the beginning Miss Johnston restricted herself to fairly routine dance reviews. Uh, after a short time, uh, she branched out to, uh, pursue more unconventional pursuits. Um, she was one of the first to recognize and write about the new forms of the medium, was one of the earliest and most sympathetic interpreters of Happenings in the theatre. Her critical writings played an integral part in the development and flowering of the Judson Dance Theatre in the early Sixties. Um, she never really specialized in so-called avant-garde or underground activities—never felt compelled to worry about what was going to be the going thing during the coming season, uh,—in fact she was often unaware of what was ostensibly avant-garde. The reason that we do pay so much attention to her tonight—and every night—is that her past writings have proved to be so prophetic that we can't really ignore her. However, during recent years, her writing has become increasingly—erotic. Her writing has become increasingly congested in style, extremely subjective in content, enormously nebulous in its logic. It would appear that she has disintegrated personally and professionally on an enormous scale. Quite long ago—as long ago as I can recall, in fact—she ceased feeling any obligation to report on dance concerts. Um, no one can blame her for not wanting to waste her time reviewing the great number of conventional dance concerts that take place in the city. However, her column had, uh, so little to do with dance—even the rather far, far-out dance that she had promoted—that it became questionable just what she was doing writing under this Dance Column. The Village Voice was as mystified as anyone else. Um, those people in that marvelous little ivory tower over on Sheridan Square who are so aware of what's going on across the street from them, um, um,—it took them a couple of years to catch on to the fact that Jill really wasn't reviewing dance at all. Around 1966 or 1967 they decided after months of contemplation to change the title of her column. They decided to call it Dance Journal—an ambiguous word that doesn't sound as if it has anything to do with criticism at all. Um, so we're here to discuss the personal and professional disintegration, um, um,—I'll begin with the personal first, which is probably more ...—maybe I should begin with professional, um, oh, um, well, ... Actually, she began writing this autobiography, um, sparing us very little of her personal life, though not giving us enough of the details to really make sense out of her column. Um, uh, her writing around the mid-Sixties began to include her sharply critical observations of people's behavior at parties and her perceptive comments on English cathedrals and lesbian movies and any number of other subjects that appeal to her. She gave up any pretense of the third-person detachment that characterizes most personal writing, and began making intensive use of the first-person singular. As she began writing about her incredible life in weekly installments, she revealed to us a cliff-hanger such as we had not seen since the Perils of Pauline. Um, her writing had always tended toward the subjective and in retrospect it was telling us how she got there, what happened to her on the way, her trouble with the taxi driver, um—she never takes subways so she spared us that—um, she obviously saw her own travelling to and from the theatre as equally important as any of the choreography that she ostensibly went to review. I don't know how many of the people here are interested in Miss Johnston's personal biography. I've made several phone calls over the last few weeks to, uh, get certain facts on her, but I think I may skip that for now. Um, I would like to say that, um, uh,—about her writing—it really is quite, uh, [something]—her writing style is comparable to water from a faucet. Um, she turns it on a few hours before her column is due at the Voice, and, um, after a couple of hours she turns it off. Uh, she makes very few revisions. In her column she talks about notebooks. You might get the impression that she takes notes. Uh, I have seen her without a notebook, although she is usually writing down very elementary things like, uh, "Max's"—M-A-X-apostrophe-S. Um, I presume that many of the people here know all about her style, so I won't go into that, because I would like to mention that Esquire magazine last year did give her one of its dubious achievement awards, giving her the "Oh, Shut Up" Prize for the sentence which reads, "'Telling it like it is' means 'telling it like it was and how it is now that it isn't what it was to the Is Now People.'" Um, I do have—I spent the last months going through Jill Johnston's columns, and I have recalled a few sentences that she has written on criticism and I would like to read them. It's a timely her September 16 column in 1965 in which she wrote, "Criticism working out is like riding a bike up and down a country hill in a race against a phantom judge. I'll take a plot of level territory and stake out a claim to lie down on it, and criticize a constellation if that's what I happen to be looking at. I also stake out a claim to be an artist—a writer—if that's what I'm doing when I get to the typewriter and decide that I like something well enough to say what I think it's all about." Um, 1968 she said, "I like to think the critic is a corporate sensibility. Ideally the critic would be a transparent medium giving off vapors of ideas and opinions, constantly clasping to its body the streams of comments of cocktail parties. To mean exactly what you say that I mean, is to say that I mean exactly what you say that you mean, or any other variations on the phrase expressing the illusion of the single mentality. Collecting marbles, and . , the critic is a scavenger of the junk gates of the mind, strung out from house to house in the telepathy of connected—connecting clotheslines, sorting our signals, selecting and conjecting, separating the pages back together is simply a compositional problem." You can see that she received ten dollars on that column. Um, in November 7, 1968, she wrote, "One of my preferences is to write about single things for each column. I like to work out a single thing into a mess of stuff about that single thing. I'm not crazy about trying to make a single thing out of a mess of stuff. Nor am I. ...." **Paul:** Na na na na very good. **David:** One of her most illuminating pieces on criticism appeared this year—January 20, 1969. "I enjoy talking for the sake of my talking, until they say, 'Shut up,' and then I start thinking which can get you in trouble, too. What I am saying is not high-handed. When I criticize, I am never talking about anybody over... in particular, actually—only myself .... except for my imagination or yours .... riding on a train ... the lost and found when I got there...." Um, then, February 20, 1969 .... the end of criticism which she recalls in a serious article about criticism, she says, "I'm a critic myself .... plants and mountains .... they're all in my head .... a picture postcard .... not an original ... and I suppose it's true .... criticism .... illustrate .. talking about it .... talking about ourselves for a change .... whatever we're talking about is ourselves .... how everyone else is doing it .... I didn't mean to be called a critic in the first place ... three years ago I said that I was a cryptic ... what I started off was as a dance-lover just like that ... a long story .... the literature aspect of it .... dancer long before I was a true book nut .... although I read plenty of book stuff long before I was an athlete and a dancer. ..." Those were just selections that I came across. There are a few questions that I would like to ask the panel on topics that I hope we will touch upon tonight, one of which is, uh—they're all so confusing, uh, uh, oh; one is "How Objective Can Criticism Be, Anyway?" .... um .... When Miss Johnston made this shift from third person to first person, uh, was she really in on something new .... um, and uh, things she doesn't want to—I forgot the vision ... where is the vision ... uh, in 1965, uh, she was under intensive care for, uh, for visions .... she had a— **Paul:** Very good .... **David:** .... she wrote that, "one aspect of my vision—" in quotes—"one aspect of my vision is in the form of a command to relinquish the role of judge." I hope that we will get on to that topic later and perhaps discuss her trip to Ann Arbor, via Houston, Santa Barbara. .... Uh, I would also like to ask members of the panel whether they think Miss Johnston represents, uh, future criticism, and what sort of criticism we can look forward to, and uh,—I did want to make a few remarks about the merits and demerits of criticism, but I think I'll let that pass for now. I'm sure it will come out soon enough. So, I'll interview the panel beginning from my left. At my extreme left we have—this is a very distinguished panel, by the way .... not as distinguished as the audience—we have to distinguish ourselves—at our extreme left we have Walter Gutman .... Walter received a great deal of fame and notoriety a few years back which caused him to be profiled in the New Yorker magazine .... I am very happy to say have been reprinted by Grove Press .... —I received my copy two days ago—a marvellous book .... I recommend it to you all—look at it—Walter is—the real reason Walter was chosen for this panel is that he was a former art critic fifty or sixty years ago, and um, also a painter and a filmmaker whose career in so-called underground films goes back .... next to Walter is Lil Picard, an artist and writer and art critic of the East Village Other .... Lil has done many Happenings lately and is into destructionist art and street works .... she has written a fascinating show for this week's East Village Other which some of you may have soon .... sitting to the

Figure 2.15 Andy Warhol's contribution to "Jill Johnston Exposed: A Life Dominated by Strange Arts, Consuming Desires, and Ego-Eroticism . . . ," special issue, *Culture Hero* (February 1970). University of Chicago Library, Chicago, IL.

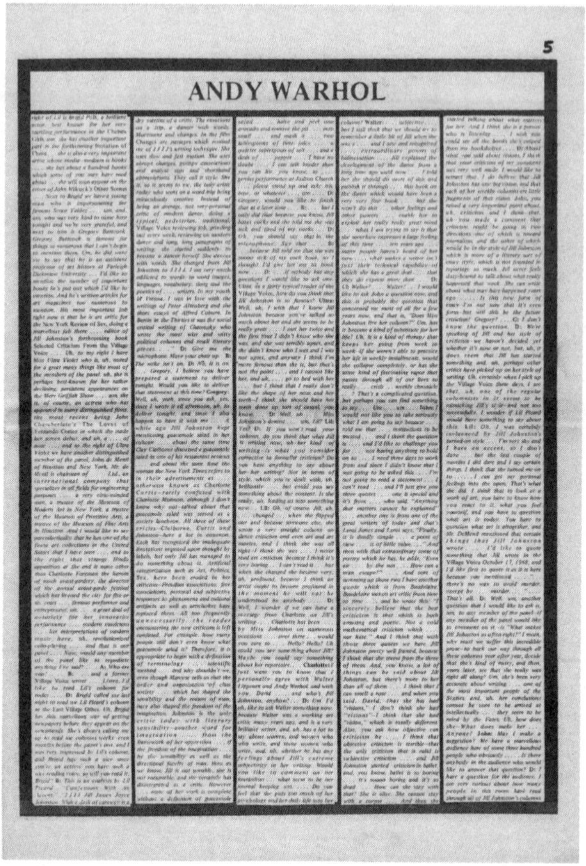

Figure 2.15 (*continued*)

*of fascinating vapor that passes through all our lives to really. . . . crisis . . .
weekly chronicle . . . ?"*

About an hour into the panel, Johnston unexpectedly rocked up to the
stage to claim a microphone and read aloud her column from that week's
Village Voice, which the editors had truncated without her permission. "She
was in her beads-vest-pants get-up, long hair flying, carrying her briefcase
'Florence,'" as Perrault describes the scene in his *Village Voice* report. "She
was smashed and all upset because her column had been cut."[68]

"How long have you been here, Jill?" Bourdon asks.

"Possibly four minutes."

"Oh! And where were you earlier?"

"I was, uh, screwing."

"Is Polly back? Jill?" Brigid Berlin interjects.

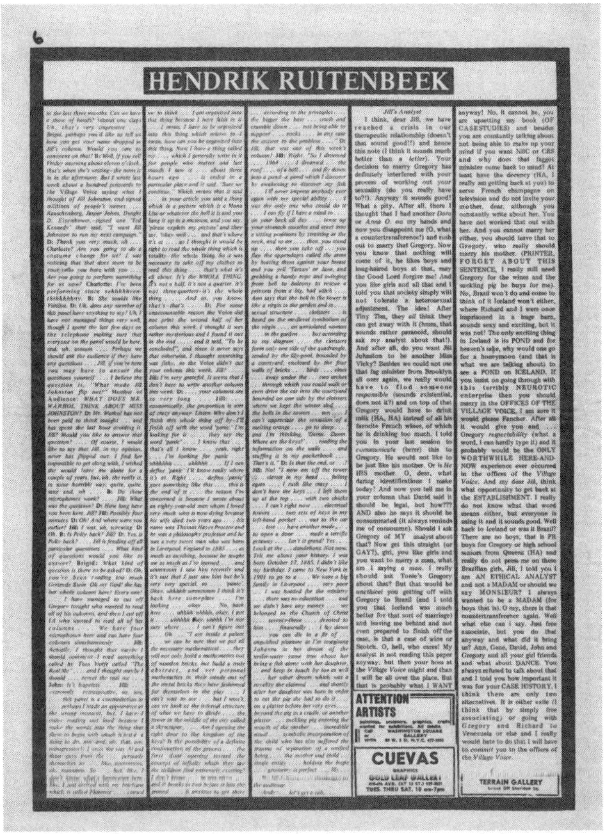

Figure 2.15 (*continued*)

"*Yes, is Polly back?. . . .*" Bourdon reiterates—acknowledging aloud the by then very open secret of Johnston's homosexuality.

"*I thought maybe I should. . . . reveal the real me. . . .*" Johnston proclaims at the microphone. To which de Menil responds, "*It's hopeless. . . .*"

"*. . . . this panel is a contradiction in. . . . ,*" Johnston continues, "*perhaps I made an appearance at the wrong moment, but, I have—I enjoy reading out loud because I make the words into the thing. So. . . . but, like, I don't know what's happening here, like, I just arrived with my briefcase which is called Florence. . . . caused me to think. . . . I got organized into this thing because I have faith in it. . . .*" As Johnston interrupts her panel to read aloud the portion of her column that had been cut from the newspaper, the language in Warhol's transcript of the panel deteriorates: long ellipses and interjections puncture Johnston's words in an auditory, now textual, performance of the disintegration she gathered everyone together to talk about and to herald as a new form of artistic expression.

"After a false start—she was trying to locate the word 'panic' which is where the column had ended—she began to read, and read, and read," Perrault reports.

"*Listen, Why don't I finish this whole thing off by—I'll finish off with the word 'panic.' I'm looking for it. . . . . they say the word 'panic.' . . . I know that. . . . that's all I know. . . . yeah, right. . . . I'm looking for panic. . . . uhhhhhh. . . . uhhhhh. . . . If I can define 'panic' I'll know really where it's at. Right. . . . . define 'panic' goes something like this. . . . this is the end of it. . . .*" And Johnston goes on and on.

"It was terrific." Perrault concludes. "The audience dropped all objections. I was moved. And so I finally understood Jill's writing. Spoken aloud all the fragments fall into place. Jill is an orator and an evangelist. She is a poet. An old-fashioned poet, but a poet nevertheless. Jill Johnston not only dances, as Lil Picard says, she also sings."[69]

On the panel, Picard made the strongest case for Johnston's status as a poet—one of the most important poets of her generation (fig. 2.16). A few days before the panel, Picard published her own "Analysis" of Johnston

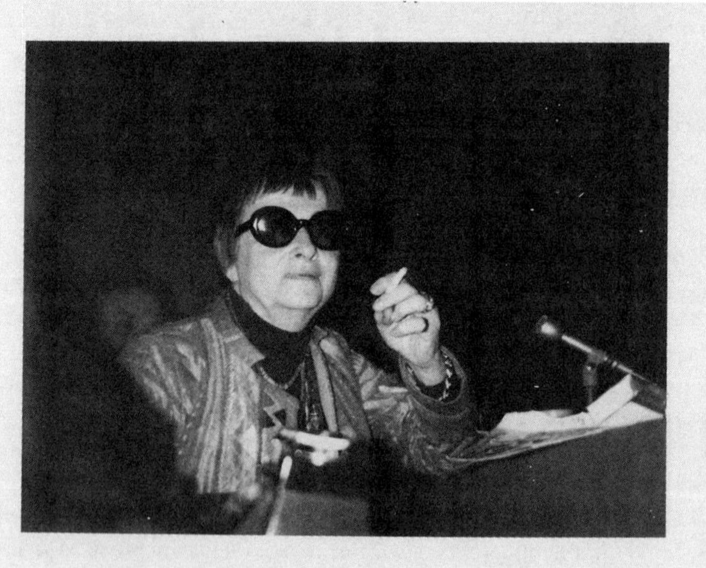

Figure 2.16 Polaroid of Lil Picard taken at the "Disintegration of a Critic: Analysis of Jill Johnston" panel at Loeb Student Center, New York University, May 21, 1969, by Andy Warhol. Lil Picard papers, Special Collections and Archives, University of Iowa Libraries, Iowa City, IA. © 2025 The Andy Warhol Foundation for the Visual Arts, Inc. / Licensed by Artists Rights Society (ARS), New York.

in *The East Village Other* titled "Confession with an Accent," which Brigid Berlin read aloud during the panel discussion, sitting right next to Picard:

"*This is an analysis by Lil Picard, 'Confessions With An Accent,'*" Berlin begins, according to Warhol's transcript. "*J J J J Jill James Joyce Johnston. With a dash of caraway is a dry martini of a critic. The emotions on a trip, a dancer with words. Movement and changes.*" And Berlin goes on and on. But the transcript of Berlin reading aloud Picard's article gets the words all wrong, which serves as a telling reminder of the errors, omissions, punctuation shifts, and homophonic slippages that occurred throughout the process of speaking, recording, transcribing, and reprinting the words of the panel discussion.

Picard's article in *The East Village Other* actually begins: "JJJJ Jill James Joyce Johnston with a dash of Kerouac is a dry martini of a critic, in motion, on a trip, a dancer with words, movement and changes."[70] Picard continues,

> She uses slow and fast motion. She uses abrupt changes. Gossiping associations and analogies in sign and shorthand abbreviations, staccato style. She is, so it seems to me, the only critic today who went on a world-trip, becoming miraculously creative. . . . What I want to say is: Jill didn't disintegrate as a critic. In fact, she got herself together and became a creative writer. I dig her. . . . I believe what happened to Jill is that she freed herself of conventions and is now on a voyage in the dream dance of words.

But for Picard, "a New York Fraulein with an accent" who lived in Berlin during Hitler's rise, the potential for freedom contained in Johnston's "dream dance of words" is overshadowed by the specter of "superfascists very soon." Picard writes, "I am dancing, too, Jill, you turned me on to it. But my dance is polluted by my memories of Europe's past, so my dance is a death dance, but I really want to be positive. A butterfly, but I can't help my negative fears."[71]

Writing for *Vogue* magazine, critic John Gruen also came away from the panel convinced of Johnston's importance as an artist and her influence as a critic. "Singlehandedly, Jill Johnston seems indeed to have invented a new form of autobiographical criticism," Gruen writes. "Through her 'Dance Journal' and through her panel discussions she has sparked an interest in altering criticism as a genre. Already, a discernible change has taken place in the writings of other young critics."[72] Battcock came away from the panel perhaps most convinced of all—convinced not only of Johnston's importance and her influence but also that she represents the future of art. In his article on the panel in *The New York Review of Sex & Politics*, he lauds her practice as an "'anti-criticism' of freedom" that "neither depends upon nor even cares about any of such traditional freedoms permitted within the capitalist class system"—an assessment that is, as he writes, "pure Marcuse without the footnote." Battcock concludes:

> As a matter of fact, it might well be the first criterion at any rate a criterion for this time and place for art that it not be recognizable, identifiable, that we not know it when we see it. That is, not know it's ART when we see it.... An "anti-art" must develop as it must accompany and more than that, it must create an over-all environment of true freedom. So must we develop an "anti-criticism" of freedom. This is terribly important. It will meet with tremendous opposition....
>
> The anti-worker has to liberate himself from prevailing terminology, classifications and categorizations. In criticism (quiticism) only Jill Johnston and Gene Swenson have so far, been able to do it.[73]

But Swenson was away at Bellevue for the last time when Johnston's panel took place. He was tragically absent. By the time Battcock published these words on July 1, 1969, Swenson had already gone back to Kansas, where he would die in a car crash just a few weeks later. Unlike Johnston, Swenson did not survive to make an enduring practice out of his disintegration. He did not gain any retrospective clarity. He did not assemble a panel of his peers to attest to his artistic achievement. He died flailing.

The "Disintegration of a Critic" panel has no easy upshot. The panelists heralded Johnston's importance as an early champion of happenings and Judson Dance who invented new language for the new art. They celebrated her literary accomplishments, stylistic innovations, and prowess as a poet. They speculated that her peculiar autobiographical turn might represent the future of criticism, a new genre of art, and a vital corrective to formalist criticism. They acknowledged her dykedom. But they were drunk, rambunctious, and sloppy. The panel garnered much critical attention in the underground papers but almost none in the mainstream art press. Warhol published a transcript of the whole panel, but it does not cohere, marred throughout by mistakes, missing words, and mistranscriptions. Which is not simply a glitch or an unfortunate limitation of the medium—rather it gets to the whole point of the "Disintegration of a Critic" panel discussion. The hard, frustrating work of reading the transcript does not reveal anything more real or stable underneath. In an almost perfectly postmodern way, the transcript attests to the reality of selfhood as being constructed in a mess of unstable language. But Johnston showed up to the panel intent to *"reveal the real me,"* as the transcript says. She bared herself to the audience, reading aloud her column, which contains an earnest, intensely personal account of searching for herself and for her past in the bell towers of England. And she emerges as "an orator and an evangelist" and an "old-fashioned poet," as Perrault put it. "Spoken aloud all the fragments fall into place." The panel does not resolve these contradictions. Rather, it attests to the unstable but fertile ground from which Johnston assembled a new kind of queer critical practice at the end of the sixties without resolution.

• • •

Swenson's last piece of writing, published posthumously, is his contribution to the special issue of *Culture Hero* devoted to Johnston. A mysterious, poetic text, it begins: "Written May 1969. How are we ever going to catch the rhythms of our time? Jill Johnston knows one of the answers: free association, automatic writing, total and post-Freudian (to dot the i) honesty. Honesty? Who, in this era of the wheeler-dealer and his successor, Mr. Empty Mind, would ever think? See how catching Jill is? Only, where I stop for punctuation, she goes on."[74]

In August 1969, Swenson stopped for punctuation with his enduring, unanswered question mark. Johnston continued on breathlessly into the seventies.

Coda: The Misteek of Sighcosis

November 30, 1972

Fast forward three and a half years.

Pick up *The Village Voice* and turn to page twelve. Johnston's weekly column—by now called Jill Johnston rather than Dance Journal to reflect its change in topic—is much longer than usual, extending over seven pages and ending with "to be continued," followed by three more pages the next week. Titled "R. D. Laing: The misteek of sighcosis," the column presents a convoluted treatise on antipsychiatry, feminism, and homosexuality.[75] Playing with spelling and syntax to assemble new language, Johnston reframes her experiences during the sixties in light of Laing's radical rethinking of psychosis not as a pathology but rather as a label that gets affixed to certain strange ways of experiencing the world that "a person invents in order to live in an unlivable situation," as Laing writes in *The Politics of Experience*, published in the United States in 1967.[76] Laing explains: "The schizophrenic is someone who has queer experiences and/or is acting in a queer way, from the point of view usually of his relatives and of ourselves."[77] Laing uses the word "queer" as a synonym for strange. Johnston's innovation at the end of 1972 was to retool Laing's theory to account for her queer experiences as a lesbian in the "patriarchal authoritative hierarchical law enforcement reality oriented materialistic sexually repressive fucked up culture in which we live," as she puts it, mincing absolutely no words.[78] In such an unlivable situation, becoming estranged from one's own queer desires and experiences, or assembling and maintaining a "false-self system," in Laing's terminology, becomes an untenable prerequisite for getting by every day.

Throughout the column, Johnston turns to her memories of Swenson. After his death and on his behalf, she recasts his "madness" as a reaction to his own unlivable situation. "I had a friend gene swenson who went on an intergalactic journey in his own space ship," she writes.

> He came back three times, and after the third time the Medical Inquisition Recovery Team and all the rest of their frogmen had at last convinced the guy that he was a "case." He was ready to take their tranquilizers forever and get a nice nine to five job filing something and wear a suit and a tie and go to a shrink very often regularly to keep himself straight. The last thing that happened was he biologically died in a carcrash in kansas with his mother. . . . I don't have any idea what the complex dynamic fuel system was that launched gene on his trips, who could ever know that, much less the chief passenger, but I do know that his life situation was basically untenable to himself and that a journey to "other regions" was in order and that as a one way ticket to bellevue he became a two-time loser every trip he took. No credibility anywhere.

It is unbearably tragic. "We didn't know what to do about ourselves," Johnston continues. "The journey solution was no big deal if you couldn't come back and seriously change the conditions of the place you found it necessary to leave. No roles for the mad."[79]

Throughout the column, Johnston lays bare harrowing details from her own confinement in Bellevue in the mid-sixties.

> I was locked into a gray walled dungeon with no way out and shot full of paraldehyde and 1000 mcs of thorazine and locked into a cell within the dungeon a room containing a peestained mattress and the dents of bludgeoning heads and trussed up to a bed and laced up into a straightjacket and left to die for the night I did and I've never been the same since I'm just beginning to get in touch with the phobias I acquired in one night's time an elevator problem is the least of it and I stand as witness for thousands like me for whom *The Politics of Experience* came like a belated vindication against our censure and invalidation by the Modern Inquisition.[80]

Johnston reframes her psychic breakdowns as difficult attempts to become whole in a "fucked up culture" that demands she be split to function normally—a kind of homeopathic process of reintegration. She explains: "schizophrenia means to me the cataclysmic brokenhearted experience of fragmentation and disintegration of those normal processes in some weird counterdynamic of a *fusion* of all those dualities."[81] Johnston describes psychic breakdown as a spontaneous journey into the estranged inner parts of oneself, often with tragic results. Tragic not because there is anything wrong with the journey, as Johnston argues, but because the world is still just as fucked up when you get back.

Throughout the column, Johnston subjects language to processes of disintegration and reintegration. She breaks phrases apart, changes words, repeats them, and recombines them into new wholes. Near the end of the column, she casts this as a feminist practice and as an explicit rejoinder to antipsychiatry's lack of feminist consciousness. "They know about the sorry state of women," Johnston writes, "but their political understanding of the world stops with socialism." She explains: "It's a mother problem all the way around. The bad mother is rampant in the Laing and Esterson book *Sanity, Madness, and the Family*. There's no analysis of how she got that way."[82] In response, Johnston reframes her own "psychosis" as a grand strategy to reinvent the world and become whole through a process matriarchal myth-making. Through her prose, she simulates the experience of psychic breakdown as a mystical way of reconnecting to the "female healing tradition proper," as she writes, snuffed out by the "patriarchal fucked up culture." She proposes to resist that culture by becoming whole in spite of it, on her own terms, and in terms that subvert normative ideas about wholeness or what it means to be an integrated subject in late capitalism. To become whole, but not like any preexisting whole. It sounds like this:

How do we get lost and become ourselves at the same time. To be both separate and the same. To be at once the mother and not the mother. To become one's own mother. Pure Mind. "In certain forms of 'psychotic' experience there is, at the height of the experience, a pure anoia in which the 'outside' becomes continuous with itself through the 'inside' so that all sense of self is lost" (Cooper). The terror of the loss of self. The madness of it. The birth of our selves from our false selves, our social selves. As Mary Barnes says, we go from false self, to madness, to sanity. The dire extremity of madness as a last ditch solution. The burning up of the masks. A little egg of a self inside a box inside. The chinese boxes. The dissolution of their walls. Going back down to the Void. The Matrix. The Chaos. . . . The law enforcement agency of the Inquisition and its older form of the Church and its new form of the Modern Psychiatric Profession is primarily an agency to keep women in their place and exter minate them if they can't. The office procedures represent the initial stages. The hospitals the final solution. I didn't mention that gene swenson was homosexual. He had an Inquisition installed in his Head. By the sights of family and state he was a Bad One. He had a normal false self system that occasionally just crumbled.[83]

Pieces of Gene.

For Johnston, however, the "dire extremity of madness as a last ditch solution" was not the end of her rope. It was one among many feminist solutions that she pursued from the early sixties through the seventies, assembling brilliant new artistic forms and modes of expression along the way.

3

lesbianlesbian
lesbianlesbian
lesbianlesbian
lesbianlesbian

Jill Johnston's Feminist Solutions

The solution to the problem of identity is, get lost.
JILL JOHNSTON, 1968[1]

Feminism is at heart a massive complaint. Lesbianism is the solution.
JILL JOHNSTON, 1973[2]

One Solution After Another

Beginning in the sixties, Jill Johnston assembled one feminist solution after another, though not all of them went by that name. Before then, things were bleak. "The fifties just sucked," Johnston later put it. "All I ever did was get fired from jobs."[3] In 1958, she entered the "final phase," in her words, of her "complete capitulation to the male corporation": she got married and had two children. "Never was a person so clearly driven into the desperate expedient of marriage as the illusory solution to a problem I didn't know was much bigger than me."[4]

Within a few years, the illusion crumbled. In 1963, Johnston left her husband and moved downtown. "Under patriarchy, I had lost my children," Johnston writes, reflecting back many years later. "It seems impossible to imagine leading the life I did during the decade 1965–75, had I not been a disenfranchised mother."[5] Already invested in the downtown world of art and dance as a critic and occasional performer, Johnston immersed herself fully in the scene in 1963, quickly becoming the "inimitable champion," in the words of Yvonne Rainer, of the new Judson Dance Theater (fig. 3.1).[6] A shifting group of choreographers, dancers, artists, and critics, the Judson Dance Theater reinvented dance in the early sixties by adopting a collabora-

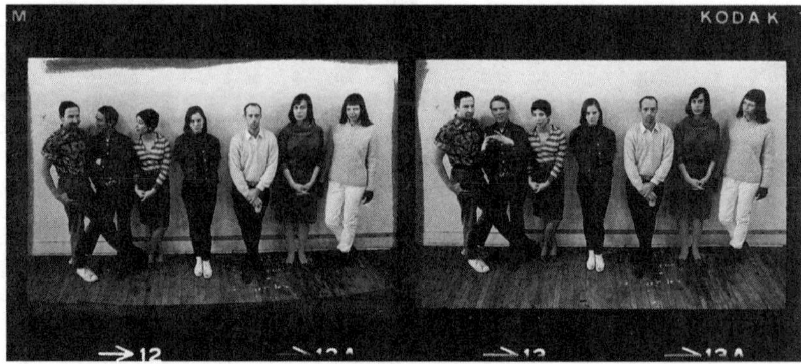

Figure 3.1 Participants in the Judson Dance Theater, 1965. *Left to right*: Robert Rauschenberg, Alex Hay, Deborah Hay, Lucinda Childs, Robert Morris, Yvonne Rainer, and Jill Johnston. Photo by Al Giese. Detail of contact sheet. Fales Library and Special Collections, New York University, New York City, NY. © 2025 Mary Hottelet (Giese) / Licensed by Artists Rights Society (ARS), New York.

tive workshop structure, embracing ordinary movements and language, rejecting conventions like narrative and crescendo, and putting undisguised bits of everyday life on full display in their art.[7]

Having found a conducive home for her own genre-bending criticism as a columnist for *The Village Voice*, Johnston assembled many feminist solutions throughout the early sixties, though she did not yet call them feminist. She experimented with language, playing with spelling, syntax, and repetition to drain words of conventional meanings and subversively redeploy them. She championed women artists. And she refused to draw sharp demarcations between life and art, personal and professional, and private and public—instead letting the stuff of life seep into her work, including difficult stuff from her life as a failed wife, mother, and woman who kept falling into bed with other women.

That tenuous balance did not hold for very long, and in August 1965 Johnston's "lives exploded in a conflagration of work and personality," as she writes in the preface to her 1971 anthology *Marmalade Me* (fig. 3.2). "I became what Timothy Leary has called a revelatory casualty and all seemed lost."[8] Throughout the mid- and late sixties, Johnston's feminist solutions mostly entailed "going crazy" and writing about it, harnessing criticism without authority as a key part of the solution. For Johnston, criticism offered space to reimagine the world and her place in it by restructuring language.

As the sixties came to a close, Johnston began "slouching toward consciousness," as she writes. "The revolution was on and I was ready."[9] In rapid, overlapping succession, she commenced practicing "the improbable

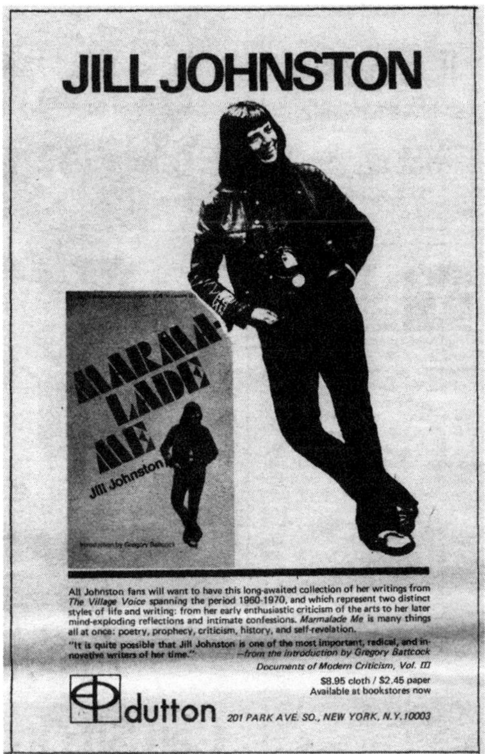

Figure 3.2 Advertisement for *Marmalade Me* by Jill Johnston in *Gay NYC*, June 21, 1971. Newspaper clipping. Courtesy of the periodical collection, Lesbian Herstory Archives, Brooklyn, NY.

art of being a public nuisance"; fucking up ("as Valerie Solanis [*sic*] said dropping out is not the answer; fucking up is"); and fucking, thereby becoming a "liberated lesbian chauvinist" ("meaning it was possible to just go to bed and have a good time and get up and share a cup of coffee or not and say goodbye and thank you quite amicably").[10] It was at this juncture, as her new feminist solutions were ramming into old ones, that Johnston prodded everyone in the art world to talk about her—first at the "Disintegration of a Critic" panel discussion in front of a packed audience, then on the pages of Les Levine's underground paper *Culture Hero*, in a special issue devoted entirely to her.

Soon these solutions would give way to Johnston's grand proclamation that a separatist lesbian nation is *the* feminist solution. Hence, of course, the iconic title of her 1973 book *Lesbian Nation: The Feminist Solution* (fig. 3.3)—a freewheeling anthology composed of *Village Voice* columns published between 1970 and 1972, several new retrospective writings, and

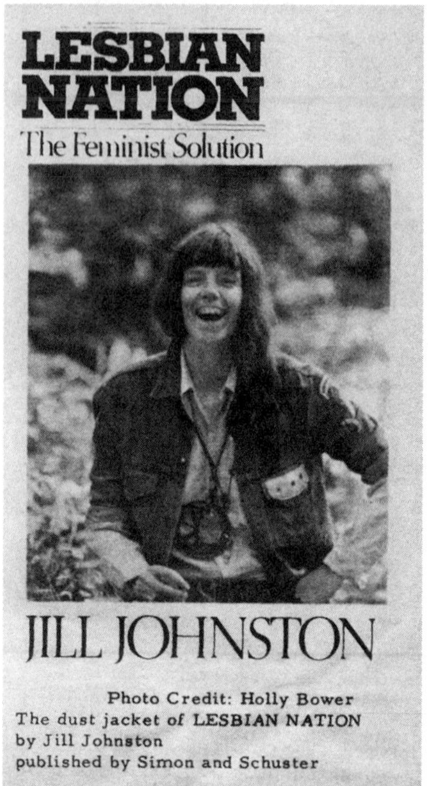

Figure 3.3 Advertisement for *Lesbian Nation: The Feminist Solution* by Jill Johnston in *Sister* (June 1973). Newspaper clipping. Courtesy of the periodical collection, Lesbian Herstory Archives, Brooklyn, NY.

entries from her journals. "The solution is getting it together with other women," Johnston proclaims. "Or separatism."[11] She argues that "the lesbian is *the* revolutionary feminist and every other feminist is a woman who wants a better deal from her old man."[12]

When *Lesbian Nation* came out in 1973, Johnston had already been an outspoken lesbian for over two years. On March 4, 1971, she published the first part of a grand manifesto-like column titled "Lois Lane Is a Lesbian," which extended over three issues of *The Village Voice*.[13] A month later, on April 30, 1971, she appeared (yet again) on a panel discussion in front of a packed New York audience, this one moderated by Norman Mailer at Town Hall and titled "A Dialogue on Women's Liberation."

For Johnston, a separatist lesbian nation was never actually a practical feminist solution. It was a "cosmic plan," as she put it, a fantasy "to somehow buy up a lot of space and establish a chain of lesbos on the mainland

and invite the lesbian population and introduce the rest to the mysteries and just forget about the men."[14] But the fact that it was always a fantasy has not made Johnston's lesbian separatism any more salutary in the decades since as a feminist goal, a queer goal, or, for that matter, an artistic goal. In narratives of feminism's progress, Johnston's book *Lesbian Nation* often gets invoked as a kind of bad object that had to be surpassed. It tends to get mentioned or alluded to as evidence of the excesses of second-wave cultural feminism: its essentialism, whiteness, frivolity, and emphasis on lifestyle. Writers on avant-garde art and dance have, by and large, dealt with this problem by dismissing Johnston's lesbian feminism without engaging it, instead simply relegating it to someone else's discipline. For example, Sally Banes—who provides some of the most astute and sensitive analyses of Johnston's early work—claims that after Johnston "came out in print as a radical lesbian July 2, 1970, the columns became a soapbox for her evolving political ideology," and she "never again wrote arts criticism."[15] Aside from being false—I'd argue that Johnston never stopped writing arts criticism—it is also arbitrary.[16] To narrate Johnston's story as one of turning away from art to embrace bad "political ideology" is to cordon lesbian feminism off in its own realm away from art, quarantining the "l-word" and thereby reifying the same old exclusions by reproducing conventional categories.

Johnston's lesbian feminism is no more programmatic than—and certainly just as creative, performative, and genre-defying as—her earlier feminist solutions.[17] And it continued to influence artists and critics around her. Fluxus artist Geoffrey Hendricks, for one, attests to the generative importance of Johnston's lesbian writings for his own artistic practice, especially her "Lois Lane Is a Lesbian" column. "It was an article I clipped and carried around with me for a long, long time," Hendricks recalls, "because it was very incisive and seminal."[18] Likewise poet Eileen Myles attests to Johnston's importance for a whole generation of queer artists. "There was Jill Johnston," Myles proclaims in response to a question about their early influences. "So many of us came to New York because of Jill; we read her column in *The Village Voice*. The book she wrote was called *Lesbian Nation: The Feminist Solution*, and Queer Nation came from that. All the nations came from that."[19]

• • •

My argument in this chapter is straightforward: All of Johnston's feminist solutions, including a lesbian nation, belong to the history of art and performance. What this means for art history and for the history of feminism matters a great deal. For art history, it means reorienting the story of what happened to art in New York in the sixties and early seventies around Johnston's feminist solutions. The conventional narrative about how Johnston left a hostile art world to pursue lesbian feminism in a different arena transforms instead into a story about how lesbian feminism (even before Johnston called it that) became a vital resource for some of the most important and ambitious art practices of the period.[20] In this retelling, Johnston's lesbian feminist work of the early seventies represents one of the most significant art practices to grow out of the Judson Dance Theater's experimentations.

For feminist history, my argument suggests a way to tell a different kind of story about feminism's recent past—a story less burdened by a need to position Johnston on the so-called good side of contemporary theory and politics, and thus less burdened by a need to downplay or excuse aspects of Johnston's lesbian feminism that now feel inimical to the pursuit of progress.[21] If, as theorist Clare Hemmings has amply demonstrated, histories of feminism since the 1970s are "consistently told as a series of interlocking narratives of progress, loss, and return that oversimply [feminism's] complex history and position feminist subjects as needing to inhabit a theoretical and political cutting edge in the present,"[22] then this chapter provides, if not a way out of that impasse, at least a way to move obliquely in relation to it by asking different questions.

Johnston's political proclamations are imperfect and troubling; they were imperfect and troubling back in the sixties and seventies, too. But to elide or forget Johnston's practices in the name of feminist and queer progress is, as feminist theorist Kyla Wazana Tompkins argues, a "form of misogyny" that we need to consider as "real and ongoing." Tompkins poses the pointed, rhetorical questions: "Do we have to keep unciting lesbians and lesbian feminism from the daily work and theorizing of queer life? Similarly, do we have to continue foreclosing the politics that are yet to come?"[23] This chapter answers: no. By analyzing Johnston's feminist solutions as so many artistic practices, this chapter cracks open spaces to admire Johnston's ambition and her brilliance, to reckon with darkness and failures, and to linger longer in the inchoate moments that brim with the creative energy of imagining how a nation might exist otherwise.

A Convulsion of Dissolving Boundaries

Johnston began publishing criticism "just when the entire art world was entering a convulsion of dissolving boundaries," as she writes in the preface to *Marmalade Me*.[24] As a critic of both art and dance throughout the early sixties, Johnston did not draw any sharp distinctions between the two categories, becoming an early champion of intermedia performances in both arenas. Her beat spanned the Judson Dance Theater, happenings, Fluxus, avant-garde festivals, off-off-Broadway, and New York Poets Theatre, as well as gallery and museum exhibitions. Throughout her early criticism,

Johnston consistently argues that all art should approach the conditions of theater—which she theorizes to mean an implosive, hugely desirable synthesis of all the individual arts, plus all the stuff of life.[25] In an essay titled "On the Happenings—New York Scene," published in October 1962, Johnston lauds John Cage as a "pioneer" of this new approach with his productions of experimental music "in which sounds, like events in nature, would occur without premeditation." She explains, "To create an art based on this way of looking at things is to give oneself up to the possibility of anything; and this means at least a partial relinquishment of the artist's conscious intentions. It certainly means giving up the idea of art as usually practiced in the Western world. And in the end it leads inevitably to *theatre*: a field of action where anything may happen."[26]

Five years later, critic Michael Fried would famously—or infamously—attack this theory as an existential threat to art. "Theater and theatricality are at war today, not simply with modernist painting (or modernist painting and sculpture), but with art as such," Fried proclaims in his 1967 text, warning that art "degenerates as it approaches the condition of theater," becoming "corrupted or perverted by theater."[27] But, really, there was never a war between art and theater in the sixties—or, if there was, it was one-sided battle waged by the reactionary camp in an attempt to keep the individual arts separate, pure, and straight. After noting that "Fried was a frequent visitor to Judson Dance Theater" in the early sixties, where he witnessed queer practices, curator and writer Thomas J. Lax surmises: "Repulsion is a lasting archive."[28] For Johnston, who was a key exponent of the theory that art "leads inevitably to *theatre*" long before Fried excoriated it, the breakdown of barriers between the arts, and between art and life, was a fascinating development replete with exciting new possibilities.

"So now we are speaking of theater (art) in general, or of life in general," Johnston concludes her October 1962 text. "Where one begins and the other ends is one of the interesting questions posed by Happenings."[29] By the time Johnston published this claim, she had already pushed this question into an area well beyond Cage's own comfort zone after he invited her to participate in the third version of his composition *Music Walk*.[30] In *Music Walk with Dancer*, Johnston performed as the "Dancer" alongside Cage and pianist David Tudor on April 4, 1962, at the Kaufmann Concert Hall at the 92nd Street Y. At the time, she was still living her "stroller mommie" life uptown with her husband and children. Reflecting back on this episode ten years later in her 1972 *Village Voice* column "The Yearly Mellowdrama," Johnston writes,

> john cage saw me in my red woolen dress at a christmas party and asked
> me to perform with him and david tudor a number of months hence in
> a thing of his called music walk and I did and I did it in my red woolen

dress and for my noisemakers I brought all the trappings of my wonderful maternal existence a baby bottle a coffee can a blender a frying pan a vacuum an apron a plastic sink an egg beater a beater beater and a toy dog on wheels that barked like a duck when I pulled it along by its string. I had a ladder on stage too. I had all this junk and john and david had only their minimum daily requirement of sophisticated electronic equipment and a handful of three by fours containing all the brilliant and elegantly scripted hieroglyphics of instructions from the godhead: the wise decrees of chance and indeterminacy.[31]

Confronting Cage and Tudor's masculine austerity with so many accoutrements of motherhood, Johnston staged an early, exceptionally pointed feminist critique of Cage's philosophy: It's easy to blur art and life when you don't have a lot of shit to lug around. In his famous "Lecture on Something," published in his 1961 book *Silence,* Cage proclaims: "Responsibility is to oneself; and the highest form of it is irresponsibility to oneself which is to say the calm acceptance of whatever responsibility to others and things comes a-long. If one adopts this attitude art is a sort of experimental station in which one tries out living; one doesn't stop living when one is occupied making art."[32]

This "calm acceptance" works out pretty seamlessly when one's life responsibilities mostly involve tinkering around with instruments and machines. By bringing so much of her own (literal) maternal baggage to Cage's performance, Johnston demonstrates what the same Cageian attitude toward art becomes when one's "responsibility to others and things" includes a whole lot of "screaming and looking at the [TV] box and eating tuna fish and falling and getting hit and generally going crazy including being unsuccessfully in love," as Johnston put it, and also "following the kids with my eyes when they left the sandbox, and swinging them on the baby swings, and buying them popsicles and picking them up when they cried and putting them down when they didn't and wondering whether my mission in life was supposed to be fulfilled."[33] "Calm acceptance" really isn't on the table. During the rehearsal for *Music Walk with Dancer,* Johnston ruined all of her own 3 × 4 index cards by dropping them into some "domestic water," as she writes, "and I said to myself shit why should I bother with these cards anyway I'll just plant my junk around the stage."[34] Which she did, improvising the whole ten-minute performance rather than following the meticulously prepared score (i.e., those "wise decrees of chance and indeterminacy"), much to Cage's apparent chagrin.[35] As a "sort of experimental station" for living, art in Johnston's hands became chaotic and truly unplanned, filled with soggy index cards, grating household noises, and real anxiety about what comes next.

Already in 1962, then, Johnston had conceived a feminist solution that was ahead of the avant-garde art she was championing. She lauded the breakdown of barriers between arts and the blurring of art and life. But she went further, embracing the fundamental—and also, I argue, most profound and potentially disturbing—aspect of this avant-garde turn: Once you open art up to life, you open it up to the possibility that "anything may happen," in Johnston's words.[36] And for Johnston, anything meant *everything*, including the chaos and crumbles of marriage and motherhood. In this early feminist solution, Johnston's brilliance consists in the way she compels the audience at Cage's performance to countenance and endure what she faces every day—a feminist strategy she would return to again and again, building upon it until it would become at times unbearable.

• • •

However, this feminist solution was still quite provisional in April 1962. At the time, Johnston focused most of her creative energy on writing rather than performing, honing her craft as a critic. For Johnston, "giving up the idea of art as usually practiced in the Western world" never signaled art's demise but rather pointed to its transformation into new modes of creative expression that can (and of course did) coexist with older forms. As Sally Banes argues, Johnston's early criticism evinces "a rigorous, analytical, yet generous approach to the avant-garde that still found room to acknowledge the contribution of the old guard."[37] And contra Fried's strange assertion that "concepts of quality and value . . . are meaningful, or wholly meaning ful, only within the individual arts,"[38] Johnston argues for new values and for sensitive new ways to describe quality in works that elide individual arts, focusing her attention on that group of ambitious young artists who would soon become known as the Judson Dance Theater.

In a *Village Voice* column published March 15, 1962, Johnston heralds "Fresh Winds" blowing, as she puts it in the title of her review. Analyzing dance works by Fred Herko and Yvonne Rainer presented at the Maidman Playhouse under the auspices of the New York Poets Theatre, Johnston describes how Herko "kept switching tactics, and if you think about it, which I am doing, it really was a mishmash of styles, events, media . . . that seemed to move forward and backward, or skip all around in time, and to have no origin, no destination, and no Simple Simon meanings."[39] With her finger to the wind, a few months later Johnston reviewed Rainer and Herko's performances in a "Concert of Dance" presented at Judson Memorial Church on July 6, 1962—a "democratic evening of dance," as Johnston writes, with "14 choreographers and 17 performers."[40] That evening launched the Judson Dance Theater, with Johnston emerging as a key catalyst, witness, and participant.

Without recourse to "Simple Simon meanings" in her careful critical prose, Johnston teaches *Village Voice* readers how to watch, how to feel, and what to value in these new performances that were notoriously "hard to see," as art historian Carrie Lambert-Beatty argues, following Yvonne Rainer.[41] Johnston focuses her criticism on the total viewing situation: on the relationship between dancing bodies and viewing spectators sharing the same physical space, awkwardly, intimately, and on how performances put pressure on that physical relationship. As Lambert-Beatty affirms, Johnston's criticism "channeled with typically casual brilliance the 'seeing difficulty' that charged so much of this period's performance experimentation: an alternating current of pleasure in and resistance to dance's inaccessibility to vision."[42] Through her criticism, Johnston demonstrated how to apprehend dance differently, and she did so by writing about it differently, focusing attention on the whole room and the relationships among people gathered together.

Occasionally, she also performed. In 1963, Andy Warhol made a short film titled *Jill and Freddy Dancing* (16mm, black-and-white, silent; 4.5 min.) of Johnston and Herko dancing together on a New York City rooftop (fig. 3.4).[43] Johnston wears a long dress and holds a drink and a cigarette; Herko dances around her "executing precise balletic turns and arresting jumps," as dancer and historian Paisid Aramphongphan writes. Facing Herko, responding to his erect formal movements, Johnston "holds her own," Aramphongphan continues, "sometimes mirroring him but deliberately adding her own looser twist, at times seemingly drunk," swaying her body "to the rhythm of her own tune."[44]

In August 1964, Johnston performed a second improvisational duet, this one with Yvonne Rainer. A photo of the performance shows Johnston—wearing sunglasses, tall black boots, black tights, and a striped top—looming above Rainer, leaning over a balcony with her legs propped on the ironwork railing (fig. 3.5). Other photos show Johnston tumbling backward into Rainer's arms and straddling Rainer on the floor between her spread legs. Regarding their duet, Rainer recalls that Johnston "fortified herself with frequent guzzles from a bottle of vodka during the hour before the performance." "Jill and I converged at several points," she continues. "I saw her waving around on the balcony, maybe hanging over the railing and I rushed over and tried to chin myself on the railing. Another time she was standing with her legs spread and I may have dived thru or twined around them. . . . What else was there to do with someone's spread legs? Jill later said that she was very surprised at my trying to 'relate' to her; she had really never expected anything like that."[45]

In both duets, Johnston moves in relation to the dancer but awkwardly, so as not to merge into anything like an elegant whole. By performing out of sync, she strains the relationship between her body and the dancer's,

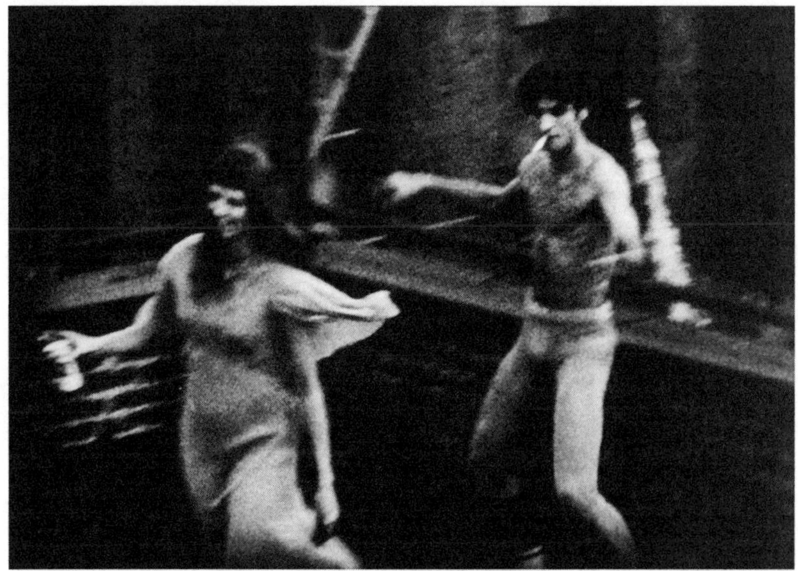
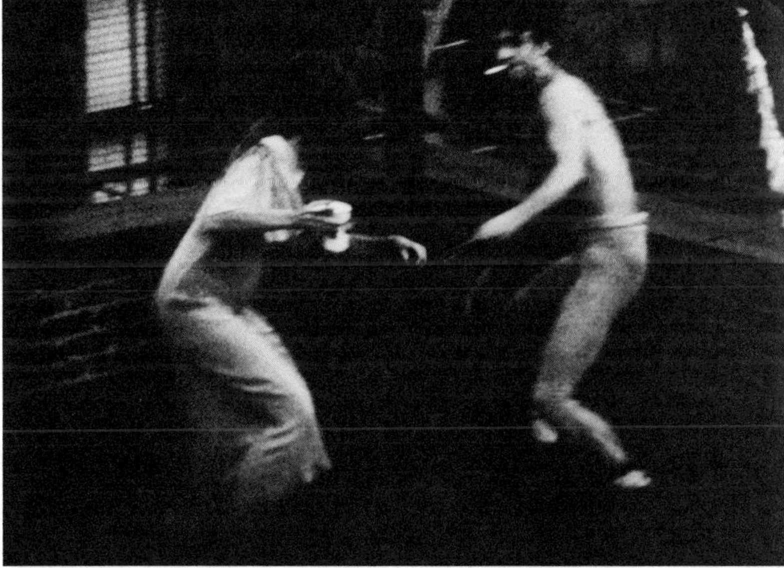

Figure 3.4 Andy Warhol, *Jill and Freddy Dancing*, 1963. 16mm film, black-and-white, silent, 4.5 minutes at 16 frames per second. Film stills courtesy of The Andy Warhol Museum. © The Andy Warhol Museum, Pittsburgh, PA, a museum of Carnegie Institute.

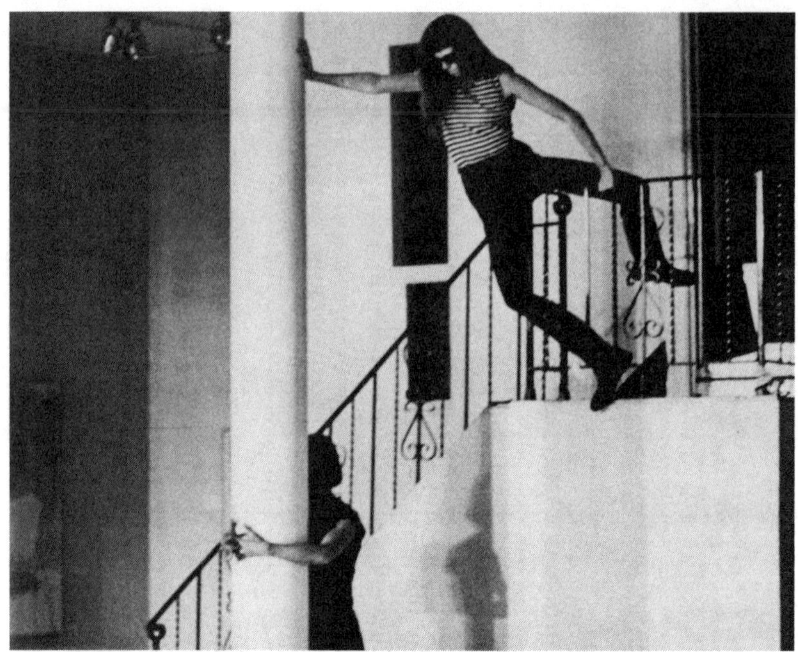

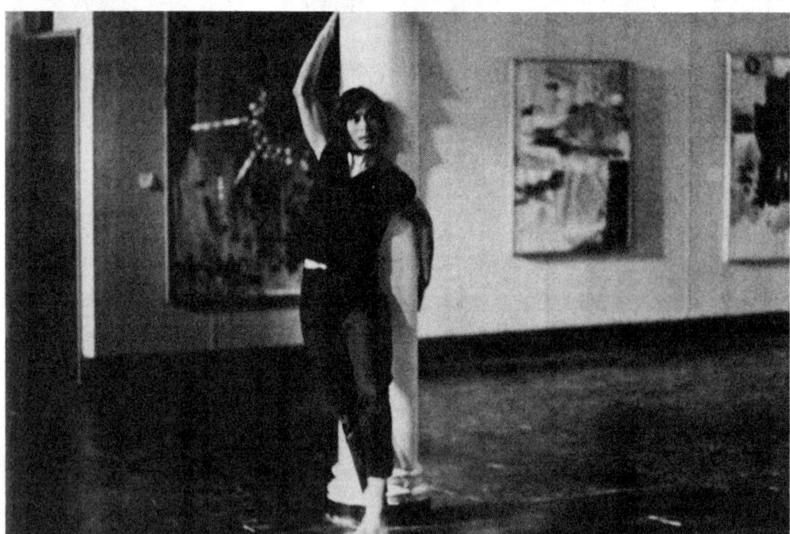

Figure 3.5 Jill Johnston and Yvonne Rainer performing *Improvisation*, Washington Square Galleries, 1964. Photographs by Peter Moore. © Northwestern University.

thereby drawing attention to that relationship. She invites the anxious possibility that anything may happen: be it a fall from a ledge or an erotic encounter. Much like in her criticism, Johnston aggrandizes the joys and perils of the total viewing situation that brings bodies together in space, often intimately and uncomfortably. But whereas performing did not work as a tenable creative solution for Johnston (she was, after all, drunk for both dances), writing criticism did. And in the realm of writing, Johnston pursued daring experiments and formal innovations.

From the outset, Johnston touted Rainer as leader of the Judson Dance revolution. "I think she's the greatest thing since Isadora crossed the Atlantic, or St. Denis saw that Egyptian cigarette poster, or any other important moments you can think of in the lives of several astonishing ladies a few decades ago," Johnston playfully asserts in her review of Judson Concerts #3 and #4, claiming a prime spot for Rainer in a genealogy of great women artists.[46] In her next review of Judson Dance, Johnston doubles down on this assertion, defending it against detractors by translating it (momentarily) into the dry authoritative idiom of conventional critical judgment: "As spokesman I believe I was expressing the enthusiasm of a number of people who, like myself, have been pleasurably involved in the progress and doings of a certain group of dancers and who recognized in Miss Rainer, participating in that group from the beginning, an unusual personality of fertile imagination, with the drive and intelligence to project in objective terms an individual style, derived from the immediate past, with original modifications and advances."[47] Johnston was deeply invested in the question of how individual artists engage with formal problems thrown up by art of the recent past, as much so as any of the most rigorous modernist critics around her. The key difference being that, for Johnston, these problems were never circumscribed by any particular medium and had everything to do with embodied performance and spectatorship.

Throughout her early criticism, Johnston's brilliance consists in assembling an exquisite, dexterous vocabulary and syntax to describe formal problems (and solutions) that pull from everywhere and might go anyplace. "Whatever she wrote, her columns were the greatest single source of PR since Clement Greenberg plugged Jackson Pollock," Rainer later put it in her 1974 book *Work*.[48] In her own work, Rainer was also invested in blurring art and life, incorporating the look, movements, and emotional tenor of everyday life into her dances. For Rainer, the key formal strategy to accomplish this became repetition—and over the course of many years, in tracing how Rainer kept deploying repetition to engender new formal problems and new solutions, Johnston did likewise in her writing. Beginning with her earliest 1962 review "Fresh Winds," Johnston describes how the phrases in Rainer's dance *Satie for Two* "do not go any place; there is no connecting material, no climaxes, etc." But rather than being a "deadly bore," this repetition stimulates a kind of familiarity that generates new things to notice, as Johnston conveys by quoting Gertrude Stein: "Reading 'Lectures in America' the other night I came onto this passage, which states the case for the author's method and which could easily apply to Miss Rainer's method in 'Satie for Two': *From this time on familiarity began and I like familiarity. It does not in me breed contempt it just breeds familiarity. And the more familiar a thing is the more there is to be familiar with. And so my familiarity began and kept on being.*"[49]

When Rainer's familiarity got too crisp for Johnston ("but I have more fun when I'm confused"[50]), Rainer made things more complex; too boring, Rainer started screaming ("like looking into the eye of a harmless hurricane"[51]); too emotional ("she releases something nutty about herself"[52]), Rainer introduced a droning audio track—and on and on, like a chess game. Indulging each other's repetitions in dance and writing, Johnston and Rainer constantly provoked one another to grapple with new formal problems and assemble new responses (while, of course, also grappling with provocations from other members of the Judson milieu). Eventually, repetition for both Rainer and Johnston congealed into new forms that amounted to a breaking point for both artists by the late sixties, as well as a new starting point. For Johnston, this break entailed untethering criticism from the tasks of reporting and evaluating. But Johnston also dipped back into reportage when the occasion warranted, as it did on April 11, 1968, when Rainer presented *The Mind Is a Muscle* at the Anderson Theater—a nearly two-hour performance that represented the culmination of Rainer's practice up to that point and marked its transformation.[53] Billing her review as the "latest expanded coverage of Yvonne Rainer's *The Mind Is a Muscle*," Johnston begins,

> The work began in 1965 as a little snowball (four and a half minutes called *Trio A*) which was slowly pushed over familiar and unfamiliar territory to its present state as a huge ball containing the history of its journey. The process was accretive rather than protean. I'm sentimentally attached to it as one might be toward a baby whose birth you attended and subsequently watched in its expanding versions of itself. Trio A was the germinal origin of the dance. The woolen underwear, a pretty tough fabric, to be covered (though never obscured) by a multifaceted garment made of the same sturdy stuff with certain additional embellishments. I've seen *Trio A* a number of times and still think I haven't really seen it. The underwear metaphor isn't a good one from the view that you've never seen such intricate underwear.[54]

Johnston's columns also tend to contain the history of their journeys. Likewise accretive rather than protean, Johnston's process throughout the sixties involved assembling new words on top of already durable critical prose. Her formal innovations in language were hardy, intricate, intimate, tailored to her body, sometimes chafing—always attentive to her own position, movements, and haptic discomfort in relation to whatever she was beholding.

• • •

In 1965, Johnston's "lives exploded," as she writes. "What had happened seemed very unclear actually except that I had a new career opened up to me as a 'mental case' and eventually I decided to exploit it instead of burying it."[55] She spent a harrowing month in the psychiatric ward at Bellevue Hospital, where she penned a manifesto-like text titled "Critic's Critics," which *The Village Voice* published the same week. "It may seem extraordinary that a newspaper would print a column directly out of a mental slammer," Johnston later reflects, "but at that time the *Voice* was still an 'underground' rag."[56] Expressing resentment over her authority, she proclaims: "Criticism wears me out—it's like riding a bike up and down the country hills in a race against a phantom judge. I'll take a plot of level territory and stake out a claim to lie down on it and criticize the constellations if that's what I happen to be looking at. I also stake out a claim to be an artist, a writer, if that's what I'm doing when I get to the typewriter and decide that I liked something well enough to say what I think it's all about."[57]

Already equipped with sturdy formal and structural solutions, after 1965 she embraced full-on that most profound and scary part of the avant-garde's blurring of art and life: the possibility that anything may happen. Whereas many of the most ambitious avant-garde artists around her tended to pare life things down in their art (including Rainer), Johnston instead began to emphasize the most difficult, dark, embarrassing, joyous, and hopeful parts of her life to produce a dense art of abundance. In the next phase of her criticism after 1965, Johnston pushes her earlier feminist solutions to new extremes: embarking upon even more daring adventures in language to compel her readers to countenance the most awful, wonderful, and visionary parts of her public and private worlds.

Whatever Isn't Settled, Labeled, Canned, Caulked, Cherished, Claimed, and Consumed

And it worked. By the summer of 1971, *The Village Voice* was taking out large, page-length ads promoting Johnston's column to sell newspaper subscriptions (fig. 3.6). "Jill Johnston Every Week in the Village Voice. Keep Ahead of the Times. Subscribe Now!" the ad proclaims, quoting fellow critic Gregory Battcock's assessment: "It is quite possible that Jill Johnston is one

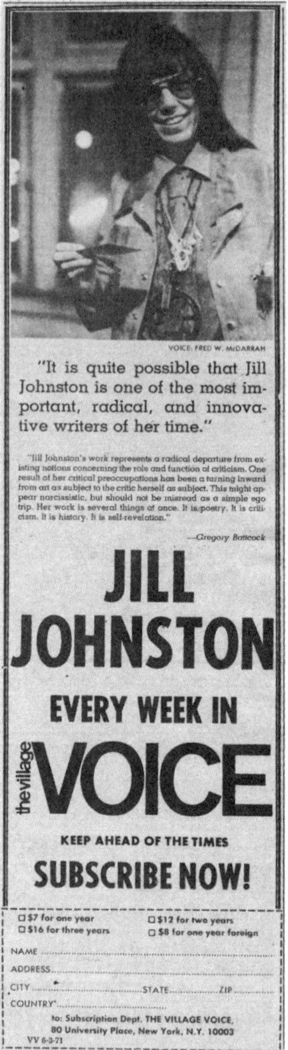

Figure 3.6 Advertisement in *The Village Voice*, June 3, 1971. Newspaper Clipping.

of the most important, radical, innovative writers of her time. . . . Her work is several things at once. It is poetry. It is criticism. It is history. It is self-revelation."[58] Johnston continued to champion other artists' genre-bending work too. "This is your local reporter," she announces in a 1967 column, "always 'looking elsewhere'—for the nonthing of the thing—for whatever isn't settled, labeled, canned, caulked, cherished, claimed, and consumed."[59] She covered the same beat as before—but rather than report on it with any semblance of objectivity, she wrote about her art experiences in conjunction with all her other experiences, exulting in breakdown and brazenly busting all sorts of boundaries. She pilfered language from everyone and revealed too much about her life and other people's lives, including all the gay and lesbian parts. "My project was to shatter and reorganize the language for myself," she explains in the 1971 preface to *Marmalade Me*. "I developed a passion for 'found' fragments—statements and exclamations heard or read—and for arranging them in the bizarre continuity of the non sequitur linked by some personal need or system of association."[60]

In a particularly poignant column titled "Holy Hurricane," published March 21, 1968, Johnston's recounting spins from having witnessed a girl acting erratically and being sexually harassed on a bus to having witnessed Aldo Tambellini's expanded cinema event *Black Zero* to having witnessed Hermann Nitsch's *Orgies Mysteries Theatre*. "I've been thinking about messes and conclusions lately," Johnston begins the column. "The world is in a mess because of its clean boundaries. A truly messy world is a consummation devoutly to be wished." But the only way to consummate this wish in the existing world of 1968 would be to go crazy, Johnston argues—which is, of course, a difficult and untenable consummation. Lifting language from Norman O. Brown's influential book *Love's Body* (1966), Johnston proclaims: "Lunacy is a perception of disintegrating boundaries. The solution to the problem of identity is, get lost"—which is to say, get lost by embracing "lunacy."[61] Like both Tambellini's and Nitsch's visions, Johnston's artistic visions often hover closer to dystopia than utopia. They are full of falling, flailing, and failing to find affinity and assert solidarity in ways that could extend out into the world.[62] Describing Nitsch's gruesome *Orgies Mysteries Theatre* as a "holy hurricane of blood," Johnston concludes the column by declaring: "This is the eye of insanity of the dissolution of boundaries. A consummation devoutly to be wished. Inferno Purgatorio Paradiso."[63]

A month later, Johnston would offer up Gene Swenson as another instance of insanity in dissolution. As we saw so vividly in chapter 2, in her April 25 column titled "Pieces of Gene," Johnston embeds news of Swenson's exploits in a long string of nightmarish non sequiturs pulled from everywhere. Without diagnosis or explanation, Johnston simulates through her writing how Swenson's wish for a "truly messy world" becomes a kind of terrifying psychic breakdown—ending the column with an image of "pieces of Gene on the sidewalk outside the UN."[64] The photo of Swenson in the winter of 1968 facing the art world alone with only his giant question mark becomes the enduring image of this unconsummated wish (see fig. 2.9). Or, rather, of a wish consummated only in the tragic disintegration of a critic. As Johnston would later explain in *Lesbian Nation*: "Going crazy has always been a personal solution in extremis to the unarticulated conflicts of political realities."[65] Swenson died flailing.

Throughout the mid- and late sixties, Johnston enacts her own version of this "personal solution in extremis." Week after week, she pulls readers into the vortex, ensnarling them in a linguistic net and compelling them to trawl the darkness with her. Images of women (often Johnston herself) trapped, disoriented, frightened, and plummeting punctuate her *Village Voice* columns during these years, often embedded within fragments of a world coming apart:

> She could be hanging herself—one arm stretched above hunched shoulders, head and neck pressed with tortured tension against the left clavicle. . . . The torso and head thrown back, held there a moment, the arms angled, bent at elbow and wrist, up over the face, to reinforce the ecstatic arch. The romantic attitude is nowhere so clear as in the fall from that effort, for while the legs take the weight of the body into the floor, the arms remain stretched, the gaze follows the arms, and the torso sinks to one side, still hoping for the impossible. (August 15, 1968)

> My head was a windstorm. My body a silent lake. This is not good. Unless you want to die. My legs were stopping still as a rock that isn't falling anywhere. So I tensed up my neck and my upper back and decided to suffer. (January 23, 1969)

> I can't breathe. I've got claustrophobia bad. My palms are clammy. From reading the information on the walls. From stealing a picture and stuffing it into my pocketbook. From climbing when I should be resting. I'm into a panic. I yell up the tower up the stairs an echo of a hollow man all headpiece jammed with straw the metal the clapper in my head I'm falling again . . . (May 22, 1969)

> I see where I am. It's not real. I'm at the top of the world. I'll fly away and never be heard of again. I can't look. Endless chasms of light struck valleys. Really giddy from this. Scared out of my skull. Start yelling. HALLO HALLO HALLO. That hose does connect to something. Up a high embankment, up up to a dilapidated looking stone structure. HAAAAALLOOOOOO. And I'm desperate, struggling up the embankment my voice echo bouncing off the goddam mountains. (November 13, 1969)[66]

As a consummation of Johnston's earliest feminist solution of opening art up to life, these passages push to the surface what so much avant-garde art and criticism around her in the late sixties sought to subdue: visceral, terrible moments when things unravel and life verges on unlivable. By then, Johnston had experienced some of the darkest depths imaginable:

laced in a straitjacket and locked in the basement of Bellevue Hospital, hemorrhaging alone after a botched abortion.[67]

But Johnston clambered out of the abyss, again and again. Throughout the late sixties, she devised other solutions in tandem with "going crazy"—so that the "dire extremity of madness as a last ditch solution," as she would put it in 1972, was not her last stand.[68] As discussed in chapter 2, in January 1969, she drove west on a grand road trip with her lover Polly in a VW Squareback, having escaped "the clutches of the psychiatric profession and its penal colonies." Convinced at last that the world was "fucked up" and that she "had to be a dyke but how," Johnston devised her new solution in the form of her "very slow calculated but unrelenting exposure of myself in the guise of literary code hopefully so challenging and fascinating and entertaining and difficult to read that any premature retaliation from a hostile society would be discouraged," as she writes. "I had tried absolutely everything there was to try and the only thing that sort of worked was writing."[69]

Through her writing, Johnston invented a "melodramatic genealogical solution"[70] that she would continue to embrace (in various guises) throughout the rest of her life. Rather than "going crazy," or perhaps through those "purgatorial fires of a mind exploding experience,"[71] Johnston set about imagining a world without clean boundaries—a "great re-integration" as she calls it. In another manifesto-like column titled "Untitled," published October 10, 1968, and reproduced as the first entry in *Marmalade Me*, Johnston writes: "Every genealogy is a fiction. There's no such thing. There's only one genealogy. It takes place in our dreams. Every specific genealogy is a fiction. . . . We're dead as soon as we're born with a name. We make ourselves new again by changing our names, by dreaming ourselves back into our real or pseudo genealogies. Or we make ourselves new not by changing the name but by repeating it and repeating it into a magical transcendence of itself. It becomes meaningless by becoming so much itself."[72] For Johnston, criticism offered a way to reorder the world by reordering language. Through repetition, Johnston dislodges established definitions. She plays with the sound of every word, evokes how it has been used in the past, and dwells on what it means—all at the same time. She writes in multiple dimensions. Meaning slips in and out of focus as the same sequences of words come together differently via resonance and rhythm, via allusion to other sources, and via multiple shifting definitions. And through this artistry, Johnston makes language newly available for imagining a truly messy world.

"The end of importance," she continues in "Untitled." "The end of politics. The end of hierarchies. The end of families. The end of groups. The end of earth as a penal colony (Burroughs).—No end to what there can be an end of in the great re-integration: the intermedia of the cosmic village, the intermedia of the genealogy as a vast prolific dream . . ."[73] Johnston goes on and on. In terms of metaphors, Johnston recasts genealogy not as a tree but rather as a paramecium: "one of the most illegal of organisms, nothing but pleasure in an orgy of self-reproduction."[74] Throughout the late sixties and early seventies, visions of this "genealogy as a vast prolific dream" punctuate Johnston's writings, often entangled with images of women trawling the darkness, all embedded within an intricate literary code filled with queer disclosures.

Culture Heroine

As all of these solutions—psychically breaking down, imagining a "great re-integration," inventing a new literary code, and slouching toward lesbian feminist consciousness—were colliding around 1969 through the early seventies, Johnston made herself extremely visible and extremely vulnerable. After offering her name as a "sort of sacrifice" at the "Disintegration of a Critic: An Analysis of Jill Johnston" panel discussion of May 21, 1969, Johnston collaborated with artist Les Levine to produce a special issue of his short-lived underground paper *Culture Hero: A Fanzine of Stars of the Superworld* devoted to her. She wrote letters to a host of other stars in New York's art world requesting they contribute 1,500 words about her, along with a photo. Lil Picard managed to save her letter—a childlike document written in pink felt-tipped pen on a giant piece of pink tissue paper (fig. 3.7).

The issue hit newsstands February 1970 with the titillating tabloid title "Jill Johnston Exposed: A Life Dominated by Strange Arts, Consuming Desires, and Ego-Eroticism . . ." (fig. 3.8). The cover features a photograph of Johnston, fully clad, playing chess against a naked woman whose face is obscured by long brown hair—a riff on the famous 1963 photograph *Duchamp Playing Chess with a Nude (Eve Babitz)*. Whether the image represents a critic facing an artist in a game of creative one-upmanship, a liberated lesbian chauvinist facing her erotic muse, or Johnston facing an externalized version of herself remains up in the air.

Likewise, the "Jill Johnston Exposed" issue of *Culture Hero* has no easy upshot. "Because Jill has been a number one topic for gossip and discussion for many years, *Culture Hero* decided to find out if any of the assorted gossipers had anything to say about her for the record," Levine writes in a publisher's note on the first page. "Thirty-four of them did and what follows is a collection of their testimony."[75] The contributors spin in different directions, refracting Johnston's many strategies. Some contributors expose themselves, adopting Johnston's style to enact their own messy processes of slouching publicly toward consciousness; others hold Johnston's practice

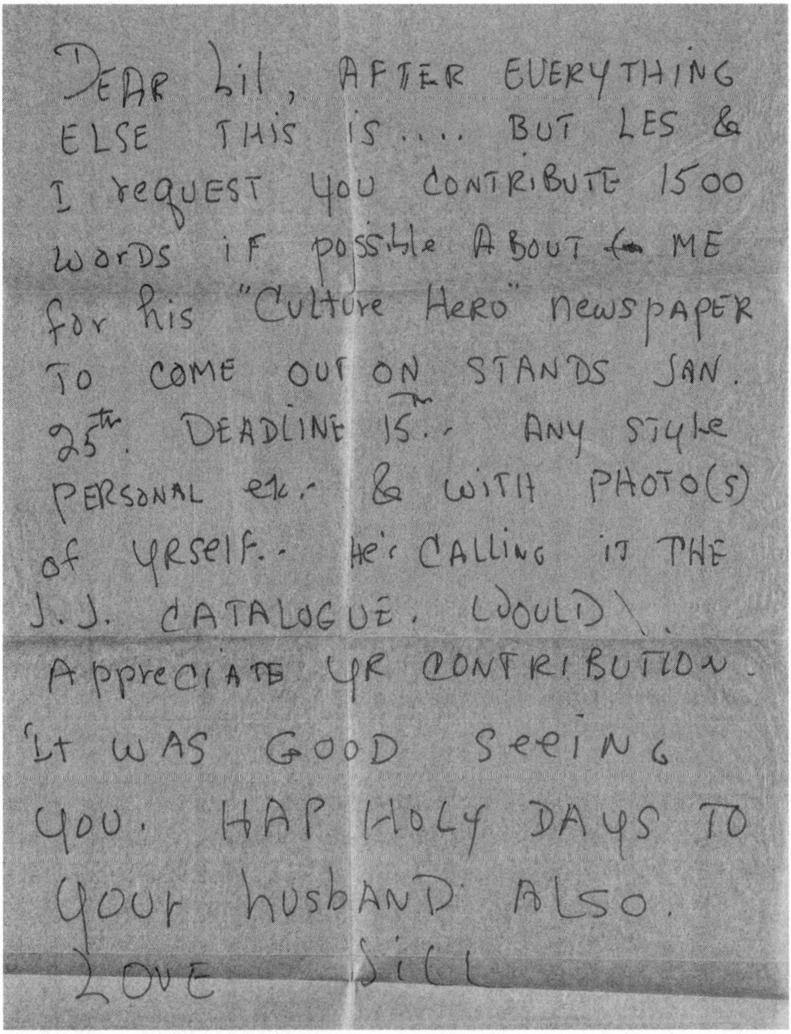

Figure 3.7 Jill Johnston's letter to Lil Picard requesting contribution to *Culture Hero*, c. 1969. Pink marker on pink tissue paper. Lil Picard papers, Special Collections and Archives, University of Iowa Libraries, Iowa City, IA.

at arm's length, analyzing its significance at a disinterested remove; and still a handful of others balk at the request, at the unseemly embarrassment of it all. *Culture Hero* thus furnishes a revealing snapshot of an art world variously impacted by Johnston's unsettled practice of criticizing, exposing herself, and slouching unevenly toward lesbian feminist consciousness all at the same time—a practice that resulted in, as Battcock put it, "the vision of a new possibility for artistic expression."[76]

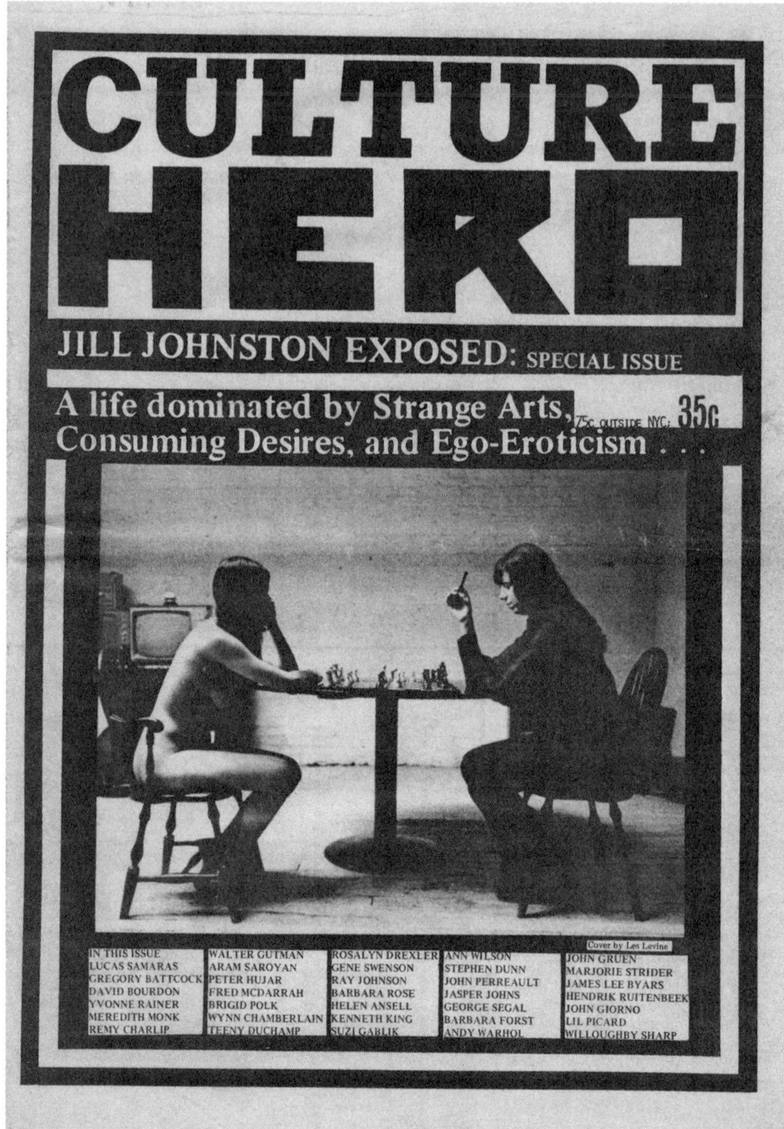

Figure 3.8 "Jill Johnston Exposed: A Life Dominated by Strange Arts, Consuming Desires, and Ego-Eroticism . . . ," special issue, *Culture Hero* (February 1970). Cover by Les Levine. University of Chicago Library, Chicago, IL. © 2025 Les Levine / Artists Rights Society (ARS), New York.

• • •

"If anyone in the future wants to find out about the Sixties, they will have to read Jill's columns," fellow *Village Voice* critic John Perrault proclaims with a great deal of prescience. "Her fractured, sometimes cut-up, confessional syntax leaps from the newsprint page. Heard aloud it is aural literature and it becomes obvious that she had been influenced by Joyce, Stein, Whitman and Ginsberg. She belongs to a venerable tradition and she adds to the tradition a madness that is all her own." "Sex too is an issue," Perrault continues. "Jill does not apologize for her unorthodox love life, in fact, she celebrates it—in print, at that, from week to week. She just doesn't give a fuck."[77] Which is not quite true. Johnston did give a fuck—she invented a whole "literary code" to stave off "premature retaliation from a hostile society"—but she celebrated her sexuality anyway.

Lesbian sex permeates *Culture Hero*, often explicitly and without shame, with fantasy and disclosure woven together. There is no consensus among the contributors to *Culture Hero* about how to deal with Johnston's "unorthodox love life" or how it matters to her criticism. Sex in the "Jill Johnston Exposed" special issue of *Culture Hero* is queer that way. Unsettled and fluid, sex exists everywhere, but nowhere is it pinned down, cordoned off, or figured out. Helen Ansell describes having sex with Johnston in steamy, pulpy prose: "She has buttoned her shirt for me to unbutton and she watches me, becoming me finding her . . . wishing she were me she says, suck me, her tongue running across my eyes and ears to be with me and the wet breast that's more mine than hers."[78] Rosalyn Drexler discloses: "Jill thinks I'm chicken because all I ever do is hug and kiss her, but never meet her clandestinely to go all the way."[79] Swenson declares: "But here she is, as erotic as a flower, a chrysanthemum all fingers and openings. Not wanting me, there is no disagreement."[80] Lil Picard writes: "I dig Jill Johnston's writing because it expresses sex, violence and a romantic, ego-erotic consciousness."[81] Ann Wilson reveals juicy tidbits about the sex Johnston has with other people: "If she can't get a woman she'll take a man in certain instances, like the night she slept with Orlovsky with Ginsberg in the next room on the phone. . . . She will proposition a girl in a bar, 'Do you feel adventurous tonight?' and make love then for seven hours like a spider in an eternal hysteria to break through sorrow—to break through the separation in living. Jill is trying to break through sorrow."[82]

Sorrow and suffering shadow sex throughout *Culture Hero*. "Jill Johnston is about violence done to the spirit and its survival of itself," Wilson concludes. "She gave up her loft and ran to Europe after an idea of love and now has no place to live. Her clothes were stolen, her car was stolen, she ran into a truck drunk with another car, she screams, she crys [*sic*] and she writes in that little black book about all of it."[83]

• • •

Of the contributors who balked at Johnston's request—including Jasper Johns and Grace Glueck, who both contributed terse, polite regrets (likely not intended for publication)—fellow critic Barbara Rose is the only one who goes out of her way to express dismay. "Dear Jill," Rose begins, "As per our New Year's Day conversation, I'm giving you a piece of my mind as promised."

> I should start by saying I used to think you were a great Culture Hero-ine. When I was a student you were a glamorous critic, and I read your column religiously. You used to talk more about art than about yourself in those days. Did you really finally decide criticism was hopeless, or meaningless or impossible? Or did you just begin to think you were more interesting than what you were looking at? As I followed your via dolorosa out of art and into life, I could never quite decide why you chose to go that way. Or as Carl Andre used to say (and he used to say many things before he too became a Culture Hero): Not all the ways out of the darkness lead into the light.[84]

While Barbara Rose certainly did not mean Andre's line as a compliment—using it instead to chastise a wayward critic—she is, I want to argue, right. As feminist theorist Jacqueline Rose contends in her book *Women in Dark Times*, "Rather than the idea of light triumphing over darkness . . . confronting dark with dark might be the more creative path. If there is such a thing as a knowledge of women, this, I would venture, is where we should go looking for it."[85] Among all the contributors to *Culture Hero*, Yvonne Rainer goes furthest in confronting Johnston's darkness with her own (fig. 3.9). Indulging their long-standing game of creative one-upmanship, Rainer's text is uncharacteristically raw and intimate, cutting through the "structural supports" and "rigorous formal means" that she tended to erect around her autobiographical disclosures at the time to conceal them in her own work.[86] It exposes a confessional aspect of Rainer's own inchoate feminism—one that embraces the painful and irrational parts of her life to give them a place at the heart of her work. The text extends over a full page and is emblazoned with a classic film still of Buster Keaton leaning over the edge of a boat with his feet propped in a ladder—a mirror image of Johnston leaning over the edge of a balcony and looming above Rainer in the photo of their 1962 duet.

Adopting a "run off at the mouth nonstop, no niggling, no erasing, no adjustments, no getting the record straight, no trial by jury . . . rough approximation of the style of JJ herself," Rainer weaves together a history of her and Johnston's intertwined lives, painful encounters, and difficult friendship. "Now that I think about it, a lot of things coincided or overlapped in our lives—JJ's and mine."

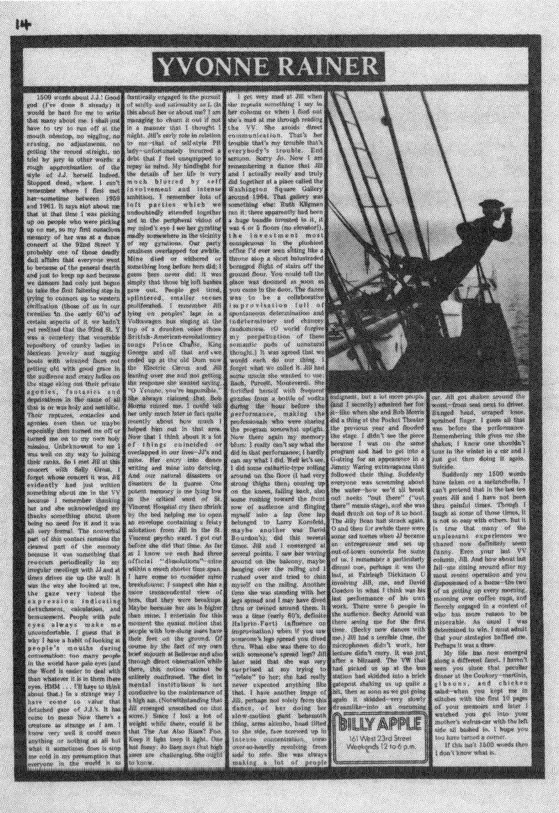

Figure 3.9 Yvonne Rainer's contribution to "Jill Johnston Exposed: A Life Dominated by Strange Arts, Consuming Desires, and Ego-Eroticism . . . ," special issue, *Culture Hero* (February 1970). University of Chicago Library, Chicago, IL.

One potent memory is me lying low in the critical ward of St. Vincent Hospital, my then shrink by the bed helping me to open an envelope containing a feisty salutations from Jill in the St. Vincent psycho ward. I got out before she did that time. As far as I know we each had three official "dissolutions," mine within a much shorter time span. I have come to consider mine break*downs*; I suspect she has a more transcendental view of hers, that they were breakups. Maybe because her ass is higher than mine.

Rainer continues on to recall a car accident she and Johnston suffered together:

Jill got shaken around the worst—front seat next to the driver. Banged head, scraped knee, sprained finger. I guess all that was before the performance. Remembering this gives me the shakes; I know one shouldn't tour in the winter in a car and I just got thru doing it again. Suicide.

Suddenly my 1500 words have taken on a melancholia. I can't pretend that in the last ten years Jill and I have not been thru painful times.... And how about last fall—me sitting around after my most recent operation and you dispossessed of a home—the two of us getting up every morning, mooning over coffee cups, and fiercely engaged in a contest of who has more reason to be miserable. As usual I was determined to win. I must admit that your strategies baffled me. Perhaps it was a draw.[87]

One year later, in October 1971, Rainer would wake up immobilized in a hospital bed after a suicide attempt, a harrowing experience she narrates in her 2006 memoir *Feelings Are Facts: A Life.* "I woke up on Thursday, six days after having tried to end my life," she writes. "It was not a sudden awakening. For what seemed an eternity I was trapped in my coma, aware of being handled, turned, and manipulated, aware of voices, clamor, bright lights, but unable to move or speak. It was a nightmare, full of terrifying hallucinations . . . there was no way out."[88]

So many dark scenes punctuate the archives of women artists from the sixties and seventies (and, I'd wager, they still do). Johnston and Rainer are not alone (or even exceptional) on this score. Images of women trapped, terrified, disoriented, and immobilized emerge from the archives with startling, terrible consistency. So do images of women doing and making fiercely brilliant things, imagining new worlds and new ways to stave off the pressure of a world that is not working. But, still, these dark scenes are hard to face. Much simpler, often, to cordon an artist's life off from her work and locate her brilliance elsewhere, away from her dark, embarrassing, anguished experiences. But this is precisely what Johnston refuses to allow as she compels readers over and over again to countenance and endure what she has to face.

The "Jill Johnston Exposed" special issue of *Culture Hero* opens a small space apart, a space for imagining otherwise, an artistic space where a vision comes into provisional focus for a "nascent, contradictory, scandalous feminist politics"—as art historian Jo Applin argues, drawing from Jacqueline Rose.[89] Focusing on Johnston's peer Lee Lozano (whose conspicuous absence from *Culture Hero* might be attributed to her *General Strike Piece* of 1969), Applin argues for the political significance of feminist practices that embrace "the darkness and failings, the emotional, psychically-charged experiences, of women." Applin asserts: "It is a feminism that may not always call itself by that name, and is important precisely because of its refusal to conform, to be reasonable and sane."[90] Embarking on this kind of feminist project means enduring the "frightening arbitrariness," as Applin writes, quoting Hannah Arendt, "inherent in any political decision-making process, in which the results cannot be known in advance."[91] *Culture Hero* thus represents a culmination of a feminist solution that Johnston had been pursuing publicly in her work since at least 1962, when she recognized the profound political consequences of the avant-garde's blurring of art and life. Johnston's brilliance consists in the ways she pursued this insight throughout the sixties, embracing the frightening arbitrariness of "anything may happen" and compelling others to respond to the darkest, most intimate and erotic—as well as the most marvelous and striking—parts of her public and private worlds. The "Jill Johnston Exposed" special issue of *Culture Hero* is an archive of such countenancing and thus an extraordinary feminist artwork.

"Oh, Jill," critic John Gruen begins his contribution, "how often I've wanted to be you, letting all my anxieties crash into people's lives, translating fifty feelings at once into words, spilling the water and wine of my emotions into those already drunk on their own!" He concludes, "You seem to have been able to transform fear itself into something very close to ecstasy. To live ecstatically, as you surely must, has always been my dream."[92] *Culture Hero* brims with instances of critics and artists redeploying language to imagine possibilities for living and relating differently, in ways that transform sorrow, fear, and anger into resources for resisting a world that is not working—even if fleetingly, only in the improbable space of a genre-bending tabloid-cum-artwork fanzine that temporarily infiltrated downtown newsstands.

It's *Always* a Dilemma

As Johnston leaned into her new role as a famous lesbian, becoming increasingly visible and vocal, so too did glib dismissals of her work and homophobic, sexist denunciations. One year after the "Jill Johnston Exposed" issue of *Culture Hero* came out, and a few months after Johnston urged everybody to "COME OUT" in her *Village Voice* column,[93] film critic Andrew Sarris published a screed in *The Village Voice* on February 4, 1971, titled (no joke) "Heteros Have Problems Too"—an acerbic denunciation of Johnston and others.[94] Accusing "Miss Johnston," as he calls her, of "publicly . . . exhorting every pretty girl in America to come out of the closet and into her bed," Sarris casts Johnston as part of a self-indulgent "phony new industry of interpersonal technology." Her "confessional gush," he writes, "is consecrated to the proposition that we must all abandon the privileged privacy of our most precious relationships, or perish from emotional constipation."[95] Responding a few weeks later with her column titled "Lois

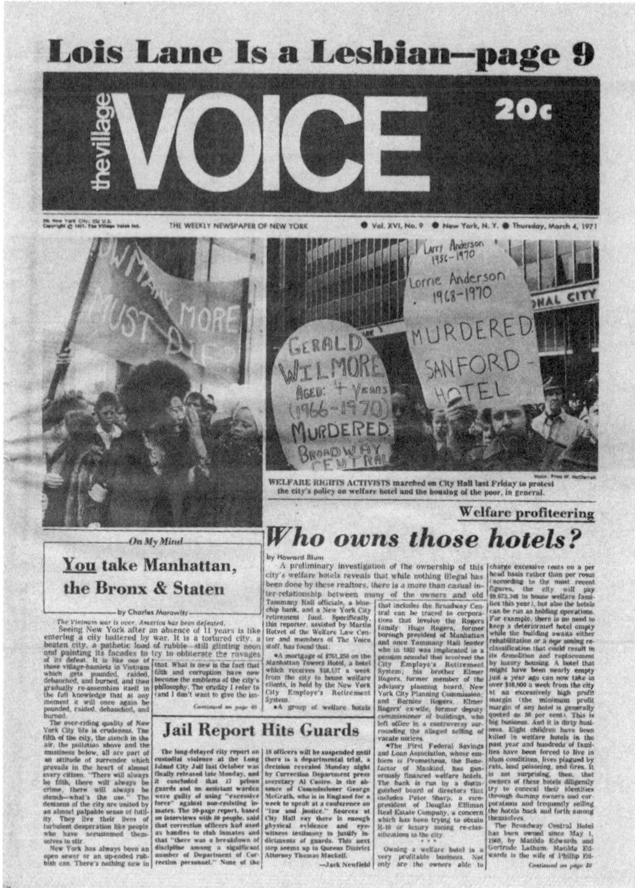

Figure 3.10 Cover of *The Village Voice* advertising Jill Johnston's column "Lois Lane Is a Lesbian," March 4, 1971.

Lane Is a Lesbian," which the *Voice* advertised prominently on the cover (fig. 3.10), Johnston snaps back, "My 'confessional gush' is consecrated to no other proposition than that of collecting all of my selves that I can raise to consciousness in the shape of current experiences into some form of literary energy at the moment I sit down most every week to write that damn column. Sometimes I get a masterpiece seizure and work very hard for a structural coup. Sometimes I'm unsuccessfully trying to merge my literary ambition with my cause concerns. It's *always* a dilemma."[96]

"Lois Lane Is a Lesbian" contains some of Johnston's most poignant political pleas on behalf of gay liberation: "My first and final line would be that if you can't walk out your door and down the street and into the park in any familiar embrace with the one you love the whole society is in trouble."[97] But the column also contains some of Johnston's most troubling and flawed political proclamations. For one, she denounces the "monstrosity of transsexualism" as "surely the most pitiful operation going, to 'help' some gullible people *not* be homosexual in a society far from convinced that all the equipment we are born with is perfectly beautiful."[98] Fighting for space to live as a lesbian in a society intent on eradicating homosexuality at seemingly every turn, Johnston accuses trans people of being dupes or shills of a hostile establishment determined to pathologize people as "transexual" in order to "cure" them, rather than simply accepting them as homosexual. It is, no doubt, a misguided accusation with capacity for real harm. Certainly "flawed by rage" (as Johnston would later put it, regarding Swenson's writings) is one way to describe Johnston's mean-spirited, firm biological essentialism. But I have no interest in excusing it here.

Johnston also claims in the column to be "more in sympathy with the black cause than ever before," but she focuses only on her incomplete attempts to get there, rather than on what such sympathy might accomplish. "My initial reaction to the black movement was hey wait a minute I didn't *choose* to be born white, and let me tell *you* about the problems of a white homosexual female in a . . . et cetera. Now I suggest you go up to a black person and say White People Have Problems Too and see what kind of response you get."[99] Skewering the premise of Sarris's complaint, Johnston does not propose any kind of alternative political formulation to express interracial solidarity in positive terms. In fact, she concludes the column by asserting her distance from *all* political movements rather than prescribing any kind of intersectional political program. "A black man once told me that LeRoi Jones and the like wanted my head on a platter," she exclaims. "The women's lib people don't like the way I swim"—a reference to the time she disrupted a speech by Betty Friedan by diving into a pool and stripping down to her underwear during a benefit for the Women's Strike for Equality.[100] "The Gay Liberation Front says I wouldn't get any support from *them*," she continues. "Both organizations think I'm a male chauvinist pig, probably because I take more girls to bed (or want to or pretend to) than I have a right to—as though nobody was ever luring *me* to bed."[101]

In a 2019 feature on Johnston for *Artforum*, critic Andrea Long Chu wryly observes, "No reader of *Lesbian Nation* will emerge without the impression that Jill Johnston, bless her, was one frisky motherfucker." Chu then poses a pair of rhetorical questions: "So what if this wasn't the revolution? Then again, so what if it was?"[102] Going with the second question, Chu argues that Johnston's brand of lesbian feminism "attained a degree of radicality never before reached in the history of progressive political movements," because it "hoped to intervene politically not just in policy or even in social practice but at the level of attachment as such."[103]

By the time Johnston published *Lesbian Nation* in 1973, she was explicit and adamant that "feminists who still sleep with the man are delivering their most vital energies to the oppressor." She explains: "Lesbianism is the solution" or the "answer to the spiritual needs of the woman deprived of herself in relation to the man."[104] But this makes for a disappointing story. Nothing much changed, and most feminists kept sleeping with men anyway because, as Chu explains, "there is no political program . . . capable of efficaciously restructuring people's attachment to things that are bad for them. . . . You simply cannot tell people how to feel, at least with the result that they start feeling the way you want them to."[105] Johnston, I'd wager, knew this, probably better than anyone. She doesn't even totally exempt herself from it. "I mean, the man is paying me to write this book," she admits in a passing parenthetical aside at the heart of *Lesbian Nation*.[106] So what can be done? It's *always* a dilemma.

Chu calls this dilemma, or impasse, the "Impossibility of Feminism." But this gives rise to a corollary, which Chu calls the "Impossibility of Not-Feminism," as in "feminism's being impossible doesn't keep us feminists from wanting it."[107] If one finds Chu's assessment of the situation compelling (which I do), then it is tempting to historicize Johnston's lesbian pronouncements and performances of the early seventies as failures: as so many examples of an impossible political project, one doomed and ill-conceived from the start, *and* as so many instances of Johnston's failure to detach herself from the misguided fantasy of a "true political revolution" in which all women become lesbians. Fair enough, but I want to propose an alternative. Rather than failures, I want to submit Johnston's lesbian pronouncements and performances as art practices that take up failure as their content. Feminism's failure to change the way women feel and what they desire is not Johnston's own personal failure. Rather, that failure, or impossibility, forms the condition of her art—a condition Johnston saw quite clearly and sought to enlarge and intensify in her work, not transcend.

On April 30, 1971, Johnston appeared on a panel moderated by Norman Mailer titled "A Dialogue on Women's Liberation" at New York's Town Hall theater in front of an audience "filled with the elite of a thousand intellectual battles," according to a write-up in *The New York Times*[108]—a capitulation to "the man" if there ever was one. "I did rather lamely agree that it was outrageous for a panel on women's liberation to be moderated by norman mailer," Johnston reflects in *Lesbian Nation*. But she participated anyway. "I was a performer and an opportunist and I couldn't think of anything more drastic and wonderful than appearing at town hall before thousands of people who lived above 14th street to tell them that all women were lesbians" (fig. 3.11).[109]

The panel was organized as a benefit to support Theatre for Ideas—a salon that *The New York Times* once gave the dubious distinction of being "New

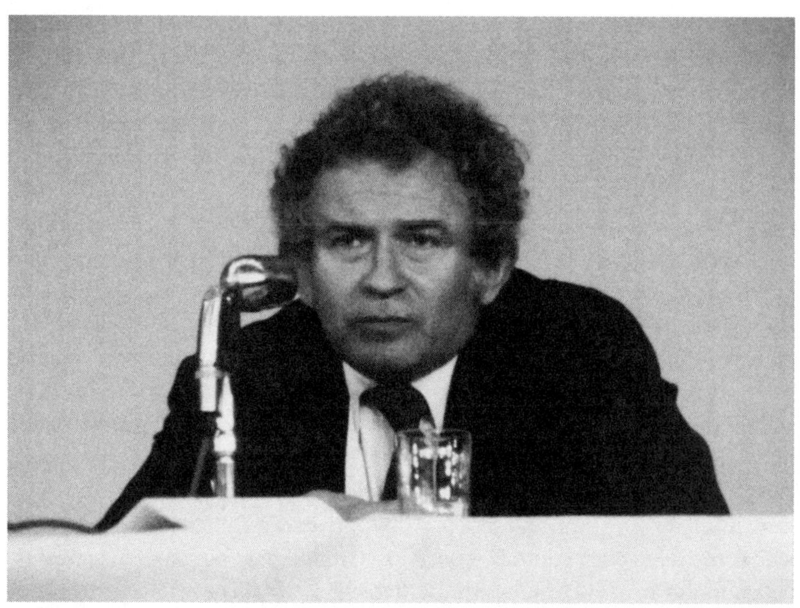

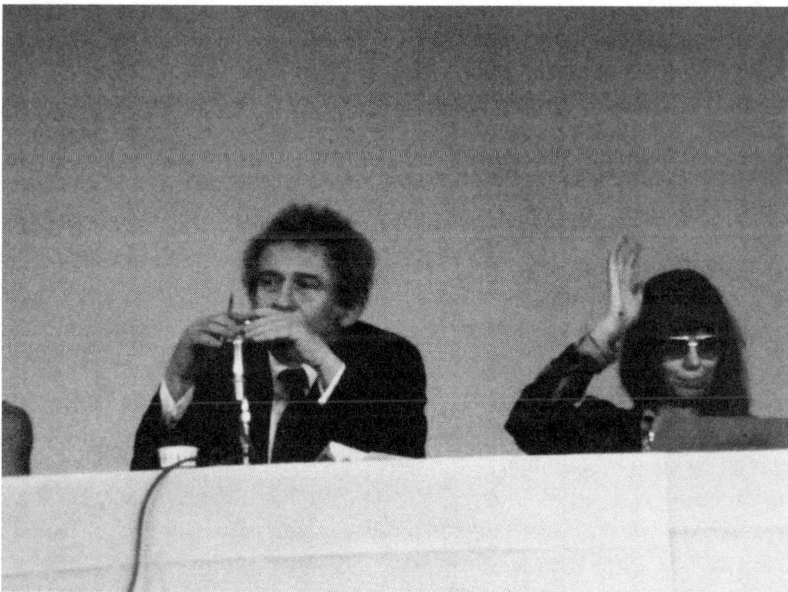

Figure 3.11 Jill Johnston and Norman Mailer at "A Dialogue on Women's Liberation," Town Hall, New York, April 30, 1971. Stills from *Town Bloody Hall*, dir. Chris Hegedus and D. A. Pennebaker (1979).

York's leading exercise in participatory autocracy."[110] Mailer, a regular at Theatre for Ideas, had just published "The Prisoner of Sex" in *Harper's Magazine*, a bombastic fifty-page rebuttal to *Sexual Politics* by Kate Millett (who did not participate on the panel). Johnston got cast in the role of radical lesbian foil to fellow panelist Germaine Greer, the glamorous "saucy feminist that even men like," according to the next week's cover of *Life* magazine.[111] The panel also featured literary critic Diana Trilling and Jacqueline Ceballos, president of the New York chapter of the National Organization for Women (fig. 3.12). Filmmaker D. A. Pennebaker recorded the event using shaky handheld cameras, and his collaborator Chris Hegedus later edited the footage into a cinema verité documentary titled *Town Bloody Hall* (1979).

The panel got off to a rocky start when poet Gregory Corso interrupted the proceedings by shouting from the balcony "All of Humanity! Not just Half!"[112]—before storming out of the theater escorted by ushers. But this time, Johnston was not "deadlocked" by "divided sympathies" as she had been three years prior when Swenson interrupted her first panel by screaming from another balcony in a remarkably similar scene.[113] This time she came prepared.

"I had the correct instinct to fuck things up but no political philosophy to clarify a course of action," Johnston writes in *Lesbian Nation*. "And had I had such a philosophy it's doubtful I would've been able to educate enough people in a short time to make a real difference."[114] Instead Johnston delivered a riotous, poetic tour de force of a performance. But she didn't call it a performance. Rather, she called it an "episode"—an ambiguous word that signals a state of animated suspension, a period of time in which *something* is happening that will eventually end, and then things will continue on as before. Episodes, according to Lauren Berlant, designate "occasions that frame experience while not changing much of anything."[115] After enduring an episode, or witnessing one, you might very well *feel* differently—perhaps relieved, elated, angry, scared, or exhausted—but it's probably not possible to predict or control how.

Mailer called Johnston to the podium third, following Greer. After kicking things off with a joke, she began: "The title of this episode is new approach." And she continued to read, and read, and read. Her text appeared in full in *The Village Voice* the next week under the heading "On a Clear Day You Can See Your Mother." It begins:

All women are lesbians except those who don't know it naturally they are but don't know it yet I am a woman who is a lesbian because I am a woman and a woman who loves herself naturally who is other women is a lesbian a woman who loves women loves herself naturally this is the case that a woman is herself is all woman is a natural born lesbian

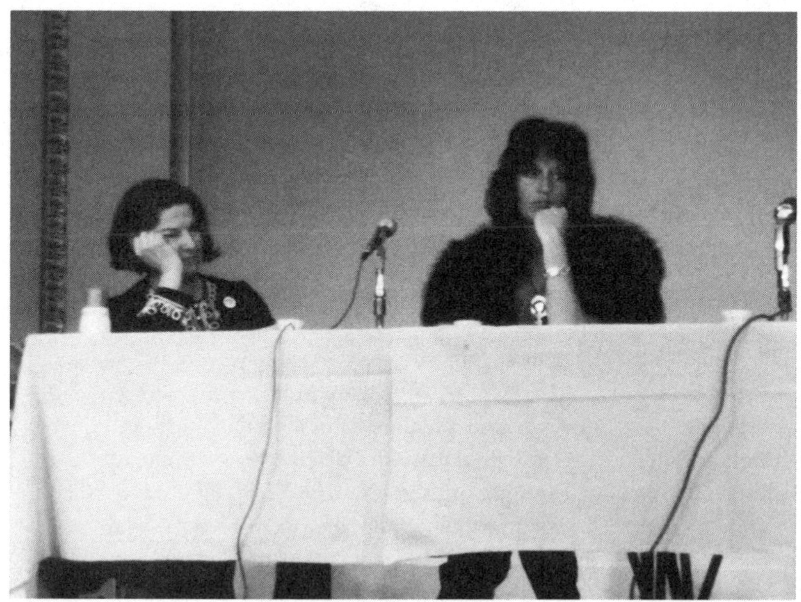

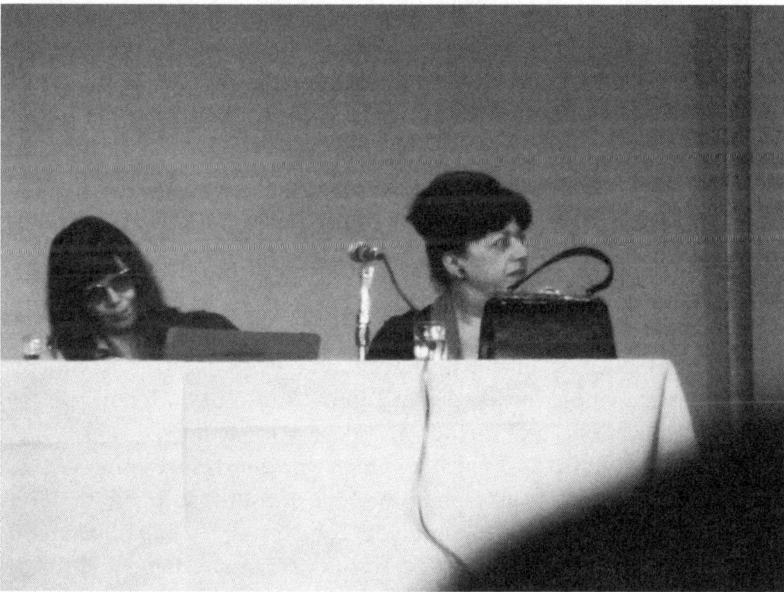

Figure 3.12 Panelists at "A Dialogue on Women's Liberation," Town Hall, New York, April 30, 1971. *Top*: Jacqueline Ceballos and Germaine Greer; *bottom*: Jill Johnston and Diana Trilling. Stills from *Town Bloody Hall*, dir. Chris Hegedus and D. A. Pennebaker (1979).

so we don't mind using the name like any name it is quite meaningless
it means naturely I am a woman and whatever I am we are we affirm
being what we are . . .[116]

The text goes on and on, punctuated by ellipses, dashes, and a few excla-
mation points but no periods. Johnston unfurls one matriarchal genealogy
after another, starting with:

> . . . but who are the daughters of Rachel and Ruth and Sarah and Re-
> bekah the rest we do not know the daughters never had any daughters
> they had only sons who begat more sons so we have very little sense,
> from that particular book, of the lineage and ligaments and legacies
> and identities of mothers and daughters and their daughters and their
> mothers and mothers and daughters and sisters who were naturally not
> lesbians if they had nothing of each other save sons so now we must
> say Verily Verily, I say unto thee, except a woman be born again she
> cannot see the Kingdom of Goddess a woman must be born again to
> be herself her own eminence and grace the queen queen-self whose
> mother has pressed upon her mouth innumerable passionate kisses so
> sigh us . . .[117]

Near the middle of the text, Johnston again proclaims, "All women are lesbians except those who don't know it of course," which she follows up with,
"which means nothing we could say it over and over again over lesbianles-
bianlesbianlesbianlesbianlesbianlesbianlesbian . . ."[118]

Close to the end of the text, she proclaims twice in italics, *Until all
women are lesbians there will be no true political revolution*"—and the
second time she clarifies, "meaning the terminus of the heterosexual institution through the recollection by woman of her womanhood her own
grace and eminence . . ." At which point she admits, "I would more properly
be as majorities would have it leaning on my sword declaring my defeat
some women want to have their cock and eat it too and lesbian is a label
invented by anybody to throw at any woman who dares to be a man's equal
and lesbian is a good name it means nothing of course so we don't mind
using the name . . ." Then she continues, ". . . Oh well . . . Lillian over and
out . . . he sd I want your body and she sd you can have it when I'm through
with it . . ." At this point in her recitation, the audience erupted into riotous
laughter. Mailer then cut Johnston off.[119]

"Jill, you've read your letter, now mail it," Mailer intoned, as a few audience members booed. "It's not fair to the other speakers. Jill's had fifteen
minutes already." That's when one of Johnston's friends mounted the stage.
With a sly nod, Johnston embraced her friend, lifting her awkwardly in a

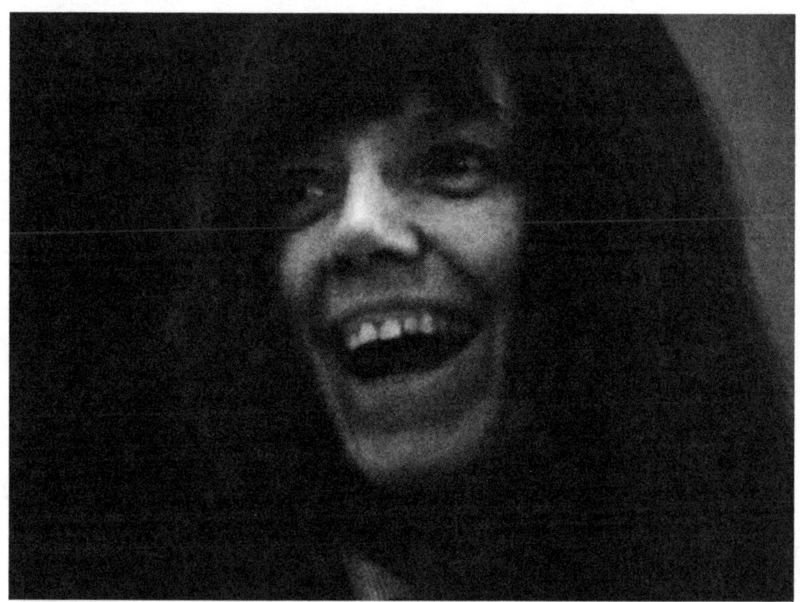

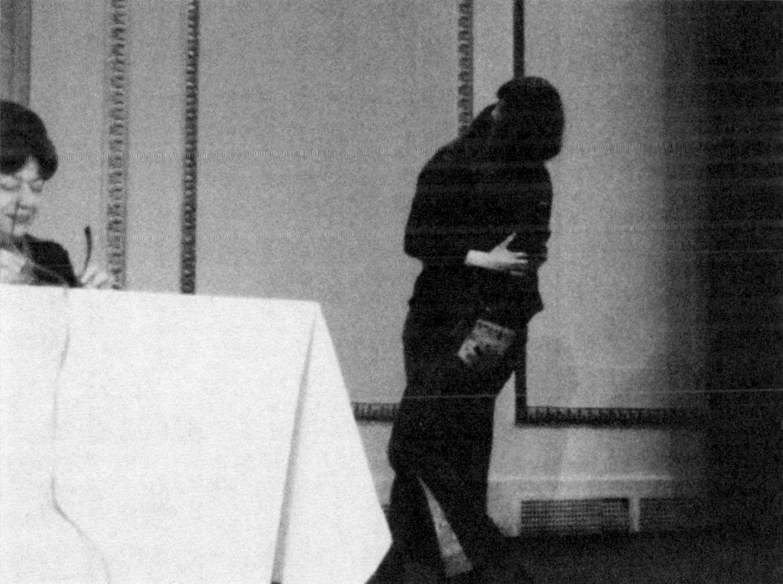

Figure 3.13 Jill Johnston making out with friends at "A Dialogue on Women's Liberation," Town Hall, New York, April 30, 1971. Stills from *Town Bloody Hall*, dir. Chris Hegedus and D. A. Pennebaker (1979).

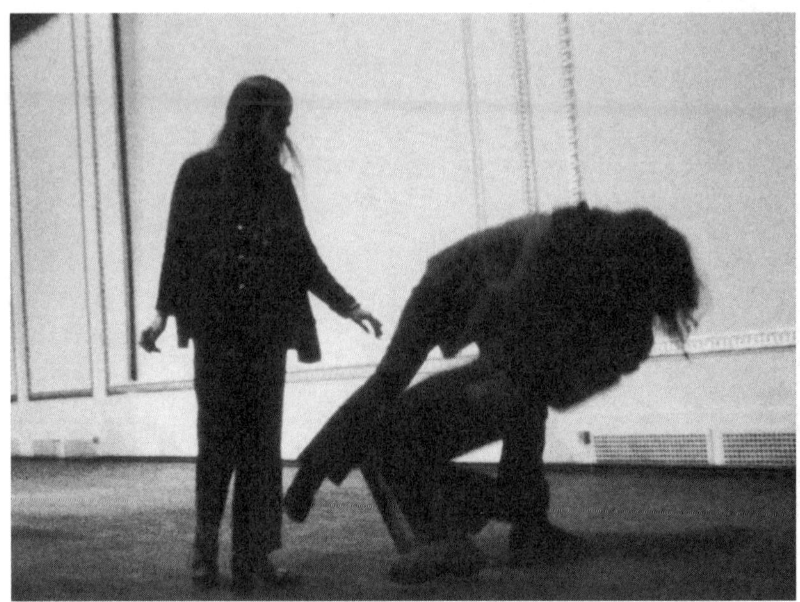

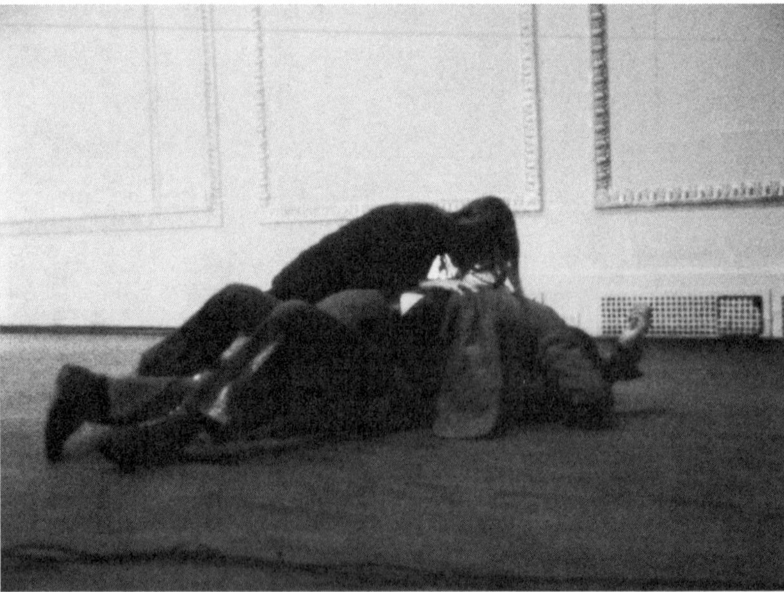

Figure 3.13 (*continued*)

handsy make-out session. Another friend climbed on stage saying, "Hey, Jill, what about me?!"—and all three tumbled to the floor (fig. 3.13).[120]

"It's great that you pay 25 bucks to see three dirty overalls on the floor, when you can see a lot of cock and cunt for 4 dollars down the street!" Mailer complained to no avail. Becoming increasingly exasperated, he eventually called a vote on whether Johnston should be permitted to finish reading. After Mailer declared the "no" votes the winners, Johnston and her pals exited the theater and did not return. Which is a shame, I think, because Johnston did not have that much more left to read. Her text in *The Village Voice* comes full circle. At the end, in the part she did not get to read aloud at Town Hall, her opening lament emerges again as an unconsummated wish that reverberates backward through the text and forward in time:

> . . . the mothers and the daughters and the great grandmothers and daughters of Rachel and Ruth and Sarah and Rebekah the rest we will know now the daughter the mothers and sisters will have daughters who beget daughters so we will have more sense, from this time, of the lineage and ligaments and legacies and identities of our mothers and daughters and their mothers and mothers and daughters and sisters who are naturally of course lesbians if they have of each other and saying Verily Verily except a woman must be born again she cannot see the Queendom of Goddess a woman must be born again to be herself her own eminence and grace the queen queenself whose mother has pressed upon her mouth innumerable passionate kisses . . . Sail away where the wind blows sweet . . . and take a sister by her hand . . . Lead her far from this barren land . . . ON A CLEAR DAY YOU CAN SEE YOUR MOTHER.[121]

•   •   •

A run-on sentence many thousand words long, Johnston's text is accretive rather than protean. Each repetition accumulates on top of the words that came before, distorting them under pressure. The whole text seems to move forward and backward, or to skip all around in time. Words get modified and remodified as each new clause echoes back, with no stable origin, no destination, and no "Simple Simon" meanings. Rather than breeding contempt, repetition dislodges conventional meanings and renders familiar words newly dynamic, alive, and available to imagine new worlds. Which is all to say, Johnston's Town Hall episode does *not* represent a departure from her earlier investments as an artist and critic. On the contrary, it engages ardently with all the formal and structural problems thrown up by avant-garde art of the recent past, and it assembles new solutions. Johnston's lesbian feminist recitation at Town Hall thus represents one (among many) culminating artistic achievements to emerge in the wake of the Judson Dance Theater.

In a 1968 article for *The New York Times*, Johnston claims that the Judson Dance Theater was a "revolution" forged in the "delirium of a sprawling rebellion" that happened at Judson Memorial Church from 1962 to 1964. "In retrospect, it was a beautiful mess," she writes—a mess that never really ended. "After a brief period of some confusion and dispersion," Johnston continues, "the movement regained its momentum and is now in the process of enlarging, elaborating, and consolidating the dimension of its early promise."[122] That early promise was *always* "inchoately queer," as Thomas J. Lax has argued more recently—"if we understand queerness to be 'a matter of the world you inhabit, not something you simply are,'" Lax elaborates, quoting art historian Douglas Crimp.[123] In Lax's retelling, the Judson Dance Theater's inchoate queerness inheres in the way artists laid bare their collaborative "sweaty, knotted labor" in their work, thereby "putting the intimate flotsam and jetsam of their daily lives onstage as part of what it meant to make art."[124] By incorporating the fraught intimacies of New York's social and cultural fabric into their work, Judson artists sought not to transcend their social situation but rather to "picture the steadfast and divisive social relations that informed their work *as the work itself.*"[125] And in so doing, they held out the promise of claiming "the intimacy of everyday life as a contestable political space," as Lax asserts.[126] Johnston was at the center of this.

With her 1971 Town Hall episode, Johnston enlarges and elaborates the queer dimension of this early promise. Pushing that dimension as far as it could go, she claims any true political revolution worthy of the name would have to fundamentally change the intimacy of everyday life. Come the revolution women would stop delivering their most vital energies to men and instead turn toward each other, love one another, and love themselves, naturally, their own grace and eminence. *"Until all women are lesbians there will be no true political revolution,"* Johnston proclaims again and again. So there won't be one. It's impossible. But rather than lean on her sword and declare defeat, Johnston amplifies the futility of the situation. Pushing her linguistic adventures to new heights of creativity, Johnston articulates in sumptuous intricate detail her wish for a true political revolution. Reclaiming the word "lesbian" from those who would use it "to throw at any woman who dares to be a man's equal," Johnston repeats it into magical transcendence. It becomes slippery and capacious and beautiful. Lesbian comes to describe a new intimacy of everyday life, where women love one another and themselves without interference from the patriarchy. Lesbian describes the new lineage and ligaments and legacies of a matriarchy filled

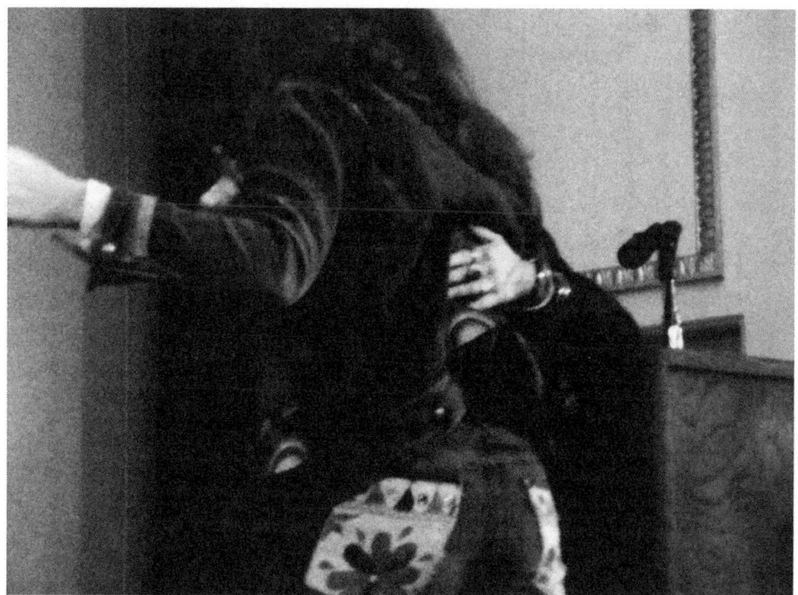

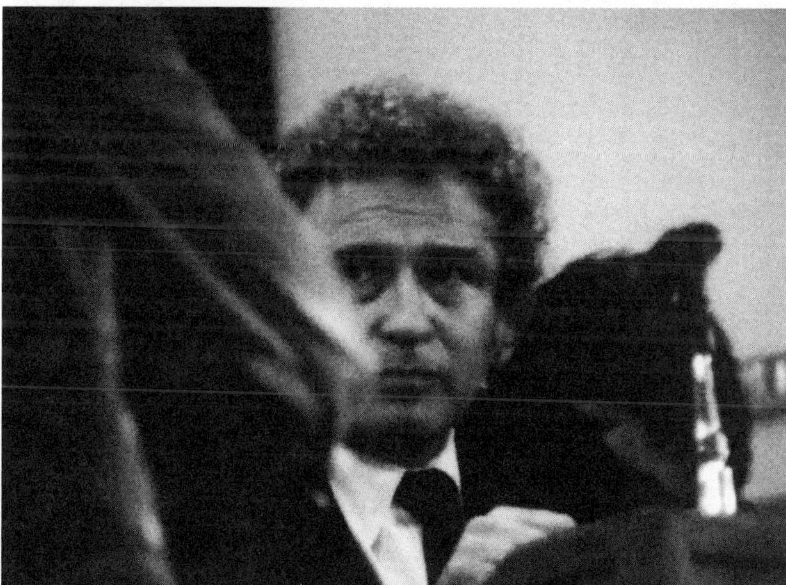

Figure 3.14 Jill Johnston and her friends leaving the stage at "A Dialogue on Women's Liberation," Town Hall, New York, April 30, 1971. Stills from *Town Bloody Hall*, dir. Chris Hegedus and D. A. Pennebaker (1979).

with laughter and innumerable passionate kisses. But, in the end, it's all just an episode—a fleeting occasion that frames experience without changing much of anything. By unfurling her wish with such lavish plentitude, Johnston also aggrandizes its impossibility. Her wish hangs in the Town Hall auditorium, unconsummated (fig. 3.14). "All women are lesbians? Get that woman outa here!" Johnston writes in *Lesbian Nation*. "And by my own volition I left."[127]

Revolutions Deferred

Apart from providing a basis for the paternalistic virtue dominant cultures claim when dissident movements fold, what does it mean for a movement, a politics, a social theory to fail? How might political breakdown work as something other than a blot, or a botched job?

. . . The aim of criticism in this light is not redemptive. It is not to perform retrospective hallowing responses to events, or to texts about events. Trying, and failing, it keeps the event open, animating, and vital. The aim is then for criticism to generate its objects, to construct unexpected scenes out of the materials it makes available.

LAUREN BERLANT, 1994[1]

This book is about things that are not sure about what they are. But, as it turns out, this book is also about unconsummated wishes. It's about revolutions deferred.

• • •

Here at the end, we're left with Swenson alone outside the Museum of Modern Art (MoMA) wielding only his giant blue question mark on a stick. Even after beseeching in print, "Why Have None of My Fellow Artists Spoken a Word in Behalf of the Revolution?" he was never met by a rallying cry in response. "This, then, is a judgement and an accusation," Swenson seethes from the pages of *The New York Free Press* on June 6, 1968. "This will, for all time, be remembered as the Season of Shame."[2] But hardly anyone was listening. Nevertheless, his friend and fellow critic Gregory Battcock encouraged him to keep writing for the *Free Press* anyway. "Nobody else would publish him," Battcock recalls in a 1971 interview, "and I thought what he had to say was very important."[3]

Upon the conclusion of his solitary protest outside MoMA, Swenson

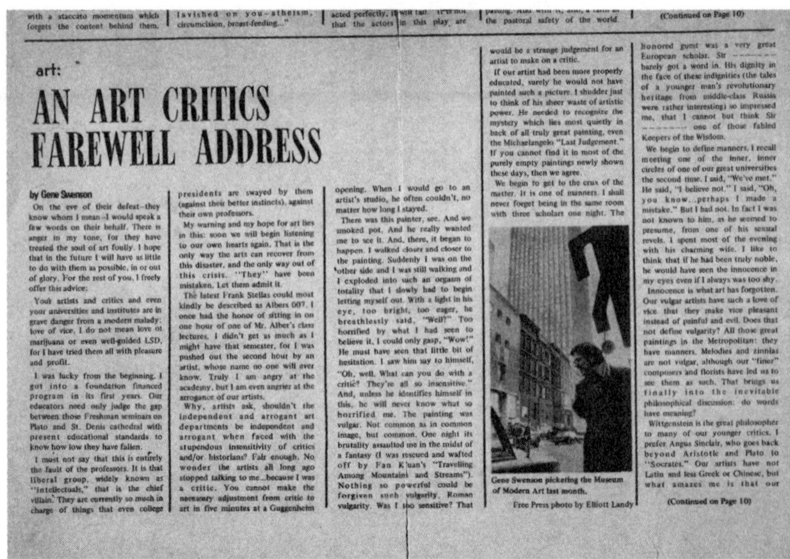

art:

AN ART CRITICS FAREWELL ADDRESS

by Gene Swenson

On the eve of their defeat—they know whom I mean—I would speak a few words on their behalf. There is anger in my tone, for they have treated the soul of art foully. I hope that in the future I will have as little to do with them as possible, in or out of glory. For the rest of you, I freely offer this advice:

Your artists and critics and even your universities and institutes are in grave danger from a modern malady: love of vice. I do not mean love of marijuana or even well-guided LSD, for I have tried them all with pleasure and profit.

I was lucky from the beginning. I got into a foundation financed program in its first years. Our educators need only judge the gap between those Freshman seminars on Plato and St. Denis cathedral with present educational standards to know how low they have fallen.

I must not say that this is entirely the fault of the professors. It is that liberal group, widely known as "intellectuals," that is the chief villain. They are currently so much in charge of things that even college presidents are swayed by them (against their better instincts), against their own professors.

My warning and my hope for art lies in this: soon we will begin listening to our own hearts again. That is the only way the arts can recover from this disaster, and the only way out of this crisis. "They" have been mistaken. Let them admit it.

The latest Frank Stellas could most kindly be described as Albers 007. I once had the honor of sitting in on one hour of one of Mr. Alber's class lectures. I didn't get as much as I might have that semester, for I was pushed out the second hour by an artist, whose name no one will ever know. Truly I am angry at the academy, but I am even angrier at the arrogance of our artists.

Why, artists ask, shouldn't the independent and arrogant art departments be independent and arrogant when faced with the stupendous insensitivity of critics and/or historians? Fair enough. No wonder the artists all long ago stopped talking to me...because I was a critic. You cannot make the necessary adjustment from critic to art in five minutes at a Guggenheim opening. When I would go to an artist's studio, he often couldn't, no matter how long I stayed.

There was this painter, see. And we smoked pot. And he really wanted me to see it. And, there, it began to happen. I walked closer and closer to the painting. Suddenly I was on the other side and I was still walking and I exploded into such an orgasm of totality that I slowly had to begin letting myself out. With a light in his eye, too bright, too eager, he breathlessly said, "Well?" Too horrified by what I had seen to believe it, I could only gasp, "Wow!" He must have seen that little bit of hesitation. I saw him say to himself, "Oh, well. What can you do with a critic? They're all so insensitive." And, unless he identifies himself in this, he will never know what so horrified me. The painting was vulgar. Not common as in common image, but common. One night its brutality assaulted me in the midst of a fantasy (I was rescued and wafted off by Fan K'uan's "Traveling Among Mountains and Streams"). Nothing so powerful could be forgiven such vulgarity. Roman vulgarity. Was I too sensitive? That would be a strange judgement for an artist to make on a critic.

If our artist had been more properly educated, surely he would not have painted such a picture. I shudder just to think of his sheer waste of artistic power. He needed to recognize the mystery which lies most quietly in back of all truly great painting, even the Michaelangelo "Last Judgement." If you cannot find it in most of the purely empty paintings newly shown these days, then we agree.

We begin to get to the crux of the matter. It is one of manners. I shall never forget being in the same room with three scholars one night. The honored guest was a very great European scholar. Sir ———— barely got a word in. His dignity in the face of these indignities (the tales of a younger man's revolutionary heritage from middle-class Russia were rather interesting) so impressed me, that I cannot but think Sir ———— one of those fabled Keepers of the Wisdom.

We begin to define manners. I recall meeting one of the inner, inner circles of one of our great universities the second time. I said, "We've met." He said, "I believe not." I said, "Oh, you know...perhaps I made a mistake." But I had not. In fact I was not known to him, as he seemed to presume, from one of his sexual revels. I spent most of the evening with his charming wife. I like to think that if he had been truly noble, he would have seen the innocence in my eyes even if I always was too shy.

Innocence is what art has forgotten. Our vulgar artists have such a love of vice that they make vice pleasant instead of painful and evil. Does that not define vulgarity? All those great paintings in the Metropolitan: they have manners. Melodies and zinnias are not vulgar, although our "finer" composers and florists have led us to see them as such. That brings us finally into the inevitable philosophical discussion: do words have meaning?

Wittgenstein is the great philosopher to many of our younger critics. I prefer Angus Sinclair, who goes back beyond Aristotle and Plato to "Socrates." Our artists have not Latin and less Greek or Chinese, but what amazes me is that our

(Continued on Page 10)

Gene Swenson picketing the Museum of Modern Art last month.

Free Press photo by Elliott Landy

Figure 4.1 Gene Swenson, "An Art Critic's Farewell Address," *The New York Free Press*, March 28, 1968. Newspaper Clipping. Gregory Battcock papers, 1952–circa 1980, Archives of American Art, Smithsonian Institution, Washington, DC.

published a column titled "An Art Critic's Farewell Address" in March 1968 (fig. 4.1), which Battcock describes as "a curious, sensitive document that isn't really a farewell address at all, but another plea for ethical reevaluation of modern esthetics, containing 'personal' experiences that were anathema to the orthodoxies of current art-writing."[4] Addressing the art world in general, and MoMA specifically, Swenson begins, "On the eve of their defeat—they know whom I mean—I would speak a few words on their behalf. There is anger in my tone, for they have treated the soul of art foully."[5] He continues,

> My warning and my hope for art lies in this: soon we will begin listening to our own hearts again. That is the only way the arts can recover from this crisis. "They" have been mistaken. Let them admit it. . . .
>
> Paul Signac once wrote a letter, anarchist that he was, praising the virtues of keeping politics and art separate. I have until now done so in my work and life. Let me, however, call upon poetry for advice in this crisis.
>
>> How sharply our children will be ashamed
>> taking at last their vengeance for these horrors
>> remembering how in so strange a time
>> common integrity could look like courage.[6]

What does Swenson find in these lines? Although he does not cite them, they come from Yevgeny Yevtushenko's poem "Talk" (1960). The poem begins, "You're a brave man they tell me. / I'm not. / Courage has never been my quality."[7] In one sense, the poem conveys resignation to a lower bar of "common integrity" and to the constant sinking feeling of living in "so strange a time" in which the modern horrors of war, brutality, capitalist greed, and so on are accepted as background noise among decent people trying to get on with the daily grind of work and leisure. In another sense, the poem conveys sad optimism in its anticipation of a near future when "common integrity" will be the rule and bravery the expectation—a future in which "children will be ashamed" when they look back on the complacency of their parents, who were unwilling to take real risks on behalf of the courage of their convictions.

But, by March 1968, hardly anybody was willing to countenance anything Swenson had to say anymore. "He wasn't listened to because what he said was said too strongly and it was too true," Lucy Lippard laments after Swenson's tragic death. "Cruelly, we accepted his sacrifice of companionship and honored him only uneasily for his generosity."[8]

•   •   •

Here at the end, we're left with Johnston on stage at New York's Town Hall proclaiming "*Until all women are lesbians there will be no true political revolution*" to an audience who sat by as Norman Mailer cut her off midsentence. The revolution never happened. On the heels of *Lesbian Nation*, Johnston published a very different anthology in 1974 titled *Gullibles Travels* (fig. 4.2)—a composite portrait of herself in motion as a flickering, fluctuating figure "in search of experiences to synthesize into an expanding succession of selves," as her friends write in the book's foreword.[9] An alternative collection of ambivalent writings from the thick of her *Lesbian Nation* years, *Gullibles Travels* is altogether less certain about the possibility of political revolution. The texts tend to turn inward, indulging the process and the act of writing. "i have some illusions left about subjects," Johnston states softly in her introductory note, writing in all lowercase. "that subjects are important, the importance of a subject seems to me to reside in how much we want to save it, is it worth saving, is the world worth saving, etc., how much concern would we lavish on the survival of the whale nations forinstance, or are we looking forward to a natural death, and given such concerns what is the proper mode for any individual of expressing them if not directly participating in the operations or politics of change."[10] That question hangs over the anthology, unanswered.

Johnston concludes *Gullibles Travels* with a text titled "Agnes Martin: Surrender and Solitude," an account of her pilgrimage to visit Martin in New

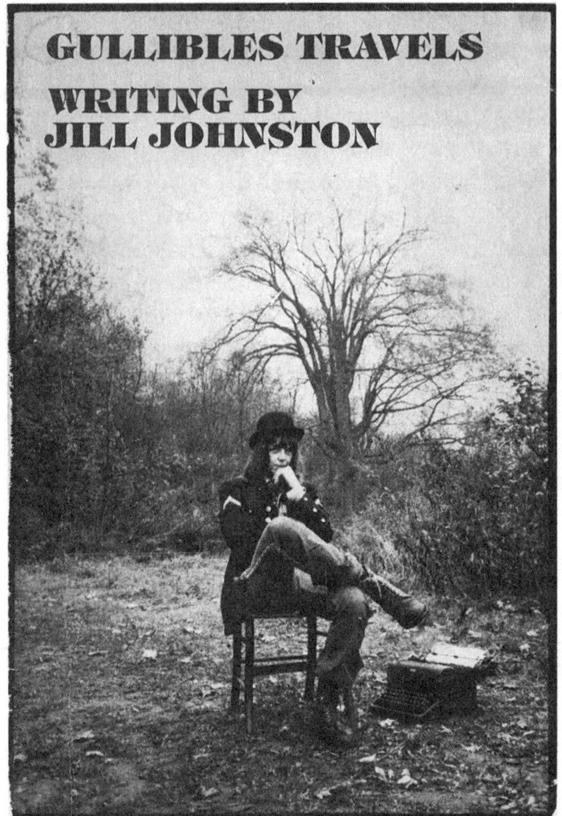

Figure 4.2 Cover of *Gullibles Travels* by Jill Johnston, 1974.

Mexico, published originally in *The Village Voice* on September 20, 1973. Quoting from Martin without quotation marks, Johnston writes,

> what does it mean to be defeated. it means we cannot move . . . but still we go on, without hope, without desire, and without dreams, then it is not i, then it is not us, then it is not conditioned response . . . without hope there is hope, we go on because there is no way to stop, going on without hope and desire is discipline, going on without scheming or planning is discipline and without striving or caring is discipline . . . defeated you rise to your feet like dry bones, these bones will rise again . . . undefeated you will only say what has already been said . . . defeated having no place to go you will await and perhaps be overtaken . . . defeated, exhausted, and helpless you will perhaps go a little bit further.[11]

But eventually, or soon, by her own reckoning, Johnston just petered out. "The book [*Lesbian Nation*] came out spring '73. By fall of that year I was in full flight from its consequences," she would reflect a decade later, in an essay titled "Lesbian/Feminism Reconsidered."

> Withdrawing from a radical position around 1975, I felt the need personally to go overboard for a time and pretend to be straight. . . . In '80–'81, returning to the big city, I could really feel the change between the old days and the new. In a conservative atmosphere, not unlike the fifties, in a place of optimum political awareness, it's possible to think about things *other* than one's sexuality. Where it was once repressed, at risk to personal health, and then flaunted, at risk to limb and survival, it can now be subsumed, or integrated, with the vital business of work and leisure. It's possible now in other words to get on with it.[12]

Getting on with it sounds a lot like getting over it. Even though this book's aim was never to inaugurate new heroes, it's hard not to be disappointed.

• • •

I did not set out to write a history of queer failure.[13] I set out to write a history of queer practices that shaped avant-garde artmaking in New York City in its heyday throughout the sixties and early seventies. Gene Swenson and Jill Johnston were, by pretty much any metric, centrally important. They both wrote about the art movements that would come to matter, often before other critics caught on: Pop, happenings, Judson Dance. Many artists around them took note, and they took notes, shaping their practices at pivotal moments in response to Swenson's and Johnston's provocations.

Swenson and Johnston were also both explicitly and unapologetically queer. And more importantly, from the early sixties on, they both used criticism as a method to figure out how to be queer in a world that did not want them to be. They wanted so much from criticism. Rather than letting it be a practice of explicating and evaluating art, they demanded that criticism become life sustaining. That it become a practice of transforming the words intended to annihilate their existence into enabling and affirming descriptors—words like "homosexual," "lesbian," "queer," "illegal," "mad," and "psychotic." They rendered their so-called nonnormative desires full of substance, full of good stuff, the stuff of building a life. They imagined new worlds where they could live out their queerness in all its freaky, fabulous fullness. Swenson envisioned a society no longer defined by Freudian repression, where everyone embraces their perversions explicitly without moralism or shame. Johnston conjured a nation outside the reach of patriarchal oppression, where women love each other without interference from laws or punishing norms. Both critics began to flesh these worlds out, imagining the end of war, the end of capitalism, the end of all oppression and repression—naïve, imperfect fantasies. And through *all* of this, they distorted criticism beyond recognition, inventing something new in the process.

Swenson and Johnston subverted protocols of interviews, panels, and protests, creating new artistic situations that resist categorization. They used writing to assemble and sustain fragile selves through cycles of disintegration and reintegration. They treated criticism as a process of writing themselves into being, over and over again. They posited unstable selves unanchored by punctuation, in Johnston's case, or anchored only by an unanswerable question mark, in Swenson's. I call all of this "criticism without authority"—an ill-fitting mantel that names a genre that never quite coheres. But as a phrase that holds things contingently together, "criticism without authority" has a descriptive force that has helped direct my own energies to dwell on instances when *something* is happening that exceeds ready-made explanation but *feels* like art: situations and episodes that remain perhaps confusing and troubling but also open, animating, and vital.

I thus wrote this book with two guiding ambitions. First, to write a history that hadn't been written of a few queer practices that were extraordinarily important on the ground in New York City in the sixties and early seventies but had eluded our disciplinary formations. Second, to argue for the significance of Swenson's and Johnston's queer practices as *art practices*. Quotes from Swenson and Johnston have long peppered art history. Their queer practices have always been visible, just not visible as performance, poetry, literature, or any other genre that would validate something as an appropriate subject for a scholarly monograph. In writing this book, I set out to demonstrate that Swenson's and Johnston's queer practices matter—not just as ancillary supporting documents but as the main event, as art that anchors a monograph. They do not sit easily with that designation—but that's the point. Recall once again Battcock's prescient 1969 claim: "The anti-worker has to liberate himself from prevailing terminology, classifications and categorizations. In criticism (quiticism) only Jill Johnston and Gene Swenson have so far, been able to do it."[14]

To restate the goal of this book: I set out to scour archives, public and private, for material traces of Swenson's and Johnston's queer practices and to generate a motley assemblage of texts, dialogues, episodes, and events. Drawing from that assemblage, I searched for language to describe not what Swenson's and Johnston's queer practices are but rather what they made possible, and what they might make possible still.

Nevertheless, in the end, we're left with two scenes of failure—two passionate pleas for political revolutions that never came. So how might political breakdown work as something other than a blot or a botched job? I think I have an answer to Berlant's tantalizingly simple question: Political breakdown *might* work as art. Swenson's and Johnston's queer practices vibrate with the creative energy of imagining new intimacies, new lives, and new worlds. As art, these situations and episodes have futures that exceed anything that we might say about Swenson's or Johnston's personal political failures. Perhaps it is not surprising that they flamed and fizzled out—the intensity with which they lived and worked and railed against the world was just not sustainable. Nonetheless, here I am surrounded by piles of queer, genre-bending books that became possible in the wake of Swenson's and Johnston's criticism without authority: David Wojnaro-wicz's *Close to the Knives: A Memoir of Disintegration* (1991), Hilton Als's *The Women* (1996), Chris Kraus's *I Love Dick* (1997), Yvonne Rainer's *Feelings Are Facts: A Life* (2006), Eileen Myles's *Inferno (A Poet's Novel)* (2010), Maggie Nelson's *The Argonauts* (2015) . . . to name just a few. Other queer practices became possible too. In 1991, Eileen Myles launched a write-in campaign for president as "a female, a lesbian, from a working class background, a poet, performer and writer."[15] "Eileen's run, in its brilliant and rebellious simplicity, demanded regard," artist Sharon Hayes would reflect many years later, right after the election of Donald Trump in 2016. "'Why not?,' the campaign seemed to ask, why can't they be president?"[16] During Myles's run, artist Zoe Leonard proclaimed "I want a dyke for president" in a typed-up, xeroxed broadside that circulated among friends in 1992, and still does, more widely. "I want a Black woman for president," Leonard continues. "I want someone with bad teeth and an attitude, someone who has eaten that nasty hospital food, someone who crossdresses and has done drugs and has been in therapy. I want someone who has committed civil disobedience. And I want to know why this isn't possible."[17] Another unconsummated wish, perhaps misguided, and definitely naïve in its utopian imagining. But still, I want to know.

". . . undefeated you will only say what has already been said," Johnston reminds us. I think she's right. ". . . defeated having no place to go you will await and perhaps be overtaken." What can be done? Swenson professes: "My warning and my hope for art lies in this: soon we will begin listening to our own hearts again." And Johnston reminds us: ". . . defeated, exhausted, and helpless you will perhaps go a little bit further." We have no other choice.

Acknowledgments

This book is the product of collaborative labor, and it carries the imprint of many friends, colleagues, and mentors. I am grateful to Jo Applin, Darby English, and Matthew Jesse Jackson, whose mentorship, encouragement, and critical feedback sustained this project over many years. Allan Doyle, Miriam Kienle, Kristine Moss, Michaela Rife, Florencia San Martín, and Caroline Schopp all read drafts of this manuscript and spent many hours talking through ideas with me—their collective brilliance has shaped this book in fundamental ways.

I am indebted to the generosity of those who knew and loved Gene Swenson and Jill Johnston. My gratitude to the late Ann Wilson and the late Henry Martin for inviting me in, sharing memories with me, and allowing me to study Gene Swenson's papers. I am also grateful to Ingrid Nyeboe, who responded generously to my email inquiries. I offer sincere thanks to many dedicated staff members at the following institutional archives: the Archives of American Art, Smithsonian Institution; the Museum of Modern Art Archives; the University of Iowa Libraries Special Collections and Archives; The New York Public Library Manuscripts and Archives Division; and the Charles Deering McCormick Library of Special Collections and University Archives, Northwestern University.

At the University of Chicago Press, I have been lucky to work with two wonderful editors: Susan Bielstein and Karen Levine. I am exceedingly thankful for Susan's early and unwavering enthusiasm for this project, and for her incisive critical edits. The book is so much richer and sharper for it. After Susan's retirement, Karen inherited this project, and I am very grateful for her continued enthusiasm and careful feedback as she shepherded the manuscript over the finish line. My appreciation for Victoria Barry's expertise and assistance at every turn cannot be overstated. And to those two anonymous peer reviewers: thank you.

As a graduate student at the University of Chicago in the Department of Art History, I found myself immersed in an intense scholarly community, filled with friends and teachers who pushed me to become a deeper and more generous thinker. I am especially grateful to my mentors Darby English, Matthew Jesse Jackson, and Rebecca Zorach. They trusted me to forge my own way, held me accountable to my convictions, and pushed me with big, difficult questions. In addition, I would like to thank many brilliant teachers and interlocutors: Adrian Anagnost, Niall Atkinson, the late Lauren Berlant, Maggie Borowitz, Claudia Brittenham, Emily Capper, Jennifer Cohen, Jadine Collingwood, Savannah Esquivel, Max Koss, Joyce Kuechler, Anna Lee, Lisa Lee, Jesse Lockard, Christine Mehring, Sarah M. Miller, Solveig Nelson, James Rosenow, Caroline Schopp, Hilary Strang, Megan Sullivan, Maggie Taft, Nancy Thebaut, Zsofi Valyi-Nagy, Leslie Wilson, and Beth Woodward. Special thanks to Leslie, Jadine, and Caroline for providing unwavering encouragement, detailed feedback, and key insights at vital moments. Special thanks as well to Bridget Madden, for her generosity in sharing image expertise. I am grateful for institutional support from the University of Chicago, including several fellowships that funded research that led to this book: a Kathleen J. Shelton Memorial Traveling Fellowship, a Humanities Division Travel Grant, a Smart Family Foundation Scholarship, and a Provost's Fellowship.

During my time as a graduate student, I received generous predoctoral fellowships from the Terra Foundation for American Art and the Smithsonian Institution's Archives of American Art. I extend gratitude to many mentors, archivists, and administrators at these institutions who shaped this research: Elizabeth Botten, Marisa Bourgoin, Josh Franco, Amelia Goerlitz, Kate Haw, Melissa Ho, Liza Kirwin, Lucy Pike, Mary Savig, Emily Shapiro, Veerle Thielemans, and Stacy Weiland.

After completing my PhD, I spent the 2019–20 academic year at the University of Arkansas as visiting assistant professor of contemporary art. For the 2020–21 academic year, I returned to the University of Chicago to serve as postgraduate preceptor for the MA Program in the Humanities, during the thick of the pandemic. For their comradery, encouragement, and critical feedback during those dark days, I am especially grateful to Allan Doyle, Oh Mee Lee, Abra Levenson, Hilary Strang, and Maggie Taft.

During the summer of 2021, I spent an idyllic two months in residence at The Clark Art Institute as a research fellow, where this project benefited greatly from in-depth conversations with Ondine Chavoya, Susan Dackerman, Julie Nelson Davis, Brigid Doherty, Caroline Fowler, Marc Gotlieb, Michael Ann Holly, Ashley Lazevnick, Keith Moxey, and Ellen Tani. The Clark, with its bucolic trails and communal dinners, provided the perfect antidote to dark uncertain times.

In fall 2021, I began a new job as assistant professor of contemporary art and theory at the University of Louisville, where I've been lucky to find myself surrounded by inspiring, engaged scholars who have provided crucial feedback as I've finished this book: Asaf Angermann, Elise Franklin, John Gibson, Chris Reitz, and Karl Swinehart. I am grateful for the support of many committed colleagues and students at the Hite Institute of Art and Design, as well as the Commonwealth Center for Humanities and Society, where I was a Faculty Fellow during the 2022–23 academic year.

At every step throughout this long journey, I've learned so much from many brilliant colleagues, friends, fellow fellows, and fellow travelers. In addition to everyone above, I thank: Jordan Amirkhani, Julia Bryan-Wilson, Sandrine Canac, Jennifer Chuong, Bruce Conklin, Sarah Louise Cowan, Nekisha Durrett, Nika Elder, Jenna Grambort, Saisha Grayson, Maggie Innes, Annika Johnson, Margarita Karasoulas, Tess Korobkin, Erin McCleary, Christina Michelon, Jennifer Noonan, Danielle O'Steen, Letitia Quesenberry, Xuxa Rodríguez, Friederike Schäfer, Abbe Schriber, Richard Taws, Alex J. Taylor, Phil Taylor, Amy Torbert, Emily Voelker, and Hannah Yohalem.

Over the course of researching and writing this book, I have benefited greatly from workshopping ideas at panels, symposia, and invited lectures at many conferences and institutions, including: the College Art Association annual conference panel, "The Difference Postminimalism Makes" (2023); Tulane University, the Sandra Garrard Memorial Lecture (2023); The Courtauld Centre for the Art of the Americas, Invited Lecture (2021); University College London, Research Seminar Series (2021); University of Chicago, Speaking of Art: Artist Interviews in Scholarship and Practice Series (2021); College Art Association annual conference panel, "The Queer Feminist 1980s" (2020); Smithsonian Lunchbag Seminars in American Art (2019); Untimely Media/Domestic Techniques Symposium, University of Vienna (2019); Hunter College, City University of New York, Invited Lecture (2018); Purchase College, State University of New York, Invited Lecture (2018); The Andy Warhol Museum, Invited Lecture (2018); Symposium of the Association of Historians of American Art (2018); and the Feminist Art History Conference at American University (2018). I extend my sincere gratitude to the many organizers, moderators, and engaged audience members at these institutions and events.

Parts of chapters 1 and 2 were published in earlier form in the *Oxford Art Journal*, and I thank Jo Applin for her guidance and two anonymous reviewers for their generous feedback. In addition, a portion of chapter 1 will appear in revised form in the catalogue for a forthcoming exhibition at the Whitney Museum of American Art titled *Sixties Surreal* (2025). I am grateful to Dan Nadel for his support.

• • •

I dedicate this book in loving memory of Leann Rittenbaum Ott. I met Leann at a meet-and-greet for art history majors at Boston University when I was a sophomore and she was a freshman. She became my dearest friend and partner-in-crime in all things art history. We sat together in class, went to museums together, studied together. With Leann, I learned to love contemporary art. Leann made everything beautiful. She created tender moments of quiet beauty that somehow pierced through her suffering. Leann died on November 1, 2018, as a result of complications from cystic fibrosis.

I reserve the last words for my family: to my parents, Ellen and Robert, and my sister Jamie. This book is a product of their love and support. And to Kristine Moss, who encourages me every day, reminds me what really matters, and dwells with me on every word: *thank you.*

Notes

INTRODUCTION

1. Gene R. Swenson, *The* Other *Tradition*, exhibition brochure (Philadelphia: Institute of Contemporary Art, University of Pennsylvania, 1966), 12. This text accompanied an exhibition at the Institute of Contemporary Art, University of Pennsylvania, January 27–March 7, 1966.

2. Jill Johnston, "Take Me Disappearing," in *Marmalade Me* (New York: E. P. Dutton, 1971), 105; published originally in *The Village Voice*, December 14, 1967. Note that throughout the sixties and seventies, Johnston frequently subverted rules of standard grammar and spelling. All quotes by Jill Johnston maintain her original spelling, syntax, and capitalization.

3. About a year after first writing this sentence, I was gratified to see how closely it resonates with Paisid Aramphongphan's excellent book *Horizontal Together: Art, Dance, and Queer Embodiment in 1960s New York*. Describing his "queer horizontal" methodological approach, Aramphongphan writes: "Yet the thrust of this project is not to find new queer heroes or further add to the heroism of known ones, but to build on efforts to bridge object-based historical and social inquiry with theoretical, speculative thinking. . . . Just as my approach to the artwork can be described as horizontal—synchronic and expansive, toward theorizing collaboration and collective endeavor—my approach to the scholarship before me is similarly open." This book, too, "dwell[s] in the space that previous scholars have opened up," as Aramphongphan puts it—in the generous space alongside *Horizontal Together*. See Paisid Aramphongphan, *Horizontal Together: Art, Dance, and Queer Embodiment in 1960s New York* (Manchester: Manchester University Press, 2021), 12.

4. Johnston began writing for *ARTnews* in March 1961. Swenson began two months later in May 1961.

5. Jill Johnston, *Paper Daughter: Autobiography in Search of a Father*, vol. 2 (New York: Alfred A. Knopf, 1985), 28–29.

6. Gene R. Swenson, "James Rosenquist: The Figure a Man Makes" (1967), *The Register of the Museum of Art, University of Kansas* 4, no. 6–7 (1971): 74; special edition published to accompany the exhibition *Gene Swenson: Retrospective for a Critic* (October 24–December 5, 1971).

7. For a historical account of Swenson's career and curatorial achievements, see Scott Rothkopf, "Banned and Determined: Gene Swenson," *Artforum* 40, no. 10 (Summer 2002): 142–45.

8. Lucy Lippard, contribution to "Gene Swenson: A Composite Portrait," *The Register of the Museum of Art, University of Kansas* 4, no. 6–7 (1971): 16.

9. Ann Wilson, contribution to "Gene Swenson: A Composite Portrait," 20–21.

10. Ann Wilson died in 2023. For an overview of Wilson's life and career, see Alex Williams, "Ann Wilson, Last Survivor of a New York Art Scene, Dies at 91," *New York Times*, March 28, 2023, https://www.nytimes.com/2023/03/28/arts/ann-wilson-dead .html. For an account of Wilson's role within the community of artists who lived and worked in Coenties Slip from 1956 to 1967, see Prudence Peiffer, *The Slip: The New York City Street That Changed American Art Forever* (New York: HarperCollins, 2023).

11. Johnston, *Paper Daughter*, 209–10.

12. Dianne Hunter and Rena Patterson, foreword to *Gullibles Travels* by Jill Johnston (New York: Links Books, 1974), xi. Jill Johnston, "More Orphan Than Not," *Gullibles Travels*, 111; published originally in *The Village Voice*, August 2, 1973.

13. Jill Johnston, *Lesbian Nation: The Feminist Solution* (New York: Simon and Schuster, 1973), 69–70.

14. For a cogent analysis of the trajectory of Johnston's career as a critic, see Jennifer Krasinski, "Jill Johnston: The I of the Beholder," in *Jill Johnston: The Disintegration of a Critic*, ed. Fiona McGovern, Megan Francis Sullivan, and Axel Wieder (Berlin: Sternberg Press and Bergen Kunsthall, 2019), 173–83.

15. Jill Johnston, "The Yearly Mellowdrama," *Gullibles Travels*, 105, 110; published originally in *The Village Voice*, October 26, 1972.

16. Johnston, *Paper Daughter*, 30.

17. Johnston, "The Yearly Mellowdrama," 106, 108.

18. Jill Johnston, *Mother Bound: Autobiography in Search of a Father* (New York: Alfred A. Knopf, 1983), 115.

19. Jill Johnston, "Introduction: Aroused is Aroused is Aroused," in *Admission Accomplished: The Lesbian Nation Years, 1970–75* (London: Serpent's Tail, 1998), unpaginated.

Regarding her children, Johnston writes in her memoir: "The shift involving the children's father occurred the year I was living alone with them, '63–'64, on Houston Street. Until then he saw them irregularly on Sundays, increasingly over weekends. Now, with a young woman who took a motherly interest in them, he suggested taking them four days a week while I kept them three. A year later the shift was complete, and I became a Sunday parent myself. There was never any legal business between us regarding money or custody, there were just plenty of bad feelings." Johnston, *Mother Bound*, 138.

20. Jill Johnston, "Judson Concerts #3, #4," in McGovern, Sullivan, and Wieder, *Jill Johnston*; published originally in *The Village Voice*, February 28, 1963.

21. Sally Banes, *Greenwich Village, 1963: Avant-Garde Performance and the Effervescent Body* (Durham, NC: Duke University Press, 1993), 67.

22. Banes, *Greenwich Village, 1963*, 1–2.

23. Here I follow Julia Bryan-Wilson in mobilizing the word "fray" as a generative description of and metaphor for queer practices that erode boundaries between artistic genres, often persisting in a state of precarity. See Julia Bryan-Wilson, *Fray: Art and Textile Politics* (Chicago: University of Chicago Press, 2017).

24. Swenson, *The* Other *Tradition*, 39.

25. Gregory Battcock, "The Art Critic as Social Reformer—With a Question Mark," in *Why Art: Casual Notes on the Aesthetics of the Immediate Past* (New York: E. P. Dutton, 1977), 30; published originally in *Art in America* 59 (September–October 1971).

26. Johnston, *Paper Daughter*, 58.

27. Johnston, *Paper Daughter*, 94.

28. Gene Swenson, "The Thought Police," *The New York Free Press*, May 30, 1968, 8.

29. Johnston, *Paper Daughter*, 214, 218.

30. Johnston, *Lesbian Nation*, 78–79.

31. Johnston, "Untitled," *Marmalade Me*, 21; published originally in *The Village Voice*, October 10, 1968.

32. Johnston, "Untitled," 19–21.

33. Johnston, *Lesbian Nation*, 11.

34. Johnston, *Lesbian Nation*, 98. See Joan Didion, *Slouching Towards Bethlehem* (New York: Farrar, Straus and Giroux, 1961).

35. Here I follow Jo Applin's feminist intervention, heeding her call to nominate Johnston (along with artist Lee Lozano) as an example of a "scandalous" or "misfit" feminist. See Jo Applin, *Lee Lozano: Not Working* (New Haven, CT: Yale University Press, 2018).

36. Johnston, "Untitled," 19–21.

37. Lucy Lippard, "An Impure Situation (New York and Philadelphia Letter)," *Art International* 10, no. 5 (May 1966): 60–65. In this essay, Lippard names for the first time "eccentric abstraction," which becomes the title of her epoch-defining exhibition and essay. Lippard adapts the title of this essay from a quote by Jasper Johns, which she includes in the middle of the column: "Johns has written: 'Sometimes I see it and then I paint it; other times I paint it and then see it. Both are impure situations, and I prefer neither'" (62).

38. Lippard, "An Impure Situation," 60.

39. Gregory Battcock, introduction to Johnston, *Marmalade Me*, 10; emphasis original.

40. Michael Fried, "Caro's Abstractness," in *Art and Objecthood: Essays and Reviews* (Chicago: University of Chicago Press, 1998), 191; published originally in *Artforum* 9 (September 1970): 32–34.

41. Clement Greenberg, "Modernist Painting" (1965), in *Modern Art and Modernism: A Critical Anthology*, ed. Francis Frascina and Charles Harrison (Harper and Row, 1982), 5, 6; published originally in *Art and Literature* 4 (Spring 1965).

42. Michael Fried, "Modernist Painting and Formal Criticism," *The American Scholar* 33, no. 4 (Autumn 1964): 642–48. Fried reprinted this essay as the introductory section to his catalogue essay for the exhibition *Three American Painters: Kenneth Noland, Jules Olitski, Frank Stella* at the Fogg Art Museum, Cambridge, MA, April 21–May 30, 1965.

43. Fried, "Modernist Painting and Formal Criticism," 648.

44. Fried, "Modernist Painting and Formal Criticism," 648.

45. Fried, "Modernist Painting and Formal Criticism," 644. Characterizing Fried's critical stance and the exclusionary effects of his emphasis on purifying aesthetic experience, Amelia Jones has written: "It is crucial, then, for the critic/art historian to claim 'pure pleasure,' to avoid acknowledging his investments in the determination of meaning: 'the loss of the subject in the object' threatens not only the interpreter's claim to authority, but his very coherence as a subject (who is implicitly masculine, white, heterosexual, upper middle class, etc.). What happens, then, when works of art solicit *impure* bodily pleasures? . . . Predictably, one of the first things to occur in such cases is the development of a renewed mode of judgement (aesthetic, political, or otherwise) to *close down* the threat of feminine openness of the theatrical." Amelia Jones, "Art History/

Art Criticism: Performing Meaning," in *Performing the Body/Performing the Text*, ed. Amelia Jones and Andrew Stephenson (London: Routledge, 1999), 39–55.

46. Michael Fried, "Art and Objecthood," *Artforum* 5, no. 10 (Summer 1967): 14–15; all emphases original.

47. Fried, "Art and Objecthood," 12.

48. Fried, "Art and Objecthood," 14.

49. Christa Noel Robbins brings this quote to light in her important essay "The Sensibility of Michael Fried." The "sculpture-theater" essay Fried references is "Art and Objecthood." The entire passage reads: "I keep toying with the idea, crazy as it sounds, of having a section in this sculpture-theater essay on how corrupt sensibility is *par excellence* faggot sensibility, and how even if the faggots didn't kill Kennedy (and I love this guy Garrison for insinuating they did) they ought to be kicked out of the arts and forced to go to work on Wall Street or something." Letter from Michael Fried to Philip Leider, March 16, 1967, Philip Leider papers, 1962–1997, Archives of American Art, Washington DC. See Christa Noel Robbins, "The Sensibility of Michael Fried," *Criticism* 60, no. 4 (Fall 2018): 429–54. See also David J. Getsy, *Queer Behavior: Scott Burton and Performance Art* (Chicago: University of Chicago Press, 2022), 18–20.

50. Fried, "Art and Objecthood," 20, 23.

51. Robbins, "The Sensibility of Michael Fried," 438.

52. Robbins, "The Sensibility of Michael Fried," 430.

53. Tina Post, *Deadpan: The Aesthetics of Black Inexpression* (New York: New York University Press, 2023), 73–74; emphasis original. Here I follow Julia Bryan-Wilson's 2024 state of the field review in which she situates Post's critique of "Art and Objecthood" as an important intervention for the field of queer US art history. See Julia Bryan-Wilson, "What Is Queer About Contemporary US Art History?," *Art Bulletin* 106, no. 2 (June 2024): 155–61.

54. Post, *Deadpan*, 70.

55. Hal Foster, *Design and Crime (And Other Diatribes)* (London: Verso, 2011), 105.

56. Lauren Berlant, *Cruel Optimism* (Durham, NC: Duke University Press, 2011), 5. Berlant uses the word "genre" to mean "an aesthetic structure of affective expectation, an institution or formation that absorbs all kinds of small variations or modifications while promising that the persons transacting with it will experience the pleasure of encountering what they expected, with details varying the theme. It mediates what is singular, in the details, and general about the subject." Lauren Berlant, *The Female Complaint: The Unfinished Business of Sentimentality in American Culture* (Durham, NC: Duke University Press, 2008), 4.

57. Berlant, *Cruel Optimism*, 6.

58. Lauren Berlant, "Big Man," *Social Text Online*, January 19, 2017, https://socialtextjournal.org/big-man/.

CHAPTER ONE

Portions of this chapter were published in a different form in "'Do You Think Pop Art's Queer?' Gene Swenson and Andy Warhol," *Oxford Art Journal* 41, no. 1 (March 2018): 59–83, and are reprinted by permission of Oxford University Press.

1. Lucy Lippard, contribution to "Gene Swenson: A Composite Portrait," *The Register of the Museum of Art, University of Kansas* 4, no. 6–7 (1971): 17; special edition published

to accompany the exhibition *Gene Swenson: Retrospective for a Critic* (October 24–December 5, 1971).

2. Robert C. Doty, "Growth of Overt Homosexuality in City Provokes Wide Concern," *The New York Times*, December 17, 1963, 1.

3. Paul Welch, "Homosexuality in America," *Life*, June 26, 1964, 66–80.

4. Lippard, contribution to "Gene Swenson: A Composite Portrait," 18.

5. See Gene R. Swenson, "What Is Pop Art? Answers from 8 Painters, Part I," *ARTnews* 62, no. 7 (November 1963): 24–27, 60–64; and Gene R. Swenson, "What Is Pop Art? Part II," *ARTnews* 62, no. 10 (February 1964): 40–43, 62–67.

6. After learning about Henry Martin's unfinished anthology, I contacted him via email at the end of 2015 to ask if he knew the whereabouts of Swenson's papers. Martin informed me that he had the papers in his possession and generously offered to let me consult them in March 2016. Working with Henry Martin and Ann Wilson, the then-executor of Swenson's estate, I helped facilitate the Smithsonian's Archives of American Art's acquisition of Swenson's papers in 2019. See Josh T. Franco, "Gene Swenson Papers," *Archives of American Art Journal* 59, no. 1 (Spring 2020): 104–5.

7. Hal Foster, "Death in America," *October* 75 (Winter 1996): 37. For Foster's account of how the "famous motto of the Warholian persona: 'I want to be a machine'" must be read "in terms of *traumatic realism*," see Hal Foster, *The Return of the Real: The Avant-Garde at the End of the Century* (Cambridge, MA: MIT Press, 1996), 127–68.

8. Gene Swenson, *The* Other *Tradition*, exhibition brochure (Philadelphia: Institute of Contemporary Art, University of Pennsylvania, 1966), viii.

9. Swenson, *The* Other *Tradition*, v–ix.

10. Irving Sandler, quoted in Amy Newman, *Challenging Art: Artforum, 1962–1974* (New York: Soho Press, 2000), 193.

11. I am grateful for Miriam Kienle's ongoing collaboration and insights in thinking through the stakes of queer archival labor for the practice of art history.

12. The "John" in question is perhaps John Giorno, Warhol's boyfriend at the time, who starred in his 1963 film *Sleep*, or the poet John Wieners, who appears in a 1963 photobooth strip alongside Warhol and Malanga. At a talk I gave at the Andy Warhol Museum on May 1, 2018, Matt Wrbican—longtime Warhol archivist and expert—identified the voice as more likely belonging to John Wieners.

13. Gustavus Stadler, "'My Wife': The Tape Recorder and Warhol's Queer Ways of Listening," *Criticism* 56, no. 3 (Summer 2014): 440. Stadler notes that Warhol procured his first tape recorder "sometime in 1964."

14. See William Berkson, "Bluhm Paints a Picture," *ARTnews* 62, no. 3 (May 1963): 38–41. Berkson describes Bluhm in almost comically butch terms: "At forty-two, Norman Bluhm has a large, swaggering, bull-like frame. With his long, black hair, narrowing eyes (behind the perfume of chain-smoked Gauloises), and long Ivan-the-Terrible nose, he appears variously as a mad Cossack-Bohemian, an Indian Chief, an off-beat trigger-man or hijacker for a Chicago (where he was born) South Side club."

15. Judith Butler, "Critically Queer," *Gay and Lesbian Quarterly* 1, no. 1 (1993): 22–23; emphasis original.

16. Gavin Butt, *Between You and Me: Queer Disclosures in the Art World, 1948–1963* (Durham: Duke University Press, 2005), 109; emphasis original.

17. Lippard, contribution to "Gene Swenson: A Composite Portrait," 16; emphasis original.

18. Swenson, "What Is Pop Art? Part I," 61.

19. Roland Barthes, "That Old Thing, Art . . ." (1980), in *Pop Art: A Critical History*, ed. Steven Henry Madoff (Berkeley: University of California Press, 1997), 372.

20. In a 2012 interview, William S. Wilson admits that he once had the early drafts of Swenson's interviews (including Thomas Hess's edits) in his possession. These, however, appear to have been lost. Wilson states: "And in fact—and I think this is important for an archive to know—at one point, I had the literal transcripts of his interviews, and I also had those transcripts as they were edited by Thomas Hess. And Thomas Hess changed the words that were—that had been spoken by Gene and by the artist. He took out anything with—that had to do with gender, and he took out anything that had to do with sexuality especially sadomasochism." William S. Wilson, interviewed by Jonathan D. Katz, 2012, Archives of American Art, Smithsonian Institution, Washington, DC. For an account of how these early drafts may have ended up in Ray Johnson's possession, see Miriam Kienle, *Queer Networks: Ray Johnson's Correspondence Art* (Minneapolis: University of Minnesota Press, 2023), 18.

21. Sometime in the 1970s, the artist Joe Raffaele changed the spelling of his surname to Raffael; however, at the time of his interview with Swenson, he spelled his name Raffaele.

22. Swenson published an edited version of his interview with Raffaele in 1966 in *Arts Magazine*. See G. R. Swenson, "Paint, Flesh, Vesuvius: Joe Raffaele Discusses the Eruptive Nature of His Post-Freudian Art with Writer G. R. Swenson," *Arts Magazine* 41, no. 1 (November 1966): 33–35.

23. Donald Judd, interviewed by Lucy Lippard, April 10–June 2, 1968, corrected transcript, Lucy R. Lippard papers, box 36, folder 39, Archives of American Art, Smithsonian Institution, Washington, DC. I am grateful to Danielle O'Steen for bringing this interview to my attention and sharing the transcript with me.

24. Gene Swenson, "The Personality of the Artist," unpublished draft of lecture delivered on the occasion of Andy Warhol's solo exhibition at the Institute of Contemporary Art in Philadelphia, which took place September 10–December 8, 1965, Gene Swenson papers, 1950–1969, Archives of American Art, Smithsonian Institution, Washington, DC.

25. Jonathan Flatley, *Like Andy Warhol* (Chicago: University of Chicago Press, 2017), 5–7.

26. Flatley, *Like Andy Warhol*, 8.

27. Swenson, "What Is Pop Art? Part I," 60.

28. Thomas Crow, "Saturday Disasters: Trace and Reference in Early Warhol" (1987), reprinted in *Modern Art in the Common Culture: Essays* (New Haven, CT: Yale University Press, 1996), 62–63.

29. Flatley, *Like Andy Warhol*, 126; emphasis original.

30. In the 2005 book *Ugly Feelings*, Sianne Ngai analyzes how "ugly feelings" produce "political and aesthetic ambiguities." Her account resonates strongly with Swenson's much earlier theorization, and it has been very helpful in validating and fleshing out the significance of Swenson's account from the early 1960s. According to Ngai, "ugly feelings" tend to produce the "inherently ambiguous affect of affective disorientation in general—what we might think of as a state of feeling vaguely 'unsettled' or 'confused,' or, more precisely, a meta-feeling in which one feels confused about *what* one is feeling. . . . Confusion about feeling's objective or subjective status becomes inherent to the feeling." See Sianne Ngai, *Ugly Feelings* (Cambridge, MA: Harvard University Press, 2005), 14.

31. Swenson uses this phrase several times throughout his published criticism. Most notably, he uses it as the title for chapter 3 of *The* Other *Tradition*.

32. Gene Swenson, "The Personality of the Artist," essay printed on a flyer to advertise Warhol's exhibition at the Stable Gallery, April 21–May 6, 1964, Andy Warhol, folder 1928–1987, Art & Artist files, National Portrait Gallery Library, Smithsonian American Art Museum, Washington, DC; emphasis original.

33. Gene Swenson, "The Personality of the Artist," unpublished draft.

34. Gene Swenson, "The Personality of the Artist," unpublished draft.

35. Swenson, *The* Other *Tradition*, 28.

36. Peter Schjeldahl, quoted in Scott Rothkopf, "Banned and Determined: Gene Swenson," *Artforum* 40, no. 10 (Summer 2002): 142–45.

37. Robert Pincus-Witten, quoted in Newman, *Challenging Art*, 192; emphasis original.

38. Several recent critical reevaluations of Surrealism in the postwar United States provide additional important historical context for Swenson's exhibition *The* Other *Tradition*. In particular, see James Boaden, "Dada, Surrealism and Their Heritage? The North American Reception of Dada and Surrealism," in *A Companion to Dada and Surrealism*, ed. David Hopkins (Malden, MA: John Wiley & Sons, 2016), 400–415; Sandra Zalman, *Consuming Surrealism in American Culture: Dissident Modernism* (New York: Routledge, 2017); Gavin Parkinson, "On 'Sensibility': Art, Art Criticism and Surrealism in New York in the 1960s," *Journal of Art Historiography* 23 (December 2020): 1–23; and Joanna Pawlik, *Remade in America: Surrealist Art, Activism, and Politics, 1940–1978* (Oakland: University of California Press, 2021).

39. Swenson, *The* Other *Tradition*, viii.

40. Swenson, *The* Other *Tradition*, ix.

41. Michael Fried, "Modernist Painting and Formal Criticism," *The American Scholar* 33, no. 4 (Autumn 1964): 644, 648.

42. Fried, "Modernist Painting and Formal Criticism," 642.

43. Swenson, *The* Other *Tradition*, 10–14. The quote comes from Clement Greenberg, "Post Painterly Abstraction" (1964), in *Clement Greenberg: The Collected Essays and Criticism*, vol. 4, *Modernism with a Vengeance 1957–1969*, ed. John O'Brian (Chicago: University of Chicago Press, 1993), 197.

44. Swenson, *The* Other *Tradition*, 40.

45. Anne M. Wagner, *Three Artists (Three Women): Modernism and the Art of Hesse, Krasner, and O'Keeffe* (Berkeley: University of California Press, 1996), 255–56.

46. Swenson, *The* Other *Tradition*, 11.

47. Swenson, *The* Other *Tradition*, 17.

48. Swenson, *The* Other *Tradition*, 32.

49. Swenson uses this phrase in an earlier essay on Warhol. See Gene R. Swenson, "The Darker Ariel: Random Notes on Andy Warhol," *Collage* 3–4 (December 1964): 102–6.

50. Gene Swenson, "Press Release for The *Other* Tradition," personal files, originally from the website for the Institute of Contemporary Art at the University of Pennsylvania, accessed circa 2018.

51. Swenson, *The* Other *Tradition*, 22.

52. Lucy Lippard, "An Impure Situation (New York and Philadelphia Letter)," *Art International* 10, no. 5 (May 1966): 60.

53. Lippard, "An Impure Situation," 60.

54. I am grateful to Tom Day for drawing my attention to the importance of this aspect of how Warhol's *Large Sleep* is lit and displayed in Swenson's exhibition. For an excellent analysis of Warhol's *Large Sleep*, see Thomas Morgan Evans, *3D Warhol: Andy Warhol and Sculpture* (London: I. B. Tauris, 2017), 77–79.

55. For an in-depth reading of Duchamp's *Large Glass*, see Linda Dalrymple Henderson, "Ethereal Bride and Mechanical Bachelors: Science and Allegory in Marcel Duchamp's 'Large Glass,'" *Configurations* 4, no. 1 (Winter 1996): 91–120.

56. G. R. Swenson, "Beneath the Skin," *ARTnews* 65, no. 2 (April 1966): 65.

57. Swenson, *The* Other *Tradition*, 23–24.

58. R. D. Laing, preface to the Pelican edition of *The Divided Self: An Existential Study in Sanity and Madness* (New York: Penguin Books, 1965), 12.

59. Swenson, *The* Other *Tradition*, 34.

60. Swenson, *The* Other *Tradition*, 32; emphasis original.

61. Swenson, *The* Other *Tradition*, 35.

62. Lippard, "An Impure Situation," 63.

63. Joseph Raffaele, quoted in Swenson, "Paint, Flesh, Vesuvius," 33–34.

64. Swenson, *The* Other *Tradition*, 35.

65. Swenson, "Beneath the Skin," 65.

66. Lippard, "An Impure Situation," 62–64. For a key analysis of how Lippard's "Eccentric Abstraction" influenced the development of art in the United States in the 1960s, see Jo Applin, *Eccentric Objects: Rethinking Sculpture in 1960s America* (New Haven, CT: Yale University Press, 2012).

67. For a feminist analysis of how Lippard's critical and curatorial labor fits within the art world of the sixties, see Julia Bryan-Wilson, "Lucy Lippard's Feminist Labor," in *Art Workers: Radical Practice in the Vietnam War Era* (Berkeley: University of California Press, 2009), 126–71.

68. William S. Wilson, interviewed by Jonathan D. Katz, 2012, Archives of American Art, Smithsonian Institution, Washington, DC.

69. Swenson, *The* Other *Tradition*, 35.

70. Swenson, *The* Other *Tradition*, 25.

71. Swenson, *The* Other *Tradition*, 27.

72. Fredric Jameson, "Postmodernism, or The Cultural Logic of Late Capitalism," *New Left Review* 146 (July/August 1984): 53.

73. Jameson, "Postmodernism," 62.

74. Jameson, "Postmodernism," 64.

75. Jameson, "Postmodernism," 71.

76. Lippard, contribution to "Gene Swenson: A Composite Portrait," 18.

77. James Rosenquist, contribution to "Gene Swenson: A Composite Portrait," 27.

78. Drafts of Swenson's essay, along with letters and telegrams from Swenson's dispute with Jean Sutherland Boggs, director of the National Gallery of Canada, are preserved in the Gallery's institutional archives. See the James Rosenquist papers, vol. 2, correspondence, box 509, folder 5, file number 12-4-360, Exhibitions in Canada, National Gallery of Canada fonds (3).

79. Gene Swenson, "James Rosenquist: The Figure a Man Makes" (1967), *The Register of the Museum of Art, University of Kansas* 4, no. 6–7 (1971): 77; special edition published to accompany the exhibition *Gene Swenson: Retrospective for a Critic*

(October 24–December 5, 1971). The quote comes from the poem "Renascence" (1917) by Edna St. Vincent Millay.

CHAPTER TWO

Portions of this chapter were published in a different form in "'Do You Think Pop Art's Queer?' Gene Swenson and Andy Warhol," *Oxford Art Journal* 41, no. 1 (March 2018): 59–83, and are reprinted by permission of Oxford University Press.

1. Jill Johnston, "Pieces of Gene," in *Marmalade Me* (New York: E. P. Dutton, 1971), 145; published originally in *The Village Voice* on April 25, 1968.

2. Gene Swenson, "The Thought Police," *The New York Free Press*, May 30, 1968, 8.

3. Martin Tolchin, "Bedlam for City Mental Patients," *The New York Times*, August 29, 1966, 1, 22.

4. Jill Johnston, *Paper Daughter: Autobiography in Search of a Father*, vol. 2 (New York: Alfred A. Knopf, 1985), 94.

5. It was not until 1973 that the Board of Trustees of the American Psychiatric Association changed its official manual of psychiatric disorders to state that homosexuality "by itself does not constitute a psychiatric disorder." The sixth printing of the *DSM-II* reclassified "Homosexuality" as "Sexual orientation disturbance (Homosexuality)," stating: "This category is for individuals whose sexual interests are directed primarily toward people of the same sex and who are either disturbed by, in conflict with, or wish to change their sexual orientation. This diagnostic category is distinguished from homosexuality, which by itself does not constitute a psychiatric disorder. Homosexuality per se is one form of sexual behavior and, like other forms of sexual behavior which are not by themselves psychiatric disorders, is not listed in this nomenclature of mental disorders." American Psychiatric Association, "Homosexuality and Sexuality Orientation Disturbance: Proposed Change in the DSM-II, 6th Printing, page 44" (Washington, DC: American Psychiatric Association, 1973), APA document reference no. 730008.

6. Lauren Berlant, "Big Man," *Social Text Online*, January 19, 2017, https://socialtext journal.org/big-man/.

7. Jill Johnston, "Cultural Gangsters," *Marmalade Me*, 158; published originally in *The Village Voice*, June 6, 1968.

8. Johnston, "Cultural Gangsters," 160.

9. Johnston, "Cultural Gangsters," 158.

10. Johnston, "Cultural Gangsters," 159.

11. Caroline Lillian Schopp proposes the term "in-action" to describe performance art in the context of postwar Vienna that stresses "dependency, incapacity, and impotence" and evinces "a failure to engage in decisive political practice and a failure to locate the missing space in which such political action might positively unfold." According to Schopp, these performances are not easily assimilated into an "art history of so-called neo-avant-gardes in North America and Western Europe after World War II." Despite Swenson's proximity to such neo-avant-garde practices, his performances are likewise not easily assimilable into a story about the "recovery of the political aspects of the avant-garde project" within the postwar United States precisely because of their failure to cohere or to become legible within frameworks of institutional critique. "In-action" thus becomes a productive concept to think with about the significance of Swenson's

contemporary performances that likewise evince certain political failures. See Caroline Lillian Schopp, "On Failing to Perform: *Kunst und Revolution*, Vienna 1968," *October* 170 (Fall 2019): 95–119. See also Schopp's forthcoming book *In-action: Viennese Actionism and the Passivities of Performance Art* (Chicago: University of Chicago Press, 2025).

12. Jill Johnston, "The Unhappy Spectator," *Marmalade Me*, 190–93; published originally in *The Village Voice*, October 17, 1968.

13. Gene Swenson, "The Question Mark," unpublished archival document, Department of Public Information: Strikes by MoMA Union (PASTA) and Protests by Outside Groups, folder 9, The Museum of Modern Art Archives, New York, NY.

14. Swenson's advertisement was printed in *The Village Voice* on March 21, 1968. For analyses of the historical significance of Swenson's protest and William S. Rubin's exhibition *Dada, Surrealism, and Their Heritage*, see James Boaden, "Dada, Surrealism and Their Heritage? The North American Reception of Dada and Surrealism," in *A Companion to Dada and Surrealism*, ed. David Hopkins (Malden, MA: Wiley Blackwell, 2016), 400–415; Sandra Zalman, "'Down with art, up with revolution': Protesting Dada and Surrealism in 1968," in *Radical Dreams: Surrealism, Counterculture, Resistance*, ed. Elliott H. King and Abigail Susik (University Park, PA: Penn State University Press, 2022).

15. Gene Swenson, "A CALL TO CULTURAL REVELATION," 1968, broadside. Gene Swenson papers, 1950–1969, Archives of American Art, Smithsonian Institution, Washington, DC.

16. Grace Glueck, "Hippies Protest at Dada Preview: 300 in Gentle Demonstration at Museum of Modern Art," *The New York Times*, March 26, 1968, 21.

17. "Wreath Sent to Statue Puzzles Metropolitan," *The New York Times*, September 1, 1967, 31.

18. James Rosenquist, contribution to "Gene Swenson: A Composite Portrait," *The Register of the Museum of Art, University of Kansas* 4, no. 6–7 (1971): 27; special edition published to accompany the exhibition *Gene Swenson: Retrospective for a Critic* (October 24–December 5, 1971).

19. Gene Swenson, "The Corporate Structure of the American Art World," *The New York Free Press*, April 25, 1968, 9.

20. Swenson, "The Corporate Structure of the American Art World," 9.

21. Gene Swenson, "Favoritism," unpublished essay dated May 1968, Gene Swenson papers, 1950–1969, Archives of American Art, Smithsonian Institution, Washington, DC.

22. Johnston, *Paper Daughter*, 222.

23. Swenson, "Favoritism."

24. According to Susan E. Cahan, the New York City teachers' strike of 1968 "polarized African Americans and Jews because the largely Jewish teachers' union, headed by Albert Shanker, was seen as standing in the way of the African American and Puerto Rican parents' desire to educate their children the way that they saw fit." Susan E. Cahan, *Mounting Frustration: The Art Museum in the Age of Black Power* (Durham, NC: Duke University Press, 2016), 75.

25. Allon Schoener, *Portal to America: The Lower East Side 1870–1925* (New York: Holt, Rinehart and Winston, 1967), 10–12.

26. Cahan, *Mounting Frustration*, 56.

27. For example, in their best-selling 1968 book *Black Rage*, activist-psychiatrists William H. Grier and Prince M. Cobbs forcefully asserted the deleterious psychological effects of racism in America and called for rage in response. As scholar La Marr Jurelle

Bruce explains, "The 'black rage' announced in their book title is at once a symptom of antiblack trauma, a defense against antiblack trauma, and a mighty force in battles against antiblackness." See La Marr Jurelle Bruce, *How to Go Mad Without Losing Your Mind: Madness and Black Radical Creativity* (Durham, NC: Duke University Press, 2021), 24. See also Jonathan M. Metzl, *The Protest Psychosis: How Schizophrenia Became a Black Disease* (Boston: Beacon Press, 2009).

28. Swenson, "Favoritism."

29. Swenson, "We Are All Nationalists—in Our Art," unpublished essay dated April–May 1968, Gene Swenson papers, 1950–1969, Archives of American Art, Smithsonian Institution, Washington, DC.

30. Darby English, *1971: A Year in the Life of Color* (Chicago: University of Chicago Press, 2016), 100.

31. Lippard, contribution to "Gene Swenson: A Composite Portrait," 18; ellipses original.

32. Berlant, "Big Man."

33. Gene Swenson, "Why Have None of My Fellow Artists Spoken a Word in Behalf of the Revolution?," *The New York Free Press*, June 20, 1968, 17.

34. As Julia Bryan-Wilson argues, the Art Workers' Coalition Open Hearing was "ideologically all over the map"—which, as Bryan-Wilson notes, Swenson's comments exemplify. "Recognizable in [Swenson's] complex, contradictory claims are both a reformist and a revolutionary drive," Bryan-Wilson writes. "These factions inevitably came into conflict with each other." See Julia Bryan-Wilson, *Art Workers: Radical Practice in the Vietnam War Era* (Berkeley: University of California Press, 2009), 20.

35. Gene Swenson, "The International Liberation Front," unpublished, hand-annotated draft dated April 1969, Gene Swenson papers, 1950–1969, Archives of American Art, Smithsonian Institution, Washington, DC.

36. Gregory Battcock, "The Art Critic as Social Reformer—With a Question Mark," *Art in America* 59 (September–October 1971): 27.

37. Lippard, contribution to "Gene Swenson: A Composite Portrait," 18.

38. Battcock, "Art Critic as Social Reformer," 27.

39. Gregory Battcock, "Museum of Modern Art Hires Guards to Keep Swenson Out," *The New York Free Press*, February 29, 1968, 6, 10; emphasis original.

40. "'Kansas' Existential," undated clipping preserved in Gregory Battcock's archive, Gregory Battcock papers, 1952–circa 1980, Archives of American Art, Smithsonian Institution, Washington, DC.

41. Lippard, contribution to "Gene Swenson: A Composite Portrait," 18.

42. Howardena Pindell, "Where Is the Art World Left?," *Art Papers*, accessed June 6, 2023, originally published in *Art & Artists*, March 1987, https://www.artpapers.org/where-is-the-art-world-left. For an important analysis of Pindell's Black feminist commitments, see Sarah Louise Cowan, *Howardena Pindell: Reclaiming Abstraction* (New Haven, CT: Yale University Press, 2022).

43. Battcock, "Museum of Modern Art Hires Guards," 10.

44. Jill Johnston, "Dance Journal: Like a Boy in a Boat," *The Village Voice*, September 11, 1969, 17.

45. Jill Johnston, *Lesbian Nation: The Feminist Solution* (New York: Simon and Schuster, 1973), 78.

46. Johnston, *Lesbian Nation*, 76.

47. Johnston, *Lesbian Nation*, 80.

48. Johnston, *Lesbian Nation*, 81–82.

49. Jill Johnston, "PRESS RELEASE: Re Panel Discussion May 21st at Loeb Student Venter of N.Y.U. 'The Disintegration of a Critic—An Analysis of Jill Johnston,'" Lil Picard papers, series II, box 15, University of Iowa Libraries Special Collections and Archives, Iowa City, IA.

50. Johnston, "PRESS RELEASE: Re Panel Discussion."

51. Johnston, "The Unhappy Spectator," 195. See Antonin Artaud, *The Theatre and Its Double*, trans. Mary Caroline Richards (New York: Grove Press, 1958), 13.

52. Lucy Bradnock, *No More Masterpieces: Modern Art After Artaud* (New Haven, CT: Yale University Press, 2020), 2.

53. Bradnock, *No More Masterpieces*, 24–25.

54. Bradnock, *No More Masterpieces*, 202.

55. My argument here builds on Bradnock's intervention. By tracing the widespread engagement with Artaud among so many artists across the United States (spanning both coasts), Bradnock argues for a much richer, more complicated historical understanding of American avant-garde artistic practice "in such a way as to trouble narratives of rupture in the shift from modernism to its reactionary progeny postmodernism." Bradnock, *No More Masterpieces*, 202.

56. Johnston, *Paper Daughter*, 217.

57. Sally Banes, "Jill Johnston: Signaling Through the Flames" (1980), in *Writing Dance in the Age of Postmodernism* (Hanover, NH: Wesleyan University Press, 1994), 9.

58. Johnston, "PRESS RELEASE: Re Panel Discussion."

59. Johnston, *Lesbian Nation*, 48.

60. Johnston, preface to *Marmalade Me*, 15.

61. Gregory Battcock, introduction to Johnston, *Marmalade Me*, 10; emphasis original.

62. Artaud, *The Theatre and Its Double*, 13.

63. John Perrault, "Art: A Sort of Sacrifice," *The Village Voice*, May 29, 1969, 14–15.

64. Gregory Battcock, "The Last Estate," *The New York Review of Sex & Politics*, July 1, 1969, 17.

65. Battcock, "The Last Estate," 17.

66. Gwen Allen, *Artists' Magazines: An Alternative Space for Art* (Cambridge, MA: MIT Press, 2011), 252.

67. Andy Warhol, contribution to "Jill Johnston Exposed: A Life Dominated by Strange Arts, Consuming Desires, and Ego-Eroticism . . . ," special issue, *Culture Hero* (February 1970), 4–6. All italicized quotes from the panel discussion come from Warhol's contribution to *Culture Hero*. All misspelled words and ellipses are preserved.

68. Perrault, "Art: A Sort of Sacrifice," 16.

69. Perrault, "Art: A Sort of Sacrifice," 16.

70. Lil Picard, "Analysis by Lil Picard: Confession with an Accent," *The East Village Other*, May 14, 1969, 13.

71. Picard, "Analysis by Lil Picard," 13.

72. John Gruen, "Vogue's Spotlight: The Underground," *Vogue*, August 15, 1969, 38.

73. Battcock, "The Last Estate," 17.

74. Gene Swenson, contribution to "Jill Johnston Exposed," 11.

75. For a cultural history of antipsychiatric and social diagnostic thinking in the

United States, see Michael E. Staub, *Madness Is Civilization: When the Diagnosis Was Social, 1948–1980* (Chicago: University of Chicago Press, 2011).

76. R. D. Laing, *The Politics of Experience* (New York: Pantheon Books, 1967), 115.

77. Laing, *The Politics of Experience*, 104–5.

78. Jill Johnston, "R. D. Laing: The misteek of sighcosis," in *Admission Accomplished: The Lesbian Nation Years (1970–75)* (London: Serpent's Tail, 1998), 198; published originally in *The Village Voice*, November 30, 1972, and December 7, 1972.

79. Johnston, "R. D. Laing: The misteek of sighcosis," 192–93.

80. Johnston, "R. D. Laing: The misteek of sighcosis," 182.

81. Johnston, "R. D. Laing: The misteek of sighcosis," 182; emphasis original.

82. Johnston, "R. D. Laing: The misteek of sighcosis," 197–98.

83. Johnston, "R. D. Laing: The misteek of sighcosis," 197–98.

CHAPTER THREE

1. Jill Johnston, "Holy Hurricane," *Marmalade Me* (New York: E. P. Dutton, 1971), 130; published originally in *The Village Voice*, March 21, 1968.

2. Jill Johnston, *Lesbian Nation: The Feminist Solution* (New York: Simon and Schuster, 1973), 166.

3. Johnston, *Lesbian Nation*, 40.

4. Johnston, *Lesbian Nation*, 70.

5. Jill Johnston, "Introduction: Aroused Is Aroused Is Aroused," *Admission Accomplished: The Lesbian Nation Years, 1970–75* (London: Serpent's Tail, 1998), unpaginated.

6. Yvonne Rainer, *Feelings Are Facts: A Life* (Cambridge, MA: MIT Press, 2006), 289.

7. For more on the history of the Judson Dance Theater, see Ana Janevski and Thomas J. Lax, eds., *Judson Dance Theater: The Work Is Never Done* (New York: The Museum of Modern Art, 2018), and Sally Banes, *Democracy's Body: Judson Dance Theater, 1962–1964* (Durham, NC: Duke University Press, 1993).

8. Johnston, preface to *Marmalade Me*, 14.

9. Johnston, *Lesbian Nation*, 97.

10. All the preceding quotes come from Johnston, *Lesbian Nation*, 39, 15, 20, 164, 157–58. For an analysis of how Johnston's queer antics and theatrics constitute "expatriate acts of joker citizenship," see Sara Warner, *Acts of Gaiety: LGBT Performance and the Politics of Pleasure* (Ann Arbor: University of Michigan Press, 2012), 135–48.

11. Johnston, *Lesbian Nation*, 181.

12. Johnston, *Lesbian Nation* 156.

13. Jill Johnston, "Lois Lane Is a Lesbian (1)," *The Village Voice*, March 4, 1971, 9–10, 64; "Lois Lane Is a Lesbian (2)," *The Village Voice*, March 11, 1971, 21, 28; and "Lois Lane Is a Lesbian (3)," *The Village Voice*, March 25, 1971, 27–28, 38.

14. Johnston, *Lesbian Nation*, 76.

15. Sally Banes, "Jill Johnston: Signaling Through the Flames" (1980), in *Writing Dance in the Age of Postmodernism* (Hanover, NH: Wesleyan University Press, 1994), 8.

16. In the 1994 republication of her 1980 text, Banes states that "Johnston began writing on dance and art again after this article was published." However, I contend that Johnston never stopped writing arts criticism, even as she turned to lesbian feminism in the early 1970s. Banes, "Jill Johnston: Signaling Through the Flames," 354n17.

17. Writing in a different context that focuses on Johnston's physical performances,

dance theorist Clare Croft also aims to "think across" the "firm line between [Johnston's] dance writing in the 1950s and 1960s and her lesbian feminist work," thereby "mess[ing] with" the strict periodization of Johnston's practice. See Clare Croft, "Lesbian Echoes in Activism and Writing: Jill Johnston's Interventions," in *Futures of Dance Studies*, ed. Susan Manning, Janice Ross, and Rebecca Schneider (Madison: University of Wisconsin Press, 2020), 117–34. Croft also provides an evocative analysis of how her research on Johnston is motivated by and entangled with her own queer desire to find and commune with lesbians in the archives, thereby reaching across time. See Clare Croft, "Not Yet and Elsewhere: Locating Lesbian Identity in Performance Archives, as Performance Archives," *Contemporary Theatre Review* 31, nos. 1–2 (2021): 34–50. See also Croft's book *Jill Johnston in Motion: Dance, Writing, and Lesbian Life* (Durham, NC: Duke University Press, 2024), which was published after the completion of this manuscript.

18. Geoffrey Hendricks and David J. Getsy, "Outing Queer Fluxus: Geoffrey Hendricks in Conversation with David J. Getsy," *PAJ: A Journal of Art and Performance* 127 (January 2021): 96. For an analysis of the importance of ambivalence in Hendricks's queer performances in the wake of the Stonewall uprising of June 1969 and his engagement with Johnston's writings, see David J. Getsy, "The Spectacle of Privacy: Geoffrey Hendricks's Ring Piece and the Ambivalence of Queer Visibility," *Art Bulletin* 104, no. 3 (2022): 117–45.

19. Eileen Myles, interview by Adam Fitzgerald, *Interview*, December 17, 2015, https:// www.interviewmagazine.com/culture/eileen-myles-1.

20. In asserting the importance of Johnston's lesbian feminism for the history of art and performance, I push back against the sharp distinction José Esteban Muñoz makes between the Jill Johnston of *Marmalade Me*, whom he claims for the history of performance, and the Johnston of *Lesbian Nation*, whom he largely disavows. He writes: "Thus I return to the Johnston of *Marmalade Me* and not the Johnston of *Lesbian Nation*—not because *Lesbian Nation* is not an admirable text and not because it is not important. The moment that Jill Johnston named herself and her sexual identity was important for the history of queer politics and thinking. Yet if we read that move alongside Johnston's refusal to name in *Marmalade Me*, we are faced with her salient question, 'What does it mean to name something? Where do we get off giving everything a legal identity?'" I argue those questions continue to be just as salient throughout Johnston's *Lesbian Nation* years. José Esteban Muñoz, *Cruising Utopia: The Then and There of Queer Futurity* (Durham, NC: Duke University Press, 2009), 115–30.

21. In arguing for the enduring significance of Johnston's lesbian feminism as full of potential, I heed Sara Ahmed's call for a "revival of lesbian feminism." She asserts, "By holding on to the figure of the lesbian as full of potential, we are not giving up on queer; rather, we are refusing to assume being queer means giving up on lesbian feminism." See Sara Ahmed, *Living a Feminist Life* (Durham, NC: Duke University Press, 2017), 213–34.

22. Clare Hemmings, *Why Stories Matter: The Political Grammar of Feminist Theory* (Durham, NC: Duke University Press, 2011), 3. I encountered Hemmings's writings through Andrea Long Chu's provocative essay "The Impossibility of Feminism." See Andrea Long Chu, "The Impossibility of Feminism," *differences: A Journal of Feminist Cultural Studies* 30, no. 1 (2019): 63–81.

23. Kyla Wazana Tompkins, "Ball Busters and the Recurring Trauma of Intergenerational Queer/Feminist Life," *Bully Bloggers* (blog), February 20, 2016, https://bully bloggers.wordpress.com/2016/02/20/ball-busters-and-the-recurring-trauma-of-inter generational-queerfeminist-life/.

24. Johnston, preface to *Marmalade Me*, 13.

25. My language here intentionally mirrors the exact terms with which Michael Fried condemns the "theatrical sensibility," dismissing it as mistaken "illusion that the barriers between the arts are in the process of crumbling . . . and that the arts themselves are at last sliding toward some kind of final, implosive, hugely desirable synthesis." Michael Fried, "Art and Objecthood," *Artforum* 5, no. 10 (Summer 1967): 21.

26. Johnston, "On the Happenings—New York Scene," *Marmalade Me*, 45; published originally in *Encore* (September/October 1962); emphasis original.

27. Fried, "Art and Objecthood," 20–21.

28. Thomas J. Lax, "Allow Me to Begin Again," in Janevski and Lax, *Judson Dance Theater*, 23.

29. Johnston, "On the Happenings—New York Scene," 51.

30. For a comprehensive history of *Music Walk*, see William Fetterman, "*Music Walk*, and *Cartridge Music*: Variations in Complex Indeterminate Notation," in *John Cage's Theatre Pieces: Notations and Performances* (New York: Routledge, 1996), 47–68.

31. Jill Johnston, "The Yearly Mellowdrama," *Gullibles Travels* (New York: Links Books, 1974), 106; published originally in *The Village Voice*, October 26, 1972.

32. John Cage, "Lecture on Something," in *Silence: Lectures and Writings by John Cage* (Hanover, NH: Wesleyan University Press, 1961), 139.

33. Johnston, "The Yearly Mellowdrama," 105–6, 110.

34. Johnston, "The Yearly Mellowdrama," 106.

35. Reflecting back much later, in 2003, Johnston recalls: "John and David were all the while fiddling with their radio dials and monkeying around with the insides of a grand piano, following instructions on their own graphically immaculate, intact—of course—cards. Everyone seemed happy with the event until afterward, when we were partying at a restaurant and I told John, with a certain misplaced glee, about my accident with the cards. Learning that I had forsaken his score, he scolded me for not giving up my ego. He meant I suppose for not giving it up to him—an ulterior design I would grow to suspect of him." Jill Johnston, "Dance Quote Unquote," in *Reinventing Dance in the 1960s: Everything Was Possible*, ed. Sally Banes (Madison: University of Wisconsin Press, 2003), 98–104.

36. Johnston, "On the Happenings—New York Scene," 45.

37. Banes, "Jill Johnston: Signaling Through the Flames," 4.

38. Fried, "Art and Objecthood," 20.

39. Jill Johnston, "Dance: Fresh Winds," *The Village Voice*, March 15, 1962, 13.

40. Jill Johnston, "Democracy," in *Jill Johnston: The Disintegration of a Critic*, ed. Fiona McGovern, Megan Francis Sullivan, and Axel Wieder (Berlin: Sternberg Press and Bergen Kunsthall, 2019), 17; published originally in *The Village Voice*, August 23, 1962.

41. Carrie Lambert-Beatty, *Being Watched: Yvonne Rainer and the 1960s* (Cambridge, MA: MIT Press, 2008), 1.

42. Lambert-Beatty, *Being Watched*, 70.

43. Warhol also made a related film titled *Jill Johnston Dancing* of Johnston dancing alone in the Factory.

44. Paisid Aramphongphan, "Real Professionals? Andy Warhol, Fred Herko, and Dance," *PAJ: A Journal of Performance and Art* 37, no. 2 (May 2015): 1. See also Paisid Aramphongphan, *Horizontal Together: Art, Dance, and Queer Embodiment in 1960s New York* (Manchester: Manchester University Press, 2021).

45. Yvonne Rainer, contribution to "Jill Johnston Exposed: A Life Dominated by

Strange Arts, Consuming Desires, and Ego-Eroticism . . . ," special issue, *Culture Hero* (February 1970), 14. Writing much later, Johnston recalls: "By the time we started I was already drowning—in alcohol, a half of a fifth of vodka as I recall. . . . Afterward I learned [Yvonne] was displeased, not with the event per se (necessarily), but with my need to perform blotto." Johnston, "Dance Quote Unquote," 96.

46. Jill Johnston, "Judson Concerts #3, #4," in McGovern, Sullivan, and Wieder, *Jill Johnston*, 21; published originally in *The Village Voice*, February 28, 1963.

47. Jill Johnston, "Yvonne Rainer: I," in McGovern, Sullivan, and Wieder, *Jill Johnston*, 24; published originally in *The Village Voice*, May 23, 1963.

48. Yvonne Rainer, *Work 1961–73* (New York: Primary Information, 2020), 9; published originally in 1974 by the Press of the Nova Scotia College of Art and Design.

49. Jill Johnston, "Fresh Winds," *The Village Voice*, March 15, 1962, 13. The quote is from Gertrude Stein, *Lectures in America* (New York: Random House, 1935), 78.

50. Johnston, "Yvonne Rainer: I," 26.

51. Jill Johnston, "Pain, Pleasure, Process," *The Village Voice*, February 27, 1964, 9, 15.

52. Johnston, "Pain, Pleasure, Process," 15.

53. For an excellent, in-depth account of *The Mind Is a Muscle*, see Catherine Wood, *Yvonne Rainer: The Mind Is a Muscle* (London: Afterall, 2007).

54. Jill Johnston, "Rainer's *Muscle*," *Marmalade Me*, 36–38; published originally in *The Village Voice*, April 18, 1968. For a beautiful account of how learning Yvonne Rainer's dance *Trio A* becomes a model for embodied queer pedagogy and the risks and rewards of writing queer art history, see Julia Bryan-Wilson, "Practicing *Trio A*," *October* 140 (Spring 2012): 54–74.

55. Johnston, preface to *Marmalade Me*, 14.

56. Jill Johnston, *Paper Daughter: Autobiography in Search of a Father*, vol. 2 (New York: Alfred A. Knopf, 1985). For an in-depth chronicle of Johnston's time at Bellevue from August 20 to September 23, 1965, see chapter 6, "Captivity," of *Paper Daughter*.

57. Jill Johnston, "Critic's Critics," *Marmalade Me*, 100–101; published originally in *The Village Voice*, September 16, 1965.

58. The ad ran throughout the summer of 1971, beginning on June 3.

59. Jill Johnston, "Take Me Disappearing," *Marmalade Me*, 105; published originally in *The Village Voice*, December 14, 1967.

60. Johnston, preface to *Marmalade Me*, 14.

61. This quote is lifted from Norman O. Brown, *Love's Body* (New York: Vintage Books, 1966), 161.

62. Regarding the failure of *Black Zero*, for example, Nadja Millner-Larsen argues that the work "ultimately undercut its own radicality." Millner-Larsen contends that despite its ambition "to undermine the supposed facticity of the racialized body" by presenting it in a disorienting, cacophonous intermedia environment, the work nonetheless also participates "in the 'hellish cycle' of anticipation and objectification internal to the representational logic of colonial modernity" (through its reliance on the voice of the Black poet). See Nadja Millner-Larsen, "The Subject of Black: Abstraction and the Politics of Race in the Expanded Cinema Environment," *Grey Room* 67 (Spring 2017): 64–99. See also Nadja Millner-Larsen, *Up Against the Real: Black Mask from Art to Action* (Chicago: University of Chicago Press, 2023), 66–99.

63. Johnston, "Holy Hurricane," 129–32.

64. Jill Johnston, "Pieces of Gene," *Marmalade Me*, 145.

65. Johnston, *Lesbian Nation*, 82–83.

66. All of the preceding quotes are from *Village Voice* columns reproduced in *Marmalade Me*, 167, 247, 287, 315.

67. Johnston, *Lesbian Nation*, 69.

68. Johnston, "R. D. Laing: The misteek of sighcosis," *Admission Accomplished*, 197; published originally in *The Village Voice*, November 30, 1972, and December 7, 1972.

69. Johnston, *Lesbian Nation*, 78–81.

70. Johnston, *Lesbian Nation*, 97.

71. Johnston, preface to *Marmalade Me*, 14.

72. Johnston, "Untitled," *Marmalade Me*, 18–19; published originally in *The Village Voice*, October 10, 1968.

73. Johnston, "Untitled," 22.

74. Johnston, "Untitled," 20, 22.

75. Les Levine, "Publisher Note," in "Jill Johnston Exposed," 1.

76. Gregory Battcock, introduction to Johnston, *Marmalade Me*, 11.

77. John Perrault, contribution to "Jill Johnston Exposed," 9.

78. Helen Ansell, contribution to "Jill Johnston Exposed," 15.

79. Rosalyn Drexler, contribution to "Jill Johnston Exposed," 9.

80. Gene Swenson, contribution to "Jill Johnston Exposed," 11.

81. Lil Picard, contribution to "Jill Johnston Exposed," 12.

82. Ann Wilson, contribution to "Jill Johnston Exposed," 7.

83. Wilson, contribution to "Jill Johnston Exposed," 7.

84. Barbara Rose, contribution to "Jill Johnston Exposed," 11.

85. Jacqueline Rose, *Women in Dark Times* (London: Bloomsbury, 2014), xiv.

86. Yvonne Rainer, quoted in Lucy Lippard, "Yvonne Rainer on Feminism and Her Film," *The Feminist Art Journal* 4, no. 2 (Summer 1975): 5–11. Writing in 1975 in *The Feminist Art Journal*, Cindy Nemser comes down pretty hard against Rainer's "convoluted, enigmatic, suggestive confusion," saying that Rainer "puts barriers of form and style between herself and any kind of open expression" and that "Rainer is indeed the epitome of the alienated artist tormenting herself with her own intellectual pretensions, unable to get back to her living source and as a result producing endless zombie-like avatars of her ongoing unresolved state." Cindy Nemser, "Editorial: Rainer and Rothschild, an Overview," *The Feminist Art Journal* 4, no. 2 (Summer 1975): 4.

87. Yvonne Rainer, contribution to "Jill Johnston Exposed," 14.

88. Rainer, *Feelings Are Facts*, 374–75.

89. Jo Applin, *Lee Lozano: Not Working* (New Haven, CT: Yale University Press, 2018), 161.

90. Applin, *Lee Lozano*, 158.

91. Applin, *Lee Lozano*, 160.

92. John Gruen, contribution to "Jill Johnston Exposed," 13.

93. In a column titled "Of This Pure But Irregular Passion," Johnston exclaims: "The gay movement is stressing the positive identity of the homosexual. The key phrase is COME OUT. Come out of hiding. Identify yourself: Make it clear. Celebrate your sexuality." She begins the column by explaining: "In support of the gay movement on the occasion of the gay celebration week: I guess yes I've been saying it in this column for a year and a half now, but always fragmentarily in the context of the literary exercises. So this will be straight on. . . . Gradually the life became the theatre became the column. The life being

everything of course included everything. Sex was especially interesting since I was in love with a beautiful girl and we were having a very good time of it at home and on the road." Jill Johnston, "Dance Journal: Of This Pure But Irregular Passion," *The Village Voice*, July 2, 1970, 20–21, 38–39, 55.

94. Sarris wrote his screed in direct response to an article in *The New York Times Magazine* by Merle Miller and took aim at Johnston too. See Merle Miller, "What It Means to Be a Homosexual," *The New York Times Magazine*, January 17, 1971, 9–11, 48–49, 57, 60.

95. Andrew Sarris, "Heteros Have Problems Too (1)," *The Village Voice*, February 4, 1971, 5–6, 62.

96. Johnston, "Lois Lane Is a Lesbian (1)," 64; emphasis original.

97. Johnston, "Lois Lane Is a Lesbian (1)," 64.

98. Johnston, "Lois Lane Is a Lesbian (1)," 10.

99. Johnston, "Lois Lane Is a Lesbian (1)," 9; ellipses original.

100. See Charlotte Curtis, "Women's Liberation Gets Into the Long Island Swim," *The New York Times*, August 10, 1970, 32. For an analysis of Johnston's performative disruption, see Sara Warner, "Expatriate Acts: Jill Johnston's Joker Citizenship," in *Acts of Gaiety*, 105–38.

101. Johnston, "Lois Lane Is a Lesbian (1)," 64; emphasis original.

102. Andrea Long Chu, "Let's Go, Lesbians," *Artforum* 57, no. 10 (Summer 2019): 248–49.

103. Chu, "The Impossibility of Feminism," 75.

104. Johnston, *Lesbian Nation*, 166–67.

105. Chu, "The Impossibility of Feminism," 75.

106. Johnston, *Lesbian Nation*, 154.

107. Chu, "The Impossibility of Feminism," 78.

108. Israel Shenker, "Norman Mailer vs. Women's Lib: 'Discussion' at Town Hall Changes Few Minds," *The New York Times*, May 1, 1971, 19.

109. Johnston, *Lesbian Nation*, 21–22.

110. Israel Shenker, "Guests at Theater for Ideas Take Up Cerebral Gauntlet," *The New York Times*, October 9, 1968, 49, 51.

111. *Life* magazine, May 7, 1971, cover.

112. Dialogue in *Town Bloody Hall*, dir. Chris Hegedus and D. A. Pennebaker (1979, Pennebaker Hegedus Films, Inc.).

113. Jill Johnston, "Cultural Gangsters," *Marmalade Me*, 158; published originally in *The Village Voice*, June 6, 1968.

114. Johnston, *Lesbian Nation*, 22.

115. Lauren Berlant, *Cruel Optimism* (Durham, NC: Duke University Press, 2011), 101.

116. Jill Johnston, "On a Clear Day You Can See Your Mother," *Lesbian Nation*, 266; published originally in *The Village Voice*, May 6, 1971.

117. Johnston, "On a Clear Day You Can See Your Mother," 266–67.

118. Johnston, "On a Clear Day You Can See Your Mother," 269.

119. Johnston, "On a Clear Day You Can See Your Mother," 271.

120. Dialogue in *Town Bloody Hall*.

121. Johnston, "On a Clear Day You Can See Your Mother," 272–73.

122. Jill Johnston, "Which Way the Avant-Garde?" *Marmalade Me*, 94–95; published originally in *The New York Times*, August 11, 1968.

123. Lax, "Allow Me to Begin Again," 23. The quote is from Douglas Crimp, *Before Pictures* (Chicago: University of Chicago Press, 2016), 11.

124. Lax, "Allow Me to Begin Again," 23.

125. Lax, "Allow Me to Begin Again," 23; emphasis original.

126. Lax, "Allow Me to Begin Again," 16.

127. Johnston, *Lesbian Nation*, 37.

CONCLUSION

1. Lauren Berlant, "'68, or Something," *Critical Inquiry* 21, no. 1 (Autumn 1994): 127, 133.

2. Gene Swenson, "Why Have None of My Fellow Artists Spoken a Word in Behalf of the Revolution?," *The New York Free Press*, June 6, 1968, 17.

3. Gregory Battcock, interview by David Bourdon, *Culture Hero: A Fanzine of Stars of the Superworld* (1971), 11.

4. Gregory Battcock, "The Art Critic as Social Reformer—With a Question Mark," *Art in America* 59 (September–October 1971): 26–27.

5. Gene Swenson, "An Art Critic's Farewell Address," *The New York Free Press*, March 28, 1968, 8. A typed, annotated draft of this text is preserved in Swenson's archive. The text was written originally as a direct address, beginning with "My Fellow Colleagues." I suspect that Swenson intended to disrupt and then deliver this "Farewell Address" at an event titled "A Symposium on the Possibilities and Responsibilities of Art Criticism" that took place at MoMA on February 14, 1968, at 8:00 p.m. and included William S. Rubin (as moderator), Thomas B. Hess, Max Kozloff, Hilton Kramer, and Philip Leider. At the time of the symposium, Swenson would have been in the midst of his question mark protest outside the museum. A recording of the symposium is preserved in the archives at MoMA (Sound Recordings, 68.3, the Museum of Modern Art Archives, New York, NY). Max Kozloff makes passing reference to the protest (though he does not name Swenson): "Actually, this whole panel and the museum itself was attacked by someone demonstrating for some time now outside of the museum as being involved in a conspiracy of the establishment. My reaction was, I couldn't imagine four people whose opinions varied as much as the people on this panel. But that may be merely an illusion, maybe they don't. Perhaps there is another art world that is really outside the kin of the people here and that in fact, willy nilly, there is an establishment. I'd like to have the views of the speakers on this."

6. Swenson, "An Art Critic's Farewell Address," 10.

7. Yevgeny Yevtushenko, "Talk," in *Yevtushenko: Selected Poems*, trans. Robin Milner-Gulland and Peter Levi (Middlesex: Penguin Books, 1962), 81.

8. Lucy Lippard, contribution to "Gene Swenson: A Composite Portrait," *The Register of the Museum of Art, University of Kansas* 4, no. 6–7 (1971): 18; special edition published to accompany the exhibition *Gene Swenson: Retrospective for a Critic* (October 24–December 5, 1971).

9. Dianne Hunter and Rena Patterson, foreword to *Gullibles Travels* by Jill Johnston (New York: Links Books, 1974), xi.

10. Jill Johnston, "Note," *Gullibles Travels*, xiii.

11. Jill Johnston, "Agnes Martin: Surrender and Solitude," *Gullibles Travels*, 280; published originally in *The Village Voice*, September 20, 1973; ellipses original. These lines

are (mis)quoted from Martin's essay "On the Perfection Underlying Life" (1973). See Agnes Martin, *Writings*, ed. Dieter Schwarz (Winterthur: Kunstmuseum Winterthur/ Edition Cantz, 1993), 67–74. I am grateful to Letitia Quesenberry for sharing this passage with me.

12. Jill Johnston, "Lesbian/Feminism Reconsidered," *Salmagundi*, no. 58/59 (Fall 1982–Winter 1983): 76–88.

13. Here I position my book in conversation Jack Halberstam's important book *The Queer Art of Failure*, drawing a distinction between my project and the utopian thrust of their project, with its emphasis on redeeming queer failure as artful. Halberstam argues that queer failure "allows us to escape the punishing norms that discipline behavior and manage human development" and "provides the opportunity to use negative affects to poke holes in the toxic positivity of contemporary life." See Jack Halberstam, *The Queer Art of Failure* (Durham, NC: Duke University Press, 2011).

14. Gregory Battcock, "The Last Estate," *The New York Review of Sex & Politics*, July 1, 1969, 16.

15. Open letter from Eileen Myles dated October 12, 1991, Leslie Scalapino papers, 1959–2011 (MSS 668), box 30, folder 1, Special Collections & Archives, University of California, San Diego.

16. Sharon Hayes, foreword to *I want a president: Transcript of a Rally*, ed. Zoe Leonard (Brooklyn, NY: Dancing Foxes Press, 2017).

17. Zoe Leonard, "I want a president" (1992), republished in Leonard, *I want a president: Transcript of a Rally*.

Select Bibliography and Further Reading

PAPERS AND ARCHIVES

Archives of American Art, Smithsonian Institution, Washington, DC
Gregory Battcock papers, 1952–circa 1980
Lucy R. Lippard papers, 1930s–2010, bulk 1960s–1990
Gene Swenson papers, 1950–1969
Charles Deering McCormick Library of Special Collections and University Archives, Northwestern University Libraries, Evanston, IL
Charlotte Moorman Archive
Fales Library and Special Collections, New York University, New York, NY
Judson Memorial Church Archive
The Museum of Modern Art Archives, New York, NY
PASTA (MoMA Union) Strikes and Protests by Outside Groups
The University of Iowa Special Collections and Archives, Iowa City, IA
Lil Picard papers

PERIODICALS AND UNDERGROUND NEWSPAPERS

Art & Artists (London, 1966–86)
Artforum (San Fransisco, 1962–65; Los Angeles, 1965–67; New York, 1967–)
ARTnews (New York, 1923–)
Arts Magazine (New York, 1926–92)
Culture Hero: A Fanzine of Stars of the Superworld (New York, 1969–71)
The East Village Other (New York, 1965–72)
The Feminist Art Journal (New York, 1972–77)
Gay NYC (New York, 1969–mid-1970s)
The New York Free Press (New York, 1968–70)
The New York Review of Sex & Politics (New York, 1969–70)
The Village Voice (New York, 1955–2019, 2021–)

ARTICLES AND BOOKS

Ahmed, Sara. *Living a Feminist Life*. Durham, NC: Duke University Press, 2017.
Allen, Gwen. *Artists' Magazines: An Alternative Space for Art*. Cambridge, MA: MIT Press, 2011.

Als, Hilton. *The Women*. New York: Farrar, Straus and Giroux, 1998.

Applin, Jo. *Eccentric Objects: Rethinking Sculpture in 1960s America*. New Haven, CT: Yale University Press, 2012.

Applin, Jo. *Lee Lozano: Not Working*. New Haven, CT: Yale University Press, 2018.

Aramphongphan, Paisid. *Horizontal Together: Art, Dance, and Queer Embodiment in 1960s New York*. Manchester: Manchester University Press, 2021.

Artaud, Antonin. *The Theatre and Its Double*. Translated by Mary Caroline Richards. New York: Grove Press, 1958.

Banes, Sally. *Democracy's Body: Judson Dance Theater, 1962–1964*. Durham, NC: Duke University Press, 1993.

Banes, Sally. *Greenwich Village, 1963: Avant-Garde Performance and the Effervescent Body*. Durham, NC: Duke University Press, 1993.

Banes, Sally. *Writing Dance in the Age of Postmodernism*. Hanover, NH: Wesleyan University Press, 1994.

Battcock, Gregory. *Why Art: Casual Notes on the Aesthetics of the Immediate Past*. New York: E. P. Dutton, 1977.

Berlant, Lauren. *Cruel Optimism*. Durham, NC: Duke University Press, 2011.

Berlant, Lauren. *On the Inconvenience of Other People*. Durham, NC: Duke University Press, 2022.

Berlant, Lauren. "'68, or Something." *Critical Inquiry* 21, no. 1 (Autumn 1994): 124–55.

Bradnock, Lucy. *No More Masterpieces: Modern Art After Artaud*. New Haven, CT: Yale University Press, 2020.

Bruce, La Marr Jurelle. *How to Go Mad Without Losing Your Mind: Madness and Black Radical Creativity*. Durham, NC: Duke University Press, 2021.

Bryan-Wilson, Julia. *Art Workers: Radical Practice in the Vietnam War Era*. Berkeley: University of California Press, 2009.

Bryan-Wilson, Julia. *Fray: Art and Textile Politics*. Chicago: University of Chicago Press, 2017.

Butt, Gavin. *Between You and Me: Queer Disclosures in the New York Art World, 1948–1963*. Durham, NC: Duke University Press, 2006.

Cahan, Susan E. *Mounting Frustration: The Art Museum in the Age of Black Power*. Durham, NC: Duke University Press, 2016.

Chu, Andrea Long. *Females*. London: Verso, 2019.

Chu, Andrea Long. "The Impossibility of Feminism," *differences: A Journal of Feminist Cultural Studies* 30, no. 1 (2019): 63–81.

Croft, Clare. *Jill Johnston in Motion: Dance, Writing, and Lesbian Life*. Durham, NC: Duke University Press, 2024.

Cvetkovich, Ann. *An Archive of Feelings: Trauma, Sexuality, and Lesbian Public Cultures*. Durham, NC: Duke University Press, 2003.

Didion, Joan. *Slouching Towards Bethlehem*. New York: Farrar, Straus and Giroux, 1968.

English, Darby. *1971: A Year in the Life of Color*. Chicago: University of Chicago Press, 2016.

Farinati, Lucia, and Jennifer Thatcher, eds. *Theorising the Artist Interview*. New York: Routledge, 2024.

Flatley, Jonathan. *Like Andy Warhol*. Chicago: University of Chicago Press, 2017.

Foster, Hal. *Design and Crime (And Other Diatribes)*. London: Verso, 2011.

Foster, Hal. *The Return of the Real: The Avant-Garde at the End of the Century*. Cambridge, MA: MIT Press, 1996.

Fournier, Lauren. *Autotheory as Feminist Practice in Art, Writing, and Criticism*. Cambridge, MA: MIT Press, 2021.

Fried, Michael. *Art and Objecthood: Essays and Reviews*. Chicago: University of Chicago Press, 1998.

Fried, Michael. "Modernist Painting and Formal Criticism." *The American Scholar* 33, no. 4 (Autumn 1964): 642–48.

Getsy, David J. *Queer Behavior: Scott Burton and Performance Art*. Chicago: University of Chicago Press, 2022.

Getsy, David J. "The Spectacle of Privacy: Geoffrey Hendricks's Ring Piece and the Ambivalence of Queer Visibility," *Art Bulletin* 104, no. 3 (2022): 117–45.

Greenberg, Clement. *The Collected Essays and Criticism*. Vols. 1–4. Chicago: University of Chicago Press, 1986.

Halberstam, Jack. *The Queer Art of Failure*. Durham, NC: Duke University Press, 2011.

Hemmings, Clare. *Why Stories Matter: The Political Grammar of Feminist Theory*. Durham, NC: Duke University Press, 2011.

Janevski, Ana, and Thomas J. Lax, eds. *Judson Dance Theater: The Work Is Never Done*. New York: The Museum of Modern Art, 2018.

Johnston, Jill. *Admission Accomplished: The Lesbian Nation Years, 1970–75*. London: Serpent's Tail, 1998.

Johnston, Jill. *Gullibles Travels*. New York: Links Books, 1974.

Johnston, Jill. *Lesbian Nation: The Feminist Solution*. New York: Simon and Schuster, 1973.

Johnston, Jill. *Marmalade Me*. New York: E. P. Dutton, 1971.

Johnston, Jill. *Mother Bound: Autobiography in Search of a Father*. New York: Alfred A. Knopf, 1983.

Johnston, Jill. *Paper Daughter: Autobiography in Search of a Father*. Vol. 2. New York: Alfred A. Knopf, 1985.

Joselit, David. "An Allegory of Criticism." *October* 103 (Winter 2003): 3–13.

Kienle, Miriam. *Queer Networks: Ray Johnson's Correspondence Art*. Minneapolis: University of Minnesota Press, 2023.

Kraus, Chris. *I Love Dick*. Los Angeles: Semiotext(e), 2016.

Laing, R. D. *The Divided Self: An Existential Study in Sanity and Madness*. New York: Penguin Books, 1965.

Laing, R. D. *The Politics of Experience*. New York: Pantheon Books, 1967.

Lambert-Beatty, Carrie. *Being Watched: Yvonne Rainer and the 1960s*. Cambridge, MA: MIT Press, 2008.

Lippard, Lucy. *Changing: Essays in Art Criticism*. Documents in Modern Art Criticism. New York: E. P. Dutton, 1971.

McGovern, Fiona, Megan Francis Sullivan, and Axel Wieder, eds. *Jill Johnston: The Disintegration of a Critic*. Berlin: Sternberg Press and Bergen Kunsthall, 2019.

Metzl, Jonathan M. *The Protest Psychosis: How Schizophrenia Became a Black Disease*. Boston: Beacon Press, 2009.

Millner-Larsen, Nadja. *Up Against the Real: Black Mask from Art to Action*. Chicago: University of Chicago Press, 2023.

Muñoz, José Esteban. *Cruising Utopia: The Then and There of Queer Futurity*. Durham, NC: Duke University Press, 2009.

Myles, Eileen. *Chelsea Girls: A Novel*. New York: HarperCollins, 2015.

Nelson, Maggie. *The Argonauts*. Minneapolis, MN: Graywolf Press, 2015.

Newman, Amy. *Challenging Art: Artforum, 1962–1974*. New York: Soho Press, 2000.

Ngai, Sianne. *Ugly Feelings*. Cambridge, MA: Harvard University Press, 2005.

Peiffer, Prudence. *The Slip: The New York City Street That Changed American Art Forever*. New York: HarperCollins, 2023.

Post, Tina. *Deadpan: The Aesthetics of Black Inexpression*. New York: New York University Press, 2023.

Rainer, Yvonne. *Feelings Are Facts: A Life*. Cambridge, MA: MIT Press, 2006.

Robbins, Christa Noel. "The Sensibility of Michael Fried." *Criticism* 60, no. 4 (Fall 2018): 429–54.

Rose, Jacqueline. *Women in Dark Times*. London: Bloomsbury, 2015.

Rothkopf, Scott. "Banned and Determined: Gene Swenson." *Artforum* 40, no. 10 (Summer 2002): 142–45.

Schopp, Caroline Lillian. *In-action: Viennese Actionism and the Passivities of Performance Art*. Chicago: University of Chicago Press, 2025.

Stadler, Gustavus. "'My Wife': The Tape Recorder and Warhol's Queer Ways of Listening." *Criticism* 56, no. 3 (Summer 2014): 425–56.

Staub, Michael E. *Madness Is Civilization: When the Diagnosis Was Social, 1948–1980*. Chicago: University of Chicago Press, 2011.

Swenson, Gene R. "James Rosenquist: The Figure a Man Makes" (1967). *The Register of the Museum of Art, University of Kansas* 4, no. 6–7 (1971): 53–81. Special edition published to accompany the exhibition *Gene Swenson: Retrospective for a Critic* (October 24–December 5, 1971).

Swenson, Gene R. "The New American 'Sign Painters.'" *ARTnews* 61, no. 5 (1962): 44–47, 60–62.

Swenson, Gene R. *The* Other *Tradition*. Philadelphia: Institute of Contemporary Art, University of Pennsylvania, 1966.

Swenson, Gene R. "What Is Pop Art? Answers from 8 Painters, Part I." *ARTnews* 62, no. 7 (November 1963): 24–27, 60–64.

Swenson, Gene R. "What Is Pop Art? Part II." *ARTnews* 62, no. 10 (February 1964): 40–43, 62–67.

Tobin, Amy. *Women Artists Together: Art in the Age of Women's Liberation*. New Haven, CT: Yale University Press, 2023.

Wagner, Anne M. *Three Artists (Three Women): Modernism and the Art of Hesse, Krasner, and O'Keeffe*. Berkeley: University of California Press, 1996.

Warner, Sara. *Acts of Gaiety: LGBT Performance and the Politics of Pleasure*. Ann Arbor: University of Michigan Press, 2012.

Wojnarowicz, David. *Close to the Knives: A Memoir of Disintegration*. New York: Knopf Doubleday, 1991.

Index

Note: Page numbers in italics refer to figures.